TACKLING RUGBY

TACKLING RUGBY

*The Changing World of
Professional Rugby*

Gareth Edwards
with
Peter Bills

headline

First published in 2002
by HEADLINE BOOK PUBLISHING

10 9 8 7 6 5 4 3 2 1

British Library Cataloguing in Publication Data
is available from the British Library

ISBN 0 7472 5276 9

Typeset in Times New Roman by
Letterpart Limited, Reigate, Surrey

Printed and bound in Great Britain by
Mackays of Chatham plc, Chatham, Kent

HEADLINE BOOK PUBLISHING
A division of Hodder Headline
338 Euston Road
LONDON NW1 3BH

www.headline.co.uk
www.hodderheadline.com

Jacket photographs:
(*front*) Gareth Edwards at the Millennium Stadium, Cardiff and
(*back*) at the home of Glamorgan Wanderers, Ely, Cardiff © Robin Matthews

ACKNOWLEDGEMENTS

The authors would like to thank everyone who has given their time so generously to assist in the preparation of this book. Those whom we interviewed are too many to name individually but their thoughts are included in the pages which follow.

In the production process, we would like to thank everyone at Headline, especially Ian Marshall and Lorraine Jerram who did so much to master the entire exercise. Thanks also go to Jane Butcher, our copy editor, and Kate Truman, the proof reader.

We would also like to thank Malcolm Hamer for his help and useful advice at every stage of the process.

Contents

Introduction   1
1   The Modern-day Player   3
2   The Old Players' View   21
3   The Agent   47
4   The Club Benefactors   67
5   Structure and Administration   87
6   Woe in Wales   109
7   The Influence of Rugby League   123
8   The Lions   151
9   The Overseas Players   163
10   The Referees   183
11   Junior Rugby   207
12   The Media   237
Summary   257
Index   269

Authors' Note

The authors would like to point out that they do not necessarily endorse the individual views and opinions put forward in this book, bar those expressed by Gareth Edwards himself.

Introduction

Yes, it may be 1978 since I experienced international rugby in the best, the only place to know it – on the field as a member of one of the teams. Nothing else in life can match that supreme moment when you run out for your country, proudly wearing your national jersey. But I have not been in the rugby wilderness for those intervening years. I have commentated upon it, written about it and also watched it, at all levels from internationals, to professional club games, to Colts and to juniors. The fact is, rugby is in my blood and always will be.

Since the game went professional, much has happened in rugby football. Not particularly concerning Gareth Edwards but of immense consequence for clubs such as Selkirk in Scotland, or Stow-on-the-Wold in England or Ponsonby in New Zealand. The radical changes have affected the senior players who now earn handsome livings out of the game, and have changed the lives of referees who have had to adapt to the demands of a professional sport. And they have altered how the game itself is played and conducted at all levels.

I wanted to take an in-depth look at rugby today, circa 2002, as it contemplates a new century. I wanted to see what people thought about those professional years, how the game had changed, whether changes had been for the better or the worse, whether any aspects of the game were in crisis and needed urgent assistance.

I live rugby still and I talk about it to all manner of people – in hotels, on railway stations, at airports, even when I am on holiday. I love discussing the old game with them and hearing their views. It therefore seemed natural to extend that informal series of conversations into a proper, informative book in which I could discuss all elements of the modern-day game with people from all kinds of backgrounds within it. On the pages that follow, you will find the views of administrators at the very top of the sport, international players who have become household names all around the world, international referees, leading coaches, financial investors in clubs, former top players, agents and others. You will also hear the views of some you will not have heard of, players from the world of junior rugby who carry on, week in week out, giving their time freely for the good of their local club. As one of them put it, 'It is simply a labour of love' and I talked to them because I know that 95 per cent of the game is not about Harlequins, Cardiff, Edinburgh and Munster but about small, largely unknown clubs in all the rugby-playing countries of the world.

What is more, I found these views fascinating. I agreed with many, disagreed with some. But what I wanted was to create a forum, a debate if you like, in which I could bring together in one book almost a definitive collection of thoughts about just where this great game has got to. I wanted to discuss not only where it is now and should be going in the years to come but also what has been the cost of what one can only term the traumatic changes brought about by professionalism.

To all those who gave generously of their time, I would like to say a special thank you for their extremely valuable contribution which will, I hope, be carefully considered by those in authority who might turn the pages of this book in a comfortable chair, and ponder in a quiet moment whether some of what follows may assure the future health and prosperity of the game.

I do not pretend to present a panacea for all the game's ills. What I have sought to do is to raise questions, air issues and put all these views in front of people so that they can absorb them, discuss them with friends and, if relevant, press to introduce them as viable solutions to some of the difficulties. But before then, I trust the reader will be animated, intrigued and challenged by the thoughts put down here by a wide variety of people. All, I believe, had only one thing in mind – the future success of rugby union football.

CHAPTER 1

The Modern-day Player

They say you can't keep a good man down. And when it comes to a get-up-and-go Irishman with a wicked sense of humour, it is especially difficult. As I found out to my cost the day I met up with Keith Wood to chew the cud about the modern-day game.

The first surprise was to see Keith dolled up in a very smart, elegantly cut suit. It bore the famous pink bow tie logo of the successful Paris-based Eden Park clothing company, run by former French international three-quarter Frank Mesnel and a few pals. Under powerful lights, Keith was doing a 'shoot' for the company, the pictures to be used in Eden Park's stores in London, Paris and Dublin. But whether he is on the rugby field in the green jersey of his beloved Ireland or in a suit for a fashion company brochure, Keith Wood is the consummate professional.

Keith is also one of those marvellous men whom you would probably choose as a companion if you had to go into the trenches: someone who confronts any physical challenge without batting an eyelid, someone who is quite happy to lead from the front where all the trouble is and yet who remains cheerful with a quip and a joke always to hand. Keith would be your man.

Mind you, Keith's jokes can land fairly and squarely on yourself if you don't watch out. There I was, pouring a cup of coffee for us both amid the comfortable surroundings of a hotel in Richmond, Surrey where Keith lives, when his ready wit flashed to the surface. I imagine you've had the same problem – those newfangled coffee flasks, with two or three buttons or whatever on the top and when

3

you press one, the coffee doesn't always come out where you had expected. Which is exactly what happened in this case, so that I was suddenly holding a saucer, not a cup, full of coffee!

'Jaysus,' said a voice behind me from the only Irishman in the room, 'Oi knew yer were a golden oldie but are yer drinking out of a saucer nowadays!' Many thanks, Mr Wood. But then, Keith has the ability to go right to the heart of an issue, and also right to the heart-strings of those who have ever played this great game of rugby.

Of course, so much has changed from when I played rugby to the present day when Keith is excelling for Harlequins, Ireland and the British Lions, that you honestly wonder if anything has remained the same. Today, we have professionalism which means money, Monday to Friday daytime training sessions, proper preparation on and off the field for everyone involved. But, I asked Keith, are you still in love with the game? Would you play it for nothing today?

Keith's reply was emphatic. 'I still love it. I would play it for nothing, no doubt about it because it's a grand life being involved with rugby. You count yourself lucky all the time. And remember, it's not that long ago that I did. I enjoy it more now because I think more about it than I used to. I see more of it and I see more possibilities now even though it is hard and often stressful at times on the field. It is much harder now. There's no way you could do all you do today and not be paid. Winning continues to create a real high for me, even thought that 'high' may only last about ten minutes nowadays because you are so shattered. But it's still worth it even for just those ten minutes.'

Keith was dead right in that respect and that attitude certainly took me back to my own playing days. I sometimes came off the field feeling completely wrecked, especially when we had played one of those tough French international sides in the 1970s. But the high was great. I'd love to play today (if I were twenty-one again, and had some decent knees).

It was good to hear that Keith's love for the game remained as strong as ever. But that didn't prevent him raising some most interesting views about rugby in the modern era. And, in the same way he plays the game on the field, Keith confronted everything with a tough, no-nonsense approach. Frankly, it's the way the man lives his life and I'm sure it is one of the reasons why he is so

4

popular wherever he plays the game, unlike, for instance, the attitude of some young players who earn a very nice wage out of rugby but don't give the impression that they are always prepared to give lots back in return.

Some modern-day players, said Keith, lived a life through rugby that they thought would always be there. He warned, 'It won't be. When I was twenty, I had only a small sum in the bank and I had to work for everything I got. Young players today are getting handsomely paid for playing a game they love but they have to realise the commitment they must make in that sort of deal. It's not all one way.'

But that's not to say everything in the game today is a bed of roses, that every aspect of the sport is smoothly operated and ideally planned. Because plainly it's not. For example, said Keith, playing and training remained a problem. 'We do a bit of rugby training during the week but it's limited because the number of matches is so high and they are so intense. Your actual fitness work is not as good as it should be. The younger guys that come through should be a lot fitter. If you look at Australia, New Zealand and South Africa, their younger guys are total powerhouses. Here, some are very good at Under-18 level and often fantastic at Under-21. But at the next step up, they get the **** kicked out of them because they haven't got the hardness, due to the fact that they have not done all the hard work.

'The Australian Academy is very good. They highlight tall guys for the line-out, smaller squat guys for the front row, fast breakaways for playing at flanker, etc. Then they specialise on every aspect of their game. That involves a lot of work with them. But certainly young fellows should be the fastest and fittest, they should be everywhere.'

Keith thought the Lions tour in the summer of 2001 was a big eye-opener for the Celtic nations as to how fit and powerful England's players were. He detected a significant difference. Throughout the England squad, and even outside it, he said, there were young players maybe with two years' senior experience that had pushed themselves to the hilt. There was, he felt, a good structure in England. At times, the level of training of a player like Iain Balshaw during the Lions tour was what he described as 'remarkable'. Then he encountered what he said was 'the tunnel vision' of someone like Jonny Wilkinson. 'God, is that guy focused? I am definitely not as focused as him, only in my own fashion. Yet it's not always necessarily a good thing to be that focused. But peak fitness is essential and the guys now are incredibly fit. So much so that it's not even a factor you tend to think about any more. It's just huge how much fitness levels have gone up.

'Wilkinson is the new breed of player who has come into the game. He has known nothing but professionalism. I don't know whether these guys, who are now twenty-four to twenty-five, actually enjoy the game. I wonder whether they are aware of what we're saying when we talk about the fun we had out of the game and the great times we shared with colleagues and opponents. It is such a different world now.'

But how did the fitness aspect apply to Ireland, I wondered. Because there was plenty of evidence to suggest that, a few seasons back, the Irish boys just weren't as fit as some of their opponents on the international field and you could see that demonstrated time and again in matches. Typically, Keith did not duck the issue.

'I am pleased to say that Ireland have worked harder on their fitness since the game went professional. I am still unbelievably disappointed we did not beat New Zealand at Lansdowne Road in November 2001 because we should have won, and we had another chance when we lost narrowly to them, 15–6, in Dunedin in June 2002. But at least we are properly fit now. Going back a few seasons, I accept we weren't. We would play for sixty minutes and then die. We had passion in spades but it wasn't enough when we lacked basic fitness. Now that has changed and we are also aware of the balancing act between passion and being clinical. Sometimes you need to temper the passion a little, to be more cold and clinical to win a game.'

I thought back to my own time playing against Ireland at Lansdowne Road. You knew what to expect when you went there, no matter whether the teams were at the top or bottom of the old Five Nations Championship table. You just took it for granted that the passion would come pouring off the terraces and out of every straining sinew from the Irish boys on the field. You always knew this passion would be directed at you wherever you met them, but especially in Dublin. I felt that when Ireland beat England there in the autumn of 2001 to deny England the Grand Slam, there was a sense of passion, pride and determination. How did Keith assess that? Was it chiefly passion or other qualities?

'Well, we did well but you're aware that you don't want to go beyond the sensible levels of passion. Yes, passion is still a very important facet of the game for us. But we don't have the strength in depth [in numbers of available players] so a lot of work is needed to create that extra strength in reserve. But until we have it, an Ireland team must rely on hard work, togetherness and, of course, passion. An Irish team can lose, as we did against New Zealand, but if you lose and don't display any passion, you will get booed. There is a minimum level of passion that is expected by the fans. But improved fitness levels have helped and they have become the responsibility of the Union, who have devised training programmes. They are not left up to the individual. That is the way it should be. Yet no one should think Ireland are now supreme in any sense. Our defence was quite poor that day against England, but there were individual feats of heroism, like Peter Stringer our scrum half tap-tackling Dan Luger, the England wing. That was a little heroic act which could have turned the whole game.'

And then, in the 2002 Six Nations, came Ireland's 45-point defeat by England at Twickenham and their heavy defeat by France in Paris. Both were disappointing results for the Irish after they had put 54 points on Wales earlier in the season.

But, I reminded him, were we not talking after a season in which the northern hemisphere countries had done well against the southern hemisphere sides? There were surely plenty of signs that several of the European nations had improved significantly, so much so that any southern hemisphere team that came visiting knew that it faced a very tough test.

Keith agreed. 'Yes, by and large they did do well. England and France both beat Australia and South Africa and we did well for an hour against New Zealand. Two years ago, there was a thought that southern hemisphere countries were in a class of their own but that thought has gone. We should have beaten Australia when we last played them, too. Ireland have been close to all three leading southern hemisphere countries in their most recent matches, but of course being close is not good enough. I know one thing, we were shattered when we lost to the All Blacks. But if we continue to make progress and make a damn sight more in the next year or two, I believe an Ireland win over a Tri-Nations team is not going to be far away. We will do it sooner rather than later. But if we rest at this stage, thinking we have climbed the mountain, we will be in serious trouble.'

Keith Wood first played international rugby for Ireland in 1994, on their tour against Australia in Brisbane and Sydney. But he had sat on the bench back in 1992. What were the main differences about the game nowadays? 'Since then, the game has changed extraordinarily. For a start, there is nil space at international level. Perhaps that is why I love looking back to your era, Gareth. The rugby was scintillating. Of course, it is trite to compare eras, that just doesn't work. There was time and space then in which players could operate. Today, I suppose the biggest change in the game would be in organised defence. And of course, fitness levels then were nowhere near what they are today.'

I know you can't look back and compare like with like. But were there, I wondered, aspects of the modern game which Wood thought had gone too far?

'I don't like all these substitutes coming on the field. For me, it is against the spirit of any sport. If you work for sixty minutes to overcome your opponent, you work your guts out. And you can get on top of him. But your "reward" for that now in the modern game is to see three big puppies come trotting on to take the places of the front row your opponents started with. It's like having a heavyweight fight and after ten rounds with just two left, your opponent goes out and a new guy comes in to take you on. That is unfair and I am very definite in my views about this. Suddenly, you are confronted by a fresh, whole new front row who may be just as good as the trio who have been taken off. If everyone can do it, then it's perhaps justified but countries like Ireland could not remove all their first-choice players and have exactly the same strength replace them. So we're working at a disadvantage. This law is just not right.'

I think this is a very valid point. I was reluctant to see substitutes allowed for non-injured players and of course now that you have this system, everyone wants to steal a march. Substitutes were first allowed during my playing career, 1969 it was. I remember Barry John broke his collarbone during the British Lions tour of South Africa but you didn't have substitutes in their rugby gear on the touchline, ready to peel off a tracksuit and just come on. Mike

Gibson of Ireland had to sit in the stand in his Lions blazer and trousers, complete with white shirt and tie, and then go down to await the medical verdict of the doctor as to whether the injured player could continue. If he couldn't, the doctor told the replacement player he was allowed to change. That was the beginning of it, but by the 1974 Lions tour again in South Africa, the substitutes were already in their playing gear and ready to go on much sooner. But they could only come on if an injured player was unable to continue.

A little smile then lit up Keith's face. Sometimes, he said, it was hard to say when that had happened, wasn't it?

He was right. I remember in one match France played, against England at Twickenham, one of their forwards who was being overwhelmed in the line-outs suddenly found he had a terrible leg injury and he went straight off. The match was only about twenty minutes old! The replacement was far better and that changed the whole game. It was a cynical act.

Keith wondered how you could get around that. But he had an idea. 'My ideal would be to have maybe one utility player on the bench for the backs and one for the forwards. For a start, you would get better footballers, more capable players. But the system as it is at present discriminates against countries without huge reserves of back-up talent. Sides like England, Australia or New Zealand who have loads of talent can have six or seven world-class subs. By contrast, countries like Ireland, Scotland and Wales don't enjoy that same strength in depth so we get penalised by the system. It is unfair.'

Of course, Keith Wood is renowned as one of the greatest hookers in world rugby, if not even the best. He gives his all in the tough exchanges up front, hammering into the rival front row at set scrummages, and working hard on ensuring his delivery of the ball into the line-outs is as accurate as possible. The latter has become one of the key areas of the game and no hooker can afford literally to throw the ball away to the opposition. But Keith's work doesn't finish there. He is one of the best forwards in open play, fast, committed and with good handling skills. At times, he resembles more a breakaway forward than a hooker, but he contributes so much to the team effort, as a general player and talisman, that you sometimes wonder where Ireland would be without him. What were

9

his views on his position as it relates to the modern game? Did he go on the field as a hooker or as a player?

'You still have to have your basics. I remember one wizened old Irish forward giving me some advice years ago to the effect that I should not stay out in the backs, I could hide in the rucks! You can imagine my retort. Because, if the ball is won, there is no point still being in among the pack. If it has gone and you are good at sport and can contribute in open play, you should utilise that ability. It is OK to concentrate on the prime functions of being a hooker in the first phases – scrum and line-out. But I don't think it's a good idea to have eight ball carriers in the forwards – you need four specialist ball winners and four grafters.'

I myself have some major concerns about the modern game. Firstly, was it better for most clubs to become professional? I think it's a good question. There has been a price to pay all round. But has it raised standards? I am not so sure it has. It has raised the competitive streak and produced sides that are more difficult to beat. But I'm not at all convinced it has produced more skilful sides or a game that is necessarily better. It's certainly faster, but better? I don't think so. I look at quite a lot of rugby and I can honestly say that some skills have not improved at all. A lot of the passing and kicking isn't as good as it was years ago. People are only developing skills which are relevant to the modern game, like forwards making far better use of the ball. But when you compare the passing and kicking of the backs today with those players of yesteryear we so admired – people like Mike Gibson, David Hewett, Jo Maso, André Boniface, Jeff Butterfield, Cliff Morgan, Ken Jones, Gerald Davies, Tony O'Reilly, Pierre Villepreux, Ollie Campbell, John Rutherford and so many more – well, what you see today just isn't as good. It's as simple as that. Another weakness is that even at the highest level, some players cannot assess a situation at all. They don't 'read' a game particularly well and when it comes to decision making, it isn't anything like what it was. By and large, players have lost the skill of being able to think quickly for themselves. I might add that there is also a widespread failure to do the basics properly, such as running, passing, tackling and handling the ball.

Another concern of mine is that there seems to be a risk of losing one of the basic principles of rugby: being a game for all shapes and sizes. Has this concept not been seriously undermined by changes allowed by the IRB (International Rugby Board)? Because my fear is that we are developing a game like rugby league but played by fifteen guys. Some people believe the southern hemisphere countries are driving this type of game and maybe the IRB is being strongly influenced by those southern hemisphere nations. I questioned Vernon Pugh, Chairman of the IRB, who told me, 'We have a key document called a Charter of the Game which sets out the principles by which the IRB thinks the game should be played. It should be a game for all shapes and sizes, even at the top level. All the Unions buy into that but how they interpret it is a bit different. It's not even a northern/southern hemisphere split. Put in its most basic form, there is a school of thought that the most important thing is what they call the "product" and it's something lots of people will find very easy to understand, will want to watch, and therefore TV people and sponsors will pay huge amounts of money to the Unions. So the product therefore goes down to the lowest common denominator: continuity. But others believe it is rugby as a complex game of checks and balances, and a fair contest for the ball, that should define what the product is and believe that people will still find it fascinating and interesting, it will attract the audiences, and the broadcasters and sponsors will buy it.

'My view is that we don't need to change our game much if at all because it is already a very attractive one. People bought into rugby not for how it might look on TV in the future but because it was already a great team game and spectacle, and for the other things it offered. It is a terrific sport and a game with a very good social benefit. It is drug free, classless, and its players have respect for referees, things like that. It offers something different. OK, you have to make some changes but you don't sell your soul to get another 10,000 people tuning in to watch it on TV. What is more important – getting another 10,000 watching on TV or another 5000 playing the game? I know what is more important to me.'

That is all well and good. But I persisted with the point. 'But when you see these teams lined up opposite each other are you satisfied this is where you want to see the game going? Are you concerned?' I asked.

'Personally, I find the athleticism and skill of the modern players generally, of all shapes and sizes, very exciting. You were one of the early ones who was supremely fit as a player and an athlete but now almost everybody at the top level is. The best players are all fantastic athletes. Having said that, I accept we are starting to lose the shape of the game and, by not having enough commitment to aspects of the play which require and encourage players to involve in phases that leave space elsewhere, I agree we are in danger of becoming like rugby league. For example, by allowing people to go to ground not only in the tackle but also with the near certainty of retaining possession and so the opposing players hang off, yes, we are more like rugby league. All I can say is it has been a huge debate in the International Board for three years. In my view, we are still at some risk of having a game that doesn't have enough midfield space and therefore not being recognisable as different from rugby league.'

Could Pugh therefore see the two games merging? 'I don't think so. The line-out is still fundamental to rugby union and referees have also got better and have helped to make it more of a contest for possession. The uniqueness of rugby union has been the different ways in which defence can be broken down, giving scope for ingenuity and individual talent to create the unexpected.

'I would say there has been a fault within the IRB in that we haven't been strong enough to ensure the laws are always complied with. It is partly our fault that now a number of coaches take the safety-first option, making sure they just don't lose a game, but I think this is starting to change.'

Was he concerned the game was getting so complex most people couldn't understand it? No, he said. He felt the tackle law had always been a problem area. He went on: 'At the moment, we have probably not got it right but the game is evolving in this respect. We need to make the tackle even more contestable and increase the benefits of mauling and rucking – of concentrated unit play and space being left for the outside players. The maul was partly addressed with an amendment to the law at the start of the new northern hemisphere season in September 2001. We are trying to ensure release of the ball by the tackled player and stopping the third man going to ground. There has to be encouragement for players to pass before being tackled and to stay on their feet.

'One thing I feel about rugby union is that it is a game played and coached by clever people. Therefore, it is only a matter of time before a bright coach finds a way of breaking tight defences, even within the present laws framework.'

Well, I thought to myself, we do have the grubber kick and that has always put defences under pressure because they have to turn and defend. Vernon's view was that if people used their skills and tried various ways, they would always come up with something that would prevent the game becoming predictable, which appeared to be the case to a certain degree. My opinion is that it is a thin dividing line between constantly mucking around with the laws, which creates all manner of difficulties and potential confusion and misunderstanding, and doing nothing about elements of the game which clearly need addressing. It isn't easy and I don't pretend it will be in the future, either. It's just important that the IRB are constantly on top of situations and that they are pro-active, rather than reactive.

I was keen to get the views of others on this matter. Phil Larder, the former rugby league coach who now organises the defensive work for Leicester, England and the British Lions, said, 'As for the differences between rugby league and rugby union, players have immensely different body shapes and mobility. Take the Leicester front row. You don't get anybody in league like that! But that's one of the beauties of union – it is for all shapes and sizes. Scrummaging and line-outs are vital parts of the union game and that won't change. That's why the two sports will never come together, they're too different. But at international level the union guys are on the same kind of programme as the league boys. I thought it would take union some time to catch up in terms of strength and power but the game is there now. You only had to look at the size of people in the 2001 Lions squad to see that.'

Well, as for Phil's belief that the two will never merge, I'm not so sure. You never know what the future holds. But I agree with Phil – the importance of union is that it is a game for all body types. That is why the game is so different. I asked the question in my last book: 'Will rugby union get rid of line-outs?' The answer is I am not convinced it won't change. It is a question of how far will anybody want to go to make the game attractive. Who can say never? When I played rugby, everybody said the game would never go professional. But the demands of my time had changed dramatically from when I started to when I finished. It became an embarrassment for everyone to ask their employer for even more time off. So beware, things do change and quickly. We only have to look at this intense focus upon defence in rugby union today to see that. Was that, I asked with a twinkle in my eye, down to the influence of the league boys in our midst? Has that influence changed the face of rugby union already? Larder argued it was like saying they wouldn't work to improve kicking skills and technique because Jonny Wilkinson would kick too many goals. The game had to progress, he felt, and therefore every aspect of it had to be developed as far as it could be. Otherwise, the northern hemisphere nations would be left behind the southern hemisphere countries, because there was no doubt they would progress.

And what of Keith Wood? Did he share my concerns? 'Yes, I do but I think we need to be flexible. The guy who took your Welsh No. 9 shirt, Gareth, after you had retired was Terry Holmes who was 6ft 1in tall, which was regarded as big for a scrum half. The majority of No. 9s are short and, as for hookers, they will always be like they are. So I don't know that you can lay down hard and fast rules for playing in certain positions. But I agree the game needs to go on offering positions for players of very different shapes and sizes.

'Scrummaging is not as hard now as it has been and it is infinitely safer because of the law which requires players to bind higher. For me, safety aspects have to be paramount in that debate. I know all about the potential dangers of scrums. I once dislocated my shoulder when a scrum collapsed largely because of bad scrummaging by my tight-head prop. Rugby is also infinitely cleaner now than it once was. There is very little punching. With every passing year it gets cleaner which is fantastic for the game in general. But some aspects of the game have almost gone, and I dislike that. For example, I am a huge fan of rucking and I still believe it would tidy up the biggest problem: namely, players lying all over the loose ball on the ground to stop a side winning quick ball and releasing their backs. A player doing that is guilty of cynicism in my view but still far too many do it. The trouble is some referees think rucking means kicking. I got penalised this season for shoeing a guy but I said to the referee, "He was in my way, directly preventing my team winning fast ball. He was guilty of gamesmanship." Yet I was the one who got penalised. Allowing proper rucking would make the game an awful lot better.'

From my point of view, I think another problem is that there are too few players in the tackle area which clutters up the rest of the field. But as for rucking, Otago of New Zealand were the best side I ever played against. I remember being caught on the wrong side of a ruck a few times and got rucked out of the back. It was a hard physical match and I finished the game covered in weals and cuts. But it wasn't dirty, just hard.

Keith acknowledged the difference. 'I think that is all acceptable and it gets rid of the frustration of the players if a guy who has been lying all over the ball to kill it is seen being rucked out of the play legally. You don't want players being kicked, that is excessive. But fair rucking is legal and should be allowed by all referees. I know that the change in attitude to rucking has affected New Zealand rugby badly. It's upset their game. The trouble is, for every single ruck, there are seven or eight potential indiscretions which makes it very hard to put rucking into your game plan. But when we played England and Neil Back, their wing forward, was lying on the ball, we shoed him off it and the referee allowed it. But I have to say that is not a majority view of referees. Most referees are under such pressure that they are becoming increasingly pedantic. It is very difficult for them and I fear rucking will happen less and less now.'

I asked Keith, would he think about taking up refereeing when he retired?

He gave me a little quizzical look, as if to say: what a curious notion. His reply was clear. 'Not at all. After playing at this level you need to get away from the game for four or five years when you retire. So the chances of taking it up after that sort of break are virtually nil. I can't see many ex-professional players taking it up for that reason. I reckon by the time you retire, you will feel you have been eating, sleeping and drinking rugby for years and you want to do something different for a period of time.' Which is rather what happened in my case and, like a lot of others, I then returned to the game after a gap away and began to do things to help put something back. I'm sure Keith will be just the same.

Certainly by the time Keith finishes, he is going to need a good long rest from physical activity because his body will have taken and inflicted so much punishment. What were his views on the physical element of the game? I particularly sought his thoughts on the area of the forward game where you see huge forwards accelerating towards a ruck to take out guys hanging around the fringes. It is called 'clearing out the opposition' and in some cases where opponents may be trying to prevent quick release of the ball, they do need getting out of the way. All the same, it is a pretty fearsome sight when you see guys of 6ft 7ins and around 18 stone hitting someone at full speed. *You* shudder, so what happens to the guy who has been involved in the collision, heaven knows. I get terribly afraid when I see those guys standing at the back or sides of rucks and mauls and suddenly someone hits them from nowhere to clear them out of the way. There is a lot of taking people out and if a player is hit very hard without any warning, it has to be dangerous even if the challenge is technically legal. Was that a concern to Keith?

'My view is that if you turn your back to the opposition at a ruck or maul – even for half a second – you are being lazy and deserve what you get. It is dangerous if you are not attached to the ruck but if you are, you can usually see people coming. But I accept, you need to have tough kidneys if you play rugby today. It's hard but I don't believe it is too physical.'

'Can you play a week later, even after the hardest games?'

'You can, yes, but the problem is you are not getting enough time to recover. Also, you need two and a half months' training in the summer to be properly ready for a season but we rarely get that because of overseas tours. People don't factor in tours to this equation, they seem to forget them. We also need one month's rest, as a holiday. I think you need to have four weeks total down-time after a tour or at the start of the summer, to refresh yourself. Then you want two and a half months for preparatory training for the new season. Certainly, you need a big gap in playing during the off-season. If you could train for seven weeks with even just three weeks off, you would be pretty happy with that kind of summer arrangement.'

Mind you, I thought to myself, it was all a bit different to the sort of training my old front-row pals from the Pontypool club were used to. Never mind the fitness assessment and seven weeks building up to a season. The summers then were just a better chance to have a few more quiet pints in peace, without having to worry about being on the training ground next day. What dreadful days those old amateur days were!

By the time Keith Wood got home from the 2001 Lions tour, July was coming to its final days and already the Lions' club colleagues had been hard at work in pre-season training with the London club Harlequins. At a time when the international stars should have been with them, they were in fact trying to come to terms with a season that had been going on for almost exactly twelve months solid, when you add on pre-season training. Which brought us on to the number of matches the top guys are playing and the demands this made upon them. What would be a realistic number of matches in a season?

'Thirty-two is about right, providing you get a proper off-season. I played twenty-six or twenty-seven last season but I missed quite a few through injury,' said Keith. 'I know one thing – players' careers will be much shorter if they keep playing forty or fifty matches a season. And that would be very sad. What was it Martin Johnson played a couple of years back – fifty-four in a season? Madness. If you play about thirty games a season your body can take it. It's not easy, but you can live with that. Many more becomes difficult. One area they should cut back on is internationals – we play too many. The Six Nations is a great competition and the buzz it creates is fantastic. Other countries in the southern hemisphere are jealous of it and I can see why. But on top of those five internationals in the New Year, we should play only two summer internationals and two more in the autumn, not three. Nine in total is right, not too bad. Any more and the players start to suffer. When you get some countries playing twelve to fifteen internationals in a twelve-month spell, which has happened quite recently to a few nations, it gets ridiculous. For every international, it is an extraordinarily special feeling for a player to pull on his international jersey. Nothing should be done to weaken that effect.'

Wood's words reminded me just how special it always felt to me, too. I agree with him – nothing should be done that would imperil that special feeling. But what about the plan to condense the Six Nations into a shorter span of the season? Wales rejected it but France and England were very keen on the idea when it was first raised last season.

Wood had very strong opinions on this one. 'To play the Six Nations every weekend will again be very biased against the smaller nations. If they were to lose their best players through injury, they would not be able to replace them in time. Countries with great strength in reserve like England and France could easily. Therefore, these countries would dominate the tournament every year. Also, you need a week to train and time to refuel the tanks after an international. To have them one after another will be too much.'

I am sure that we have made too many decisions 'on the hoof' in rugby since it went professional. There has been insufficient attention to thinking through the implications of momentous decisions. Many have been rushed and later regretted. So I believe the debate should continue on this one. But I see Keith's point clearly and, if what he says did occur, that countries like England and France dominated the tournament because of their superior playing numbers, then that would hardly benefit the future of this wonderful event.

There were a few other issues I wanted to raise with our man before the end of the conversation. One was the question of overseas players coming into domestic rugby and Keith felt that in England, anyway, there were too many imported players and it needed sorting out. You would always have a couple of Irish, a few French and Welsh, that sort of thing, he said. But some clubs had filled their side with Australians, Argentinians, Samoans, Frenchmen etc. That, he felt, was too much and I agreed, although I continue to insist that a few 'outsiders' are very good for a club because it gives them another perspective.

'Some clubs are better than others. Harlequins have a lot of English qualified guys and that is right. Ideally, I would restrict it to two or three non-English qualified guys but of course under the European laws now, I don't believe that is possible. Talking of Europe, some of the European Cup matches have been absolutely brilliant. So much so that the English League has looked a tad tired this year.'

'What about a European League, would you like to see that happen?'

'No, I don't think so because I think the Heineken Cup is good enough and there is enough rugby being played anyway. I totally disagree with the Celtic League in its present form. There are too many matches. It's fine if the international players don't have to play every week but people rightly want to see them and that adds up to too much rugby.'

But what about the game in general? Wasn't it true that 95 per cent of the sport wanted to return to amateurism and should be allowed to do so without further delay?

Keith absolutely agreed. 'The only professional teams should be your international side, and provincial or top club teams. The rest should all be amateur. Where you are asking guys to dedicate themselves to fitness and preparation, it's only right and fair that they get paid. But most of the game isn't like that and never will be. When the game went professional, suddenly players started getting paid even at the smaller clubs. But it led to a lot of unease because what about the guy who wheeled a machine up and down the pitch to mark it out before each match? He was getting nothing but some players were being paid. And you could say why doesn't the tea lady get paid, too?

'It is important to remember that the great strength of rugby clubs was in the community spirit. That was the entire gelling factor of the game. Everybody was even, they were all in it together. The doctor and the docker could play rugby together. I believe that with *that* gone we have lost some of that community spirit.'

Keith and myself sing from exactly the same hymn sheet in that respect. Lots of people I speak to want to see this happen so that most junior clubs abandon any form of professionalism. He reminded me that it is happening in Ireland already but they are doing it step by step.

I asked him who were his favourite players. He thought about it for a moment and then came up with something unexpected.

'Maybe it's a strange choice but the ex-France and Harlequins flank forward Laurent Cabannes was always a guy I admired. He had something – I don't quite know what it was – that I certainly never had as a skill. He was wheelchair bound in the early 1990s after breaking his shoulder or arm in a car crash and suffering other injuries. I remember when he joined Harlequins, we played in one match in which he hit the ball at pace as he took it and his hands almost seemed to hit the ball faster than his body was moving. Sounds daft, maybe, and I couldn't figure it out, then or now. But I remember thinking to myself when I saw it happen in the middle of the pitch "Gee, I could never do that." In real time, it was something special.

'As a player, I also like Robert Howley of Cardiff and Wales. He is extremely talented. He has probably the best pass of all the No. 9s in the modern game. He also has great gas and interests the back row. They have to wait to see if he is going to break on his own so there is more room for those outside him.'

And finally, what of the young ones who have come to the game in recent times and are starting to understand all about its great attractions, its charms and its traditions? What advice would he give to young players today? Would he want his son to play the game?

He smiled, for Keith Wood seldom does not have a nice smile upon his face. 'I would. But I would not limit it to rugby. I played everything as a young fellow – hurling, Gaelic football, soccer, rugby, tennis . . . whatever was going. Even show jumping. I remember jumping over ten fences in the garden one day – you just did what was on TV! If you play several other sports, you develop a much better hand-eye coordination.'

And that, you could just say, is a useful quality in the land where Guinness was invented!

CHAPTER 2

The Old Players' View

You just can't please some people. The date was Monday 20 January 1975 and a young rugby player named Graham Price had just walked into the dressing-room at his club, Pontypool, for the regular Monday evening training session.

Graham, or 'Pricey' as he was known by the time he had earned the last of his forty-one caps for Wales in 1983, had just spent one of the great weekends of his life. Not only had he won his first cap for Wales in 1975, against France at the Parc des Princes, Paris, but Wales had finished winners by 25–10. Better still, Graham had scored an unbelievable try for a prop forward, booting the ball downfield and winning the race for the touchdown after a chase of 70 yards or more. I should know, I was some way back downfield puffing in a vain attempt to keep up with this marauding prop forward.

You couldn't have asked much more than that from a new cap, especially as he'd more than held his own against one of those traditional grizzled French front rows. But if Pricey thought there'd be back-slapping and cheers of encouragement once he got home to Pontypool Park, he could think again.

Pontypool in those days were coached by one of the legends of Welsh rugby, Ray Prosser, a man, as someone once said, who made nails seem as soft as butter. 'Pross' as everyone called him, had been a real hard nut in his playing days, and he was good enough not only to play twenty-two times for Wales between 1956 and 1961 but also to go on the 1959 British Lions tour of New Zealand. This man could play and he could speak from experience.

The locals up at Pontypool Park joked that if 'Ponty' scored more than three tries in a game, Pross would have them in for extra, gruelling training the next day as a punishment for spreading the ball too far from his beloved pack. To Pross, the game began and ended up front, and the backs were there either to kick for position so that the pack could get hold of the ball again, or just turn it back inside and make their tackles. Woe betide any three-quarter who missed a tackle there, too.

Anyway, Pricey had no sooner got into the dressing-room that evening, than someone joked about his try. Alas, Ray Prosser was standing beside him. 'Pooh,' said Ray, 'that prop you were marking must have been bloody useless, if you had all that energy left to run around the field.'

But things were different then. Take Bobby Windsor's experience when he got home from the 1974 British Lions tour of South Africa, a trip on which he played so well he even kept out of the Test side the supposed No. 1 hooker, Ken Kennedy. Bobby remembers it all vividly. 'We weren't even known then, really. When I got back in 1974, I sat in my house and thought "Right, I'm going down the pub for a pint of Welsh bitter." When I walked into the pub, the landlord said, "Hullo, haven't seen you for some time – where have you been?" '

Bobby used to work at the local steel mill, a regime of starts at the crack of dawn on winter mornings when your body froze the minute you left your house. 'Aye, I used to go to work every day on the push-bike and it was freezing at six o'clock on winter mornings. Then one day I got a call at home from someone called Brian Lewis at Howell's garage. He said he wanted me to go down to Cardiff but I said I couldn't see the point, I didn't have any money for a car. Luxuries like that were unheard of in my life then. He said, "Well, it's to your advantage" so off I went.

'When I got there, he said they'd heard I was going to work on a push-bike and they didn't want a Welsh rugby international doing that, so they were giving me a car, rent free, to drive. So I got into this new Allegro and drove it home pleased as Punch. I'd never even been in a new car before, never mind owned one. I drove round the estate like a dog with two you-know-whats.

'A week later, I had a phone call from Bill Clements, secretary of the WRU. "We hear you have been given a new car," he said. "Give

22

it back tomorrow or you'll be a professional." And that was the end of my new car.

'So when I hear the boys today moaning about their lot and saying they have it tough as they climb into their sponsored, air-conditioned, leather-seated Mercedes or BMW, I think they should open their eyes.'

But if that was the end of Bobby's new car, it wasn't the end of the legend of the Pontypool boys. Theirs has remained a rich part of folklore that I suspect will still be intact when we're all playing matches in the next world (and Wales are again beating England almost every time they meet, just like the good old days?).

Windsor was the first of the trio (of Pricey, 'Charlie' and himself) to make the senior Welsh team, his first cap coming against Australia in 1973 at Cardiff. Not a bad match to begin with, either – Wales won 24–0! Curiously, 'The Duke' as Bobby came to be known – as in the Duke of Windsor – did exactly as Pricey was to do two years later – he scored a try on his debut for Wales. Tony Faulkner, or 'Charlie' as he was to his closest friends, was not to be outdone, getting one of the four tries Wales scored against Ireland in their 32–4 victory in Cardiff which wrapped up that season and made Wales Five Nations Champions.

'Charlie' Faulkner, like Pricey, also made his debut for Wales in the match against France in Paris, 1975. He had seen thirty for the last time and kept his exact age as close a secret as his private bank balance! For his debut, Faulkner offered his birthdate as 27 February 1945 but a few years later it had been altered to 1943. And that was as far as 'Charlie' was prepared to go.

By the time the trio first played together for Wales in that match in Paris in 1975, I was winning my thirtieth cap and was the most experienced player in the team. Not that that ever fazed Bobby and his pals. I could sense from the start that here were some special people, rich characters who also happened to know the front-row business from their eyebrows down to their toenails.

Perhaps Clem Thomas and Geoff Nicholson, those late great Welshmen, summed up the Ponty boys best, when they wrote in their book *Welsh Rugby, the Crowning Years*, published in 1980 by Collins, London:

To the Welsh public they were like the three musketeers,

intensely loyal to each other, to Pontypool and to Wales – and probably in that order. When occasionally Charlie for any reason was out of the side they grieved with him and then consoled him and each other, and whenever he re-emerged as when he flew out as a replacement for the Lions in 1977, the other two were as overjoyed as puppies who had found a lost member of their litter.

Over the years, I have continued to admire the boys. Pricey went on playing for years, for a variety of teams, and still pulling his opposing loose head all over the scrum. 'Charlie' went into coaching, worked at Cardiff and then was involved at Caerphilly. Bobby set himself up in his own business and has done well through his own hard labours. I've always enjoyed their company whenever we've got together and I don't believe that will ever change. For me, they are special people, every one of them.

Bobby Windsor, as always, has plenty of thoughts on rugby, past and present. 'Take Wales. If the last Welsh coach, Kevin Bowring, had been given the support by the Union they gave that fellow Graham Henry, he would have been a great success. He was as good as anybody and look what happened in autumn 2001. England appointed Bowring to their coaching ranks as "Head of Elite Coaching" because they said he was far and away the outstanding candidate. I think Kevin Bowring would have been a great coach if he'd been given any support by the WRU.

'I felt the nation was disgraced by having players who weren't eligible to play for Wales. Henry wanted to bring over South African players at eighteen to qualify by residence after three years here. Thank God that was stopped.

'Henry made his name coaching an Auckland team that had twenty All Blacks. It wasn't too difficult to be successful with that lot to choose from every week. How on earth could he have been chosen as Lions coach? The England side put nearly fifty points on Wales, in Cardiff, and the Lions selectors go and choose the Welsh coach. Why? The selectors went for a poorer option and the Lions suffered. Not clever. But there were plenty of other people. What about Gareth Jenkins of Llanelli?

'Then Henry persuades the WRU to spend £2 million bringing

Iestyn Harris down to Wales from rugby league. Yet they're already £47 million in debt.'

That's Bobby for you – always sitting on the fence, never willing to say what he really thinks! But I wondered whether there were not more sinister aspects to consider in the game, especially in Wales. For instance, have we lost our love of the game? Bobby Windsor was also wondering about that. 'Club gates have dropped and then they had 20,000 to see an international against Romania. That sums it up. The nation can't say they can't afford it. They watch in the pub and spend £20 on drinks at the bar.

'The thing I don't understand about players today is that they go on tour for six weeks and they're getting paid, which I don't mind. But they whinge and say, "Oh, it's so hard being away from our families." They complain they don't see enough of the wife, of their kids. But they're touring the world, being treated like lords and playing the game they love. They're being paid, too. But they keep moaning and complaining. I can't take that.

'Nobody says what a great life it is they've got, what a fantastic time they're having and how fortunate they are. No one. The fact is they're playing the game they love, earning great money and the missus is happy because there's £50,000 in the bank and she can order her new kitchen without even thinking about it. Was it easier for her when she had to go out and get some extra money by cleaning?

'As for seeing more of their families, we used to work from 7a.m. to 5p.m., go home and pick up our kit and go off training. Never saw the bloody missus or kids.'

Pricey, the quieter one, nodded his head in agreement. 'The players just don't seem to want to play today. I can't understand it. Look at the Barbarians. Their demise has been one of the worst things in rugby. When we played that was *the* thing – you wanted to play for the Barbarians more than anyone, apart from your country. If you couldn't get a cap for your country, that was a great honour, a Barbarians call-up. But today, the players make excuses not to play for the Barbarians. I think the trouble is they're training too much. They should cut the training in half and play more games. They're knackering themselves on the training ground.

'The year Pontypool won the Western Mail Championship and Bobby and I were playing for Wales, I think I played fifty-two

25

matches that season. The week we'd be playing for Wales, we would have to miss the midweek game for Ponty a few days before the international. Well, we hated that – we'd kick lumps out of each other up in the stand.

'After the international on a Saturday, you'd train Monday, play a midweek match Tuesday or Wednesday night, train Thursday and then Friday and you might get the bus after work up to Leicester or somewhere.'

The thing was, said Windsor, the old Pontypool players preferred to play a midweek game than train. It made you a better player, sharpened you up mentally, made you tougher physically, even though international players were targets for any headhunters playing the game in the valleys in those days. And, unlike today, you got no protection from linesmen because they weren't allowed to interfere in things like foul play in those days. 'Played for Wales, have you – beaten the bloody Frogs have you?' sort of thing. 'Well, try this one, we can clout harder than the Frogs.' You'd get a whack around your head. I knew all about this, because I had it as well. But you just got on with it.

Windsor felt there was only so much you could do on the training ground. 'And Christ, it gets boring. Maybe that's why they're all so boring as players these days,' he said. 'When we played in those midweek matches, we might play second row, back row, anywhere just to have a game. But despite all the training and practice, they're no more talented than in our day.

'We just wanted to play rugby 'cos we loved it so much. If a player today is happier sitting in the stand then there's something wrong with him, in my eyes.

'Pricey talked about our love of the game, our appetite for it and you have to say there's a huge difference today. Players like Scott Gibbs and Allan Bateman went north for the money at a time when Wales were in trouble. Then they came back for the money and yet they're so well thought of. Wales were in a bad way but that didn't stop them jumping ship because it suited them. I hope Iestyn Harris becomes a great player in rugby union and a great servant to Wales. But I'll tell you this, 1.5 to 2 million quid makes it a lot sweeter whatever happens.

'We loved the game more in our day, I'm convinced of that. Charlie Faulkner won his first cap at thirty-two and his last at thirty-six and he went to extremes to disguise his real age because he was so frightened they'd say he was too old for it. He wanted to go on and on, didn't he? Because he loved it so much.

'Then when we were finished at senior level, we played second-team rugby and you helped to bring on the youngsters that way. That doesn't happen these days. But these boys could do a great job helping kids at a lower level while they're still playing at some level. It's the natural process. They should step down and play without the pressure, for fun and to help others. But they just quit and that's it. Because money has ruined the game already.'

Money. Now there's the great issue of our time. Strictly amateur for over a hundred years, every rule and regulation regarding amateurism was suddenly thrown out of the window one afternoon in Paris, in August 1995, when the IRB declared the game 'open'. There are multitudes of people who would tell you that it's never been the same since. Did Graham Price agree?

'Money had to come but it was the way it was done. The WRU threw their hands up and said, "That's it, anyone can earn." It's killed the clubs and look at the problems it's caused.'

That is undoubtedly true. But I sensed none of the boys really wanted to spend our time talking about money and whether it had or had not ruined rugby. Because the danger is everyone would think we're just jealous of modern-day players earning a handsome living from a game which didn't pay us a penny for playing. We would all deny that to our dying breaths. We have no problem in seeing the world's best players earning a high salary, because the fact is, they're putting so much more into the game now in terms of time and commitment.

In my view, and I touched on this in my last book, money had to come into the game because the authorities opened the floodgates to it by their determination to bring in as many commercial partners as possible. They had sponsors of just about every competition played and if people thought all that money could come flowing into rugby without a penny going to the players, then I have to say they were very naïve. Life is not like that.

What interested me more was to hear the boys' views on the game itself today, especially in terms of the front-row part of it. Was it tougher now or easier, had scrummaging changed or were those solid techniques still essential for the quality front-row man?

Bobby Windsor smiled. 'People say it's harder now but I'll tell you this, when you scrummaged against France and stood back and charged at them from 10 feet away, you couldn't have been in more danger than that. There's nothing as hard about that phase of the game as when we played. In fact, it's softer now.

'When you played the French, there were no prisoners taken. The second rows were only there for pushing in the scrums and swinging punches as you front-row boys came in. 'Course, the ref couldn't see that, could 'e? You got booted, too, that was another part of the deal. But after the game they were great, good as gold.

'They say the game is much faster, but I don't believe that. You name me someone who was faster than Gerald Davies, or that French wing, Lagisquet. Christ, they could move and a lot like them. J.J. Williams in South Africa in '74 wasn't exactly a snail, either.

'Then there's the hooker's art of throwing. Today, his jumpers are lifted and they're hanging in the sky waiting for him to deliver it. We used to dread the throwing-in part of the job because it was a jungle then. You were throwing-in virtually into a space in the air. It's much easier now you have a clear target to hit.

'Something else I don't like to see is front-row players hanging around out in the centre. Before, you had to go where the ruck or maul was. If you weren't there, you were seen being slow and not getting there and the crowd and coach would be on your back. The front row had to be where the ball was. The backs threw the ball about and we had to be there when it went down. Now, though, players stay where they are, they hang around. That's why you sometimes see a lock on the wing which is bloody daft. My view is, if he's got the energy to get out that far, he's not doing his job up front.'

Which was doubtless a view formed in the Ray Prosser school of excellence. But what about the tight head's role today? How did Price view that aspect of the modern game?

'The first thing is, the scrums are a lot quicker now. They get down, the ball goes in and it's in the back row before you can blink. They get it away straightaway. When we played, we would be engaging the opposition with the ball not yet in the scrum. What that meant was, there was a lot more wrestling involved, a much longer period of strength testing and technique examining. It was better from a technical point of view because you were really tested in terms of how good you were.

'It's still very important for the tight head to do his job. You must have a square scrum and, for that, the tight head has to stop it slewing around. Today, the opposition try and wheel and if the scrum goes through 90 degrees, you lose possession. In my day I could do a lot to nullify the advantage of the other side by things like taking down my opponent very low. But nowadays it seems you just go in and push and try and chase the ball as quickly as possible.

'In terms of engagement of scrums, we three preferred it the old way where you stood back and hammered in. We collapsed plenty of scrums of course but from a lower position. Often, the scrum would collapse because you and your opponent were wrestling low down and the scrum didn't have to go far to collapse. Today, when it collapses, it does so from a greater height which is more dangerous in my view because players don't take it low by wrestling each other so much.

'Another thing that's very different is that non front-row men are not allowed to play in the front row. We used to have all sorts of players moved up into the front row if we had an injury. A flanker or lock might come up a row.

'Generally, though, if you saw someone tall lined up against you at prop, you'd rub your hands. You knew you'd give him a roasting because a big man is easy to handle. When you saw a small guy, that was the danger. A player like Ben Evans of Swansea and Wales would have been a dream for us, because you can get under him. I saw Matthew Madden of Llanelli destroy Evans in one match and I wasn't surprised.'

I wondered whether that kind of front-row duel had been eliminated or whether it was still important.

Charlie Faulkner felt that it was still vital. 'It's no good working with the backs on fancy moves if you're not winning the ball for them. Do the basics properly and everything else follows.

'Today, though, props don't seem to mind losing their battle in the forwards. It doesn't seem to bother them if they're getting a stuffing in the tight as long as they can run around in the loose. That's ridiculous for a tight forward. I can't understand that. To us, it was pride in bettering your opponent in the tight scrums. You wore him down and defeated him, or he did to you. If we were having trouble in the scrum you didn't run after the ball. It affected you mentally if you were off the pace and not up to it in the tight.

'My view was that if I was in the scrum and I could hurt my opponent, it would affect him mentally and could damage his whole team. It's a mental thing.'

A couple of years ago, scrummaging was almost becoming passive. But I wondered if that was beginning to change and it was becoming more important again. Faulkner agreed. 'It's definitely got better, people are putting more emphasis on it now.'

Charlie smiled. 'Aye, but it became almost passive for a while in more recent years. I began to wonder whether we would just have rugby league scrums. But the laws altered a little and the props have got to bind over the top and back-row forwards can't leave the scrum before the ball is out. Those things have helped.

'Even so, I reckon they have taken the contest out of the scrum because the referee is almost in the scrum these days. I think that's bad. The worst thing in a scrum is when you are pushing the other side back and the other team drops it so you land on your neck. But all the pressure comes from behind you, which means you can't control it. The other side that have collapsed it can find a nice safe position but with the weight coming from behind you, you can't. That's the worst thing that can happen to you.'

Another thing that amazes us today about the game is how often the players are offered water. They start the match, kick-off, and the referee blows his whistle for blocking an oncoming player trying to reach the hanging kick-off.

The side goes for goal and suddenly an army of blokes come on offering bottles of water to the players. But they've only just left the dressing-room.

That reminded Graham Price of when they trained at Pontypool Park, climbing up that hill, and they'd have to do four laps of the circuit. 'We'd want a drink pretty often so we'd slip down the steps into the dressing-room and stop for a drink. Ray Prosser got so mad about it he told them to lock the dressing-room doors. He said he didn't want water wobbling around in our guts.'

This was before sports science taught us about dehydration. But what, perhaps more importantly, of the future? What did the boys feel about the kind of format for rugby in Wales in the years to come? The topic was timely because in the first two months of the new season, 2001–2002, just about every senior Welsh club had had disappointing, some said dismal, results. Cardiff, their start wrecked by injuries, had been beaten in the Heineken Cup 37–10 at French club Montferrand and by 47–32 at Glasgow; Swansea had been hammered 38–9 at Bath and lost 24–15 at Biarritz, the eventual 2002 French champions, without having scored a single try in their first four matches in Europe. Neither club went on to qualify for the Heineken Cup quarter-finals, although Llanelli did carry the Welsh flag in that competition, splendidly reaching the semi-finals before narrowly losing to Leicester. Similarly, Welsh clubs did not make much impact in the Celtic League, which was dominated by the four Irish provincial teams, Munster, Leinster, Connacht and Ulster.

Then came news that Leighton Samuel, the financial backer behind Bridgend, was threatening to pull out of the club at the end of the season, disenchanted by the reaction of supporters. Worse still, the Welsh national side was trounced 36–6 on its own ground, the Millennium Stadium, by Ireland in mid-October 2001 in a rearranged Six Nations Championship match from the previous season. And Wales went on to suffer four defeats in their five matches of the Six Nations Championship of 2002. It was hardly a happy picture. Was it therefore time that Wales was divided into provincial sides? Bobby Windsor certainly thought so.

'I'd go down the provincial route the Irish have chosen and seem to work successfully. They have four provinces and I'd do the same. There are too few clubs now in Wales and too few decent players. Create four counties with thirty players in each county squad, the same as Ireland, and you could compete. Have it run and paid for by the Union. Let the clubs stay in leagues with younger players. They'd have more room for them then to come through.

'Whatever they do, I'd hope they'd be more generous with caps than in our day. We played for Monmouthshire and the rule was you were only awarded a county cap when you'd played six matches for them. They had no money, see, so there's about 2000 players out there who all played five matches for Monmouthshire and never got to six. The county couldn't afford to shell out for a proper cap for them so they didn't pick them any more than five times. Don't think even you'd have got in six times, Gar.

'The former Swansea coach John Plumtree said the Irish players are better than ours but that's nonsense. A good county side or provincial team will always beat a club side. Always. And you could keep out the foreign players too because you'd only choose players available to play for Wales. Look at Newport now – they have so many foreign players they keep out promising young Welsh boys. That's no good for Welsh rugby. You had a prop like Ceri Jones, a good promising boy, being kept out of most of the games by Rod Snow, a Canadian, and Adrian Garvey who is a South African. Crazy. What chance have Wales got to progress with that situation? I sometimes think there are more Tongans here than in Tonga. Now their kids are having an effect on the junior age-group levels of the game in Wales, too.

'Trouble is, the young Welsh kids don't play the top matches so they know nothing really about the role, about the tricks of the trade, about how to survive and how to prosper. They just get into the scrum and push, that's all. But that's not enough at senior level. A boy should know the tricks of the trade at twenty-one. When I left school at sixteen you could play for anybody. I went and played for Newport Saracens and you'd come up against a prop who was perhaps thirty-two. He tore you inside out and it was very hard. You got booted and punched and all that. But by the time you got to twenty-one you had learned. That was how you came through and understood the business. Then you were worth looking at from the selectors' point of view.

'I was twenty-six when I won my first cap and I knew my way round the track long before then. But boys of sixteen to twenty are no longer allowed to play against blokes of thirty, so they know nothing. There's too much protection these days.'

Bobby felt that it was quality not quantity that was needed in Wales and that was how you created it. Teach youngsters in the company of good old 'uns as they start out, and teach them correctly. Might be painful at first but they would learn and benefit from it.

Charlie Faulkner said that one system that certainly wouldn't work was the idea floated in autumn 2001 that Swansea and Neath should merge for economic and other reasons. He couldn't see that at all because of the strong identities and traditions, and he wasn't alone in that view.

My view was that the main aim was to have a strong Welsh international side. So we needed a system in place that could support that. You couldn't have nine or ten clubs with forty players in each because we didn't have the players.

Windsor argued that one of the problems was that too many clubs had disbanded their Under-16s and Under-17s sides, yet they were the kids of the future. So they went off and played golf or sat in front of computers instead. They were lost to the game. But you couldn't afford to lose them at that age. Even those who did play the game in Wales had problems. There were quite a lot of Tongans now in Wales and their sons were big boys at 12. They played at Pontypool for the Under-12s and they took up a position in front of a Welsh boy of that age because they were so big already, Bobby claimed. All the teachers and coaches looked for was size, he said. That wasn't good for Welsh rugby.

I certainly feel that money going to the clubs should be spent on supporting these young age-level teams.

But what about the $64,000 question: would the boys like to play the game today?

Charlie Faulkner certainly would. 'I think it would be easier from a prop's point of view because of all sorts of factors. Referees shout "engage" whereas in our day it was the law of the jungle. Maybe it's a good thing from a safety point of view that referees control the scrums more, but it's meant much of the contest has been lost. I suppose it went over the top too often in our day. I don't know that I ever felt frightened in a scrum but I did think I had to get my blow in first in a certain situation otherwise I'd be in real trouble. When we came together and scrummaged hard, sometimes the hooker looked like he had been garrotted. You would see him lying on the ground, his eyes bulging. He often had one prop's head under his chin and another's rammed into his Adam's apple. Christ, that was tough. But now they make you scrummage straight on, you can't bore into the hooker as easily.'

Bobby had the kind of evil expression on his face that suggested memories of past appalling deeds were fresh in his mind. 'Yeah, but you can still throw a right hook. What's wrong with that?'

There's hardly any room at all nowadays to do things like that, I told him. 'You can't clout anyone, bite or knee them these days, can you?'

Charlie chipped in. 'You can, as long as you don't break the skin. You have to get the second rows to do it now. The punch coming through from underneath into the opposing front-row man's face can never be seen. We had a couple of good boys for that, especially John Perkins. But the difference is that you might go to jail for those things now.'

Punching. Now there's a lost art in the modern game. No, honestly, I'm only joking! But seriously, I have to say it is a thin dividing line between acceptable physical confrontation and a punch. And therefore, from time to time, players can stray across that line. I believe it's inevitable.

If you have ever played the game, you know what is acceptable and what's not acceptable. I can't say I ever went into a game thinking about duffing up the opposition. Yet we all knew it was a man's game and you stood toe to toe with someone if necessary. Frankly, you wonder sometimes how some blokes didn't get put in jail. They would have been if they had done in the street what they used to get up to on the field.

But you have to be realistic about punching. When you play this hard physical game you are going to get bumps and bruises and every now and then it will get out of hand. Most of the boys I played with felt that if a fist was thrown, all right, it was part of it. What is not acceptable, and never has been in my book, is either hitting someone unseen or stamping. There is a definite danger of maiming someone by those methods and I have no sympathy for players who do it and get punished.

In that respect the game is so much better today. You can't get away with such things, and rightly so. After all, there are two touch judges and a video referee watching in major games. And I say that's better for the game. I might add, as long as the touch judges are there chiefly to look for foul play and that alone: I don't agree with moves to use touch judges for other roles because you would end up having them come on to the field too much. That is absurd.

I suppose I spent the better part of twenty years standing as close as you can get to the front rows of a pack of forwards. But I still wouldn't say I knew much about what really goes on in those dark depths of the field. Mind you, I'll never forget the lesson I was given early on about the kind of physical demands put on players in the front row.

Barry [John] and I were messing about at a Welsh training session, chucking away possession the forwards had won and generally fooling about. Clive Rowlands, the coach, took so much of it and then snapped. 'Get in that front row you two and then we'll see how much messing about you do.'

All the boys behind us in the pack did was put on a mild squeeze, nothing more. But I've never felt a sensation like it. I thought my arse was going to come out through my eyes.

Windsor smiled. 'Welcome to the world of the front-row boys, Gar. When I'd had 110 stone of the French pack coming at me, with 90 stone or so of our pack crashing in behind me, I sometimes stood up from a scrum and wondered which planet I was on. I felt like I'd been caught up in a bomb blast.

'I had sixteen stitches after being bitten in an ear against France. Windsor's ear à la carte, they said. But what's also interesting about ears is that today you see hookers with cauliflower ears and that proves they haven't learned the basic techniques of the business. If you're getting cauliflower ears as a hooker, it shows you are pushing with your head and that means you are contributing only half of what you should do.

'Hookers should scrummage with their shoulders. You went into the scrum hard to split the opposing front row apart. You scrummaged with your chest and shoulders and you were far stronger for doing that. You haven't got as much power if you scrummage with your head, it stands to reason.'

As I said, I've seen front-row play from closer up than most people because of the position I played on the field. But I don't believe anyone apart from the front-row boys themselves really know what is going on in there. Take a player like Graham Price. He liked to take his opponent down as low as possible in the scrummage to nullify his ability to disrupt the opposition scrum. If you've got a guy with his eyes almost on the ground he isn't going to be able to do very much in an attacking sense. Incidentally, there is nothing illegal in what Pricey used to do; taking a scrummage low was perfectly acceptable, it was a trial of strength. But if the scrum then collapsed, who was to blame? Had Pricey pulled it down too low so that it collapsed? Or had his opponent, under severe pressure and unable to attack, decided he fancied a re-set scrum and a chance to escape that poor position, so he fell on to the turf deliberately?

So you see, how do referees begin to apportion blame? How do they know who has collapsed it? How can they say for sure who is responsible if a scrum wheels? A scrum spins round by one of two things: either the pressure on one side of the scrum is too much for one of the props and he can't prevent it wheeling. Or, the prop finds himself under heavy pressure and deliberately lets it spin right around, hoping that the referee will not give the opposition the put-in but decide the scrum must be re-set. That often happens if the scrum disintegrates. A new law now, of course, says that if a scrum wheels more than 90 degrees, the side which has fed that scrum loses the put-in at the next scrum. But you often see a referee undecided as to who is to blame, especially if the wheel has resulted in a collapse. So he re-sets the scrum and the team feeding it gets another chance. Which means a fresh opportunity to get a better foot grip, or a higher level of concentration by the whole scrummaging pack or a better lock-in position from the first engagement. All these things are factors in the equation.

Another old trick of the trade is for the tight head of the team feeding the scrum to collapse the first scrummage. He might even collapse the second one deliberately if his ruse hasn't succeeded the first time. The ruse? Well, you see referees falling for it time and time again. No sooner has the scrum collapsed on the tight-head side, especially if it is for the second time, than the referee shoots around the back of the scrum to stand right beside the tight-head prop. The scrum is re-set and, hey presto, wonder of wonders, the scrum stays nice and steady that time because the referee is watching closely. But why do it? Well, the reason is that if the referee is on the other side of the scrum, having left the side where the scrum half is feeding it, the scrum half can slip the ball into his own second-row men's feet. It is perfectly safe from penalty because a referee standing on the tight-head side cannot see accurately where the ball is fed. So the side feeding the scrum is guaranteed to protect its own ball. This is often happening in a game, especially if a side is under pressure at the scrummage. The referee's presence may intimidate the attacking loose-head prop too, so that he may not apply the intense pressure he had been doing.

If one of Bobby Windsor's pet hates about the game today is the moaning by some players, then I should admit here and now that referees dictating the way the game is being played is what drives me nuts. They are saying stay down, do this, don't go there, don't touch him. But, for example, how much do you think refs know about what goes on in the front row?

'Some are better than others but the majority of refs haven't got a clue what's happening in there,' said Faulkner. 'The WRU should get a few training sessions together with ex-props and teach the refs.'

What has also irritated Bobby is that just about every other country has utilised the expertise of successful ex-players. But the WRU never have. Yet we'd do it for nothing. Tell us where to go, which schools to go to, which referees to teach. We even suggested it a few years back, but the WRU never even replied to our letter.

'I'll tell you something that is better about the modern game,' said Faulkner. 'The law that says back-row forwards aren't allowed to break before the ball is out. It used to be that the fly half had the opposing flanker in his face just as he got the ball. You had to be good to get away from that pressure. The new law gives scrum halves and half backs in general much more room to attack. It makes the game look better. Christ, Edwards would have scored bloody hundreds of tries for Wales if that law had existed then.'

They both agreed that good fly halves saw the chances because they were thinking about the game, whereas a lot of players today don't seem to see the opportunities right in front of them.

I remember they called Dai Morris of Neath 'the shadow', because wherever I went, he was there supporting me. Today, players are criticised for going too far on their own and losing their support, but that's plain daft – it's up to the player's colleagues to be where he is and support him at the end of a break.

Charlie felt that over-coaching may be the greatest threat to the future attraction and appeal of the sport.

'Sometimes, if a move goes wide and a gap appears in the centre, instead of taking advantage of it, players still move the ball wide. They are not making decisions on the field like they used to. We're becoming regimented by the system and the coaches. Players are frightened to think for themselves and do anything different, because if it doesn't come off they'll be criticised by their coach.'

'Yes, they get told off, all right. But the bottom line is most of them haven't got the skills,' said Bobby. He believes that a change in the rules of the game, aimed at de-powering the scrummage and instigated right across the other side of the world in New Zealand, had a profound effect upon rugby in Wales and throughout the British Isles.

'When the Lions went to New Zealand in 1977, we pushed their forwards off the field. Their scrummage was so wrecked that they put only three men in the scrum and didn't try to contest them. Then, straight after that, they wanted it all changed. They said the scrummage was dangerous and needed weakening. But it was only because they'd been so exposed in that area by a Lions pack. They didn't have the players to play that tough forward game so they got the rules changed. They never said that when they had a pack of forwards like the one in the 1960s with people like Kel Tremain, Waka Nathan, Wilson Whineray, Colin Meads, Brian Lochore and Ken Grey in it. No problems for them then.'

I have to say I think Bobby is dead right. I remember watching that 1977 Lions series on TV and being staggered at what our boys did to that All Black scrum.

Bobby agreed, but reminded me about the circumstances behind that trip. 'Aye, but the fact that you didn't come on that Lions tour or the Welsh tour of Australia the following year, cost us both series. We lost the Test series in 1977 by three to one, losing in one game by four points and the other by one point. If you'd been there, we'd have turned those defeats into wins, you bugger. Then a year later in Australia, after losing the first Test, we lost the second by just two points, 19–17.'

I find this subject interesting because when the Lions won both series in 1971 in New Zealand and 1974 in South Africa, people said it had a hugely positive influence on British rugby. Then in 1977 the Lions demoralised the All Blacks up front but didn't win the series. So the influence of the 1977 tour was lost in Britain because people saw it as an unsuccessful tour, yet the New Zealanders quickly recognised its importance. They started saying scrums were dangerous and could endanger players and that youngsters would not play the game unless the scrum was weakened.

For my part, I also remember that when we beat the All Blacks in 1971 with just 40 per cent possession, they realised they had to change their approach or be left behind. And they did. They had a tonking up front in 1977 but found a way to avoid changing again. They got the laws changed. The laws of the scrummage changed irrevocably after that because much of the old aggression was removed by the banning of certain techniques and practices, such as pulling your opponent as low as possible in the scrum. To our disadvantage, of course, in the northern hemisphere, as Bobby Windsor reminded us all. But there it was. There was, however, another aspect to the modern game which Bobby thought was a huge loss and a very significant factor. We all used to play lots of soccer as kids, as well as rugby.

'Until about the age of twelve all the boys played soccer. Gareth, I know you did; Barry John did, Stevie Fenwick, Phil Bennett, even Geoff Wheel . . . most of us. Soccer is the greatest game out for developing ball skills. But now, boys can't play soccer really because they start mini rugby at about six or seven. But when I coach or watch boys playing today, I can tell within minutes the boys who have played soccer as youngsters and those that haven't. Those who have are invariably good footballers, that's the difference. And on that theme, I'd ask "What has mini rugby done for our kids?" My view is: nothing.'

I agree with Bobby about soccer. For a kid there's nothing better than having a ball and learning skills with it. They are invaluable when it comes to rugby.

The point about mini rugby is valid, too, in my view. When I used to watch my boys playing mini rugby, the two guys in charge would keep saying, 'Don't let your man go past you, mark your man' etc. It was regimented. One of them never got the ball yet he won a medal and you wondered where that exercise had got him.

Don't get me wrong, there are good people doing a lot of things for kids at that age and I applaud their efforts. But making it too structured, too regimented, is counter-productive. And if parents are over-enthusiastic and shout at their kids, that is 'the worst thing kids need at that age,' said Bobby. 'But I come back to what they actually learn from playing that stuff. I don't feel they are taught anything much.'

I go back to my long-held view that we need basic schoolmasters teaching basic skills to kids like handling, passing, tackling and kicking. Youngsters are not getting that in mini rugby and they go straight into senior rugby without having learned the basics. Many of the privileged schools still get their masters to turn out on Saturday mornings to coach kids but there is not enough of this at state school level.

'I coach Caerphilly,' said Charlie, 'and I can see they're not as fit as we were. Now, Caerphilly's players are part-time so many of them come to training after work like we used to do. But they have this attitude that they're semi-professional and therefore they don't do anything on their own to help their fitness levels. They only do what they have to do with the club.'

But we used to do something every day to help our fitness. Bobby Windsor, for instance, remembers lunchtimes at the steelworks in Newport. When he went there, Charlie used to look after him like an older brother. They took their kit to work, even though they were sweating a lot off working at the hot furnace, and they'd go to Tredegar Park at lunchtime and do a circuit.

'We did it because we had to do it to play for Pross [Ray Prosser],' said Bobby. 'He'd tell us, and he'd be right, that it's in the second half when the cracks show in your opponents if they're not as fit as you. Then in the last twenty minutes, you've gained the upper hand and you can go on to win the game. That's what superior fitness does for you.

'Prosser kept us going through scrum after scrum when we trained. We'd beg to do some other things but he'd say, "You can only do those things if you're fit enough."

'Of course, Charlie had to do the fitness work because at that age you have to train all the time, much more than a younger man. Charlie trained like a dog. He'd even go for an hour's training on a Friday before an international.'

I'll never forget one thing about Charlie. We were due to play Scotland up at Murrayfield, and we came out of the team talk where we'd discussed the Scottish pack and the two fine props they had. They were Ian McLauchlan, the 'Mighty Mouse' they called him, and Sandy Carmichael, both of them Lions in 1971.

I remember saying to Charlie it would be a tough game and all he said was, 'Gar, we may go up, we may go down but we're not going backwards.' He didn't just say it, he meant it. That was Charlie, as tough mentally as he was physically.

Are players mentally fit enough today?

'Life is too easy generally,' said Charlie. 'They're not mentally ready to play at a high level. Too many of them can't dig deep, they can't hang on in there. When we played, we had written across our minds "My job for this team is to do this first. That's my basic job."

But players today don't seem to be able to focus as hard in that way.'

And what of defeat? Does that hurt them like it did us? Windsor didn't think so.

'When we lost, and it was pretty rare especially at home I'm pleased to say, we'd have to go to the Angel because that was where the dinner was, but we'd slip through the staff entrance and go up a back stairway to avoid facing the fans. We'd feel ashamed we'd lost, no matter who it was against.

'What used to make the game so good, I'm convinced, was its offensive-defensive style of play. I mean one minute you were defending desperately then you'd snatch possession and there would be a sweeping move upfield. All right, we used to have pile-ups that needed addressing but they have got rid of that to change to another form of stagnation, namely the crashball set-up. There's nothing worse than seeing a line of three-quarters standing 5 yards apart and hammering into each other, with someone trying to plan what to do six moves ahead. The attractiveness of the game we played was that we might be under pressure for fifteen minutes but if the opportunity came to break out and go down the other end in one movement and score, we took it. You hardly ever see that today. It's just like rugby league – one side dominates the ball for six or seven moves, then they lose it through a mistake and the other lot have a go until they lose it and give it back to the first team. The game ebbed and flowed in our day. Today, it's boringly predictable.'

Charlie Faulkner referred to our brief earlier mention of the overseas players in Welsh rugby.

Bobby said that the accepted view was that Tony Brown (chief investor at Newport) was doing a great job for Welsh rugby, but he couldn't see it, because Brown was spending most of his money on foreign players and a foreign coach and he couldn't see how that was going to help Welsh rugby. It was said there were fifty-six foreign players in the Welsh Premiership at the start of the season 2001–2002 and that was far too many in Bobby's view.

Personally, I rather disagreed. I am a great believer in having a few foreign players, because I think it helps the youngsters learn. If you bring in someone like Pieter Muller, the South African at Cardiff, you see an outstanding professional. What he has done for Nicky Robinson, Cardiff's young outside half, and indeed his brother Jamie, has been immense. The real problem is that we don't have enough good players in Wales. If we could have a Cardiff squad filled only with excellent quality Welsh players we would have.

Faulkner examined further the question of how tough the game was today. 'When you look at aspects like the line-out, it has become a sissies' game, they stand so far apart. You can't touch the player catching the ball.' The trouble is the law-makers are scared about law suits from someone getting injured. They've weakened the game in so many areas, but especially the scrummage by introducing aspects such as the shoulders of each player in the front row not being lower than the hips, and forming up from close range, rather than standing back and charging from 10 yards or more. But perhaps that was unavoidable.'

I think anyone who saw the era in which we played would say there were some fine players. But I firmly believe there are some great players in the modern game, too. The boys agreed with me on that one. So, I asked them, who do you most admire?

Bobby thought that Austin Healey of England was a great little player. 'You could play him anywhere. He's a footballer. He also reads the game – sees a gap and he goes for it. He looks like a former soccer player to me. I always say a failed footballer makes the best rugby player. He's an outstanding talent.' So too, he thought, were Fabien Galthie of France and the French wing Aurélien Rougerie.

Charlie Faulkner felt that Keith Wood was out on his own. 'He would have been tremendous in any era because he does his tight work and is also a great contributor outside the scrum. He is the best of the lot, a one-off.

'From our earlier era, Colin Deans of Scotland was a great player. I reckon we saved his career, too.

'We had played for Wales in a Five Nations international and won several tight heads. The Scottish coach was talking to us at the evening dinner and said he'd been bitterly disappointed with Deans who was too small and would probably be dropped. We told him he was mad. We said Deans was a terrific player, very quick around the field, but his pack hadn't stuck with him that day and his props hadn't helped him either. We noticed next time we played the Scots, Deans was still in but the props had changed.'

Bobby Windsor remembered a story about the time the boys'

willingness to play for an invitation side had nearly rebounded on them. Mind you, he had a glint in his eye when he told the story so I don't know whether we should shed too many tears for them.

'Charlie, Pricey and myself were asked to go up to Oxford and play for Major Stanley's XV against the University one autumn. We asked about expenses and they said what do you want to claim? We said we'd have petrol costs and they allowed us to charge for a meal, too. So we agreed on £25 each.

'Anyway, when we got to the next Welsh squad session, Keith Rowlands, one of Welsh rugby's bigwigs, called us into his office. "You've done it now – you've professionalised yourselves," he said. "Did you claim £25 expenses each to play at Oxford?" We said it was true. "Well, I know that the three of you all went in one car."

'We denied it, and they eventually accepted our explanation. In fact, Pricey had gone from a college somewhere, I'd gone from somewhere else and Charlie met us up there.

'We did a bit of homework on this, and the name of a certain player was mentioned to us as the one who'd allegedly shopped us. He turned out to be a Scottish international forward. So when we next played Scotland, we made him our no. 1 target. We zipped him up nicely with some fancy bootwork and fair do's to him, he was a good man and took it, so we didn't have any argy-bargy.

'Anyway, at the dinner that night, he came in with the stitches in his head and he came up to us to talk. "I can understand what you have done and why you did it. The only trouble is the one you want is my brother." We replied weakly, "Come and have a drink." '

Bobby also remembered the story about the flight out to South Africa with the 1974 Lions. 'I'm never likely to forget it,' he said. 'I had this prawn cocktail at the airport in London before we left. I didn't like flying, made me very nervous. So I was sitting on the plane next to J.P.R. Williams and we started having a few drinks. After an hour or two's drinking, I started sweating like hell and I couldn't move. I was burning hot, too, a terrible heat. By this time, JPR had fallen asleep and was woken up urgently by a worried stewardess who took one look at me and didn't like what she saw.

'JPR's reply was that of a great team mate: "Give 'im another beer," he said, before going back to sleep. Well, there was another doctor on the plane, Ken Kennedy, our Irish hooker. He eventually came up to see me but by then the stewardess was so worried at my raging hot body, she gave me two chunks of ice and put them in my mouth. I was lying down almost unconscious by this time and Kennedy put this thermometer or whatever it was in my mouth. I didn't know anything much about it, I was in a bad way. But when they pulled it out and the stewardess asked how I was, Kennedy looked at the thing and said, "Well, according to this, the bugger's dead." He didn't know I had a mouth full of ice.

'Anyway, we eventually got to Johannesburg and I was carried off the back of the plane on a stretcher by two black blokes and put into an ambulance to go to hospital. It turned out I had a very severe case of gastroenteritis. What happened next was like a scene from the Keystone Kops. Every time the driver slammed on his brakes, I shot down one end of the ambulance on the plastic sheet on which I was lying. Whenever he accelerated, I went flying up the other end and banged into the partition wall behind me.

'When I got to hospital, I got no bloody sympathy. Some doctor turned up and grinned: "You've got 'Bok fever – it's fear of what our boys are going to do to you." Wasn't much of a bloody prophet, was he? [The Lions were to beat the Springboks 3–0 in the Test series.]

'Anyway, I had to have a jab every four hours and I lost between one and two stones in weight in five days. And when they took the red Lions T-shirt I was wearing off me, I was covered in red, because the red dye had come off as I sweated.'

I also remember I was sharing a room with Bobby at some point during our tour, when we went to a game reserve for a few days' break. It was late, I was trying to sleep and Bobby was reading his wretched book. I said, 'For Christ's sake, put that light out, Bobby.' He put it out and I drifted off to sleep. It must have been not long after, I was woken by a terrible bloodcurdling scream, shouting and a crashing of furniture. I sat bolt upright in bed wondering what the hell was going on. All I could hear was Bobby shouting, cursing and swearing. When I opened my eyes, there he was, completely naked, kicking something around the room like a man demented. I said, 'What the hell are you doing?'

He said, 'I went to the bathroom with the light still off and on the way back I put my foot on something that was thin and long. I thought it was a snake.'

When the light went on, we looked at what he'd kicked the shit

44

out of. The fluffy Lions mascot was in a shocking state. He'd stepped on its tail!

You never knew what to expect with Bobby Windsor. We were sitting having a cup of tea one day in the week before a Welsh international and talking about one thing and another. He said, 'Just the other day, I was down in the steelworks and I saw this little sparrow. It had fallen in the oil can, and was covered in thick oil. I tried to clean him, but didn't seem to be able to, so I took him home and went round to the vet with him. He said there wasn't much they could do, so I brought him home and got out this cloth and tried to clean him up. I felt so sorry for him.'

While he was saying all this, my mind was thinking how amazing . . . Here's this hard, rugged man of rugby talking about caring for and trying to save the life of this little sparrow. I thought to myself, there's more to this guy than I knew – it's a side of Bobby I never realised existed.

Anyway, Bobby said he must have tried to clean this bird's wings for hours but he still didn't know whether he would fly. So he put him on the wall to see if he could fly away, but he couldn't.

'Well, what happened in the end if he couldn't fly?'

And he said, all matter-of-fact like, 'I got this bloody great sledgehammer and hit him on the head.'

'You did what?'

'Aye, I couldn't leave him like that.'

So I thought, that's Bobby Windsor's kindness for you. But, as Bobby said later, he was suffering and he couldn't leave him like that.

We'd chewed the cud, shared some tales and had a good few laughs. And I knew one of my stories would also raise a few smiles. I told them I'd never forget Bobby Windsor's face in a match against Scotland when he was throwing into a line-out. Our line-out calls were Welsh words. Trouble was, Bobby didn't speak Welsh.

He threw in once and the referee blew his whistle and said he wanted it taken again. I shouted 'Eto' to Bobby, which in Welsh meant 'again – throw it to the same place'.

Bobby came off the touchline, walked over to me and looked at me with an expression between complete bewilderment and panic. 'What the hell did you say?'

'Eto, eto,' I said, forgetting he didn't speak Welsh.

'And what the bloody hell does that mean?'

I can't remember who eventually won that line-out but I shouldn't think it was us. Our forwards were laughing so much they wouldn't have been able to contest a loose ball with a baby.

Bobby smiled. He often does. 'I remember it well. And it always embarrassed me that I couldn't speak Welsh. I didn't do much at school, wasn't good at anything really. But the day my son passed his GCSEs in eleven subjects I was proud enough. Both my sons speak Welsh now and I'm glad they do.'

CHAPTER 3

The Agent

Michael Alan Burton has always been infamous for doing things in life 'his way'. The man known throughout the rugby-playing world as 'Burto' has built an outstanding career, both on and off the rugby field, from the humblest of origins. So much of what Burto has done has been down to a combustible mixture of courage, character, charm and streetwise knowledge. Whenever there has been controversy, Mike hasn't been far away. Or so it has seemed.

Take the night in South Wales some years ago when Burton and Gloucester were involved in a white-hot confrontation with one of the top Welsh clubs. Burton had a reputation as a hard man, and Gloucester were hardly known as shrinking violets. When they met hardened valley sides like Newbridge or Pontypool, the sparks tended to fly.

On this particular occasion, Burton was on the receiving end of a very hard, very accurate punch which sent him reeling. When he had gathered his thoughts, the Welsh referee took him aside. 'Right, Burto,' said the official, 'I've seen what's happened and I'm giving you a free hit. But only one. Right?'

Even Burto was probably amazed to hear such news. But a deal was a deal, and Burto was more than willing to 'strike' this particular one. All of which was completely unknown to the crowd when, a few minutes later, Burton let fly an almighty punch which dropped his assailant right in the middle of a line-out. This time, it was Burton who was called over to the referee.

'Right, Burto,' said the ref once again. 'Now you know I've got to wag my finger like this at you, because the crowd want you off. We had a deal, right, but now we're quits.' And after that, what you might term 'mob justice', they all went back to the game.

I cannot remember the exact moment but I'm sure the first time I met up with Mike Burton on a rugby field, I'd have come off the pitch at the end either with a black eye or sore ribs from laughing so much.

Don't misunderstand me, Burto was no joke of a player. In fact, he was an outstandingly tough, hard, committed front-row forward who was good enough to win seventeen caps for England between 1972 and 1978 and go on the British Isles tour of South Africa in 1974, thus becoming a member of the so-called 'Invincible Lions'.

What Burto always had, besides tons of effort, enormous physical presence and, if need be, brutal determination, was a mischievous twinkle in his eye. He enjoyed the company of administrators and officialdom as much as tourists like swimming with sharks. When he was sent off in one County Championship match playing for Gloucestershire against Hertfordshire, he stopped just before reaching the main stand and performed an elaborate bow to the committee box. That was Burto at his best, although the dismissal was to cost him dear. He lost his place in the England team to play against Ireland. On another occasion, Bristol and England lock Dave Watt, who stood 6ft 6ins tall, caught Mike and broke his jaw but he played on, even though he was in agony and could not speak afterwards.

In 1975, Mike was sent off when playing for England in a Test match against Australia in Brisbane, after the game erupted in violence straight from the kick-off. Australia had begun the match with an awful explosion of violence. Fists and feet were liberally employed at the first ruck and after the initial line-out there was more trouble. Burton was first censured by the Australian referee Mr Burnett for head-butting (there were no neutral referees in those days, as is now the case) and soon after was dismissed for a late tackle. He therefore became the first England player to be sent off in an international match.

I got to know him well during that Lions tour in South Africa in which he was unlucky to suffer an early injury causing him to miss the first three tour matches and he was not chosen for a Test side. Of course, I already had a deep respect for him gained from playing

48

against him, for Cardiff and Wales against Gloucester and England. No Welsh prop to my recollection ever regarded a match against Gloucester as a nice easy day out and even though Burton played for England in an era when Wales were a formidable outfit and were collecting Triple Crowns and Grand Slams a'plenty, we never underestimated Mike.

Good judges of a front-row forward, like the Pontypool boys Graham Price, Bobby Windsor and Charlie Faulkner, would gruffly acknowledge Burton's value. In those nether regions, Burton was known as one of the best and one of the hardest men in the business. Speaking personally, I never found Mike Burton anything other than a funny bloke, a great personality and a fine footballer. But he was always that bit more besides. That's why I called him 'streetwise'. On our 1974 Lions tour, we became the first Lions party ever to play a Bantu team, the Leopards. The match was played at Mdantsane, East London on 9 July 1974 and, although the Lions won comfortably, by 56–10, there was an incident in the game which demonstrated Burton's niftiness in certain situations.

One of the Leopards' forwards bore a disturbingly similar resemblance to the former world boxing champion Marvin Hagler. No matter, the player was punched by Burton and promptly aimed a fierce, swinging punch in retribution, supposedly at Burton, who luckily for him, saw it coming and ducked. Alas, Chris Ralston, Burton's England pack colleague, was not so fortunate. The punch split Ralston's right cheek clean through. He needed fourteen stitches and did not recover consciousness until he was in the ambulance taking him to hospital. Burton looked on with the air of a completely disinterested bystander! Not for nothing did Mike entitle his autobiography, published in 1982 by Queen Anne Press, *Never Stay Down*. Perhaps he won't mind if I retell a joke about me from those pages.

Max Boyce, as ever, was the creator of the joke: the Pope, Bill Beaumont and myself had to cross a lake without a bridge. The Pope went first and went straight down to the bottom. But Bill and myself raced across the lake and reached the other side. No bother, as Bill McLaren might have said. Bill turned to me and said, 'Pity the Pope didn't know about those stepping-stones, Gareth.' To which I was supposed to have replied, 'What stepping-stones?'

Burto said he rated me not for my tries or kicking ability but for my dogged approach when the chips were down. He could have said the same about himself, except that he showed that tough approach even before the chips had had a chance to go down. Anyway, before this mutual appreciation society gets completely out of hand, let me acknowledge what an outstanding success Mike has made of the business he began and then built into a worldwide operation. Mike did it as he did most things – his way. He ignored the sly remarks and criticism from those who wondered and complained how on earth he could get hold of tickets to events, and steadily built a vibrant and financially successful company.

Today, Mike Burton's business interests span sports from rugby to tennis to horse racing to soccer. He is an officially appointed Wimbledon tennis ticket distributor, an official FIFA agent as well as representing many rugby players as an agent and he organises travel for thousands of sports fans the world over. He is also a highly popular after-dinner speaker. Who better, in fact, to discuss the modern game with, the ramifications of professionalism and influence of agents?

He sat at his large desk in a vast office in the centre of his beloved Gloucester and reflected on just where this old game that he and I used to play has got to. First, what of the role of the agent? What did he say to the accusation that professional rugby clubs have paid huge salaries to too many players who were not really good enough, principally because their agents forced large sums out of the club owners for their clients?

'Pay has gone up, that's not in doubt. But that reflects the old maxim about having the right person available at the right time. Yes, clubs have paid a lot of money for some players but it isn't my experience that players who are quite ordinary earn six-figure salaries. Maybe the top international stars but not that many of them.

'And you have to say clubs are only too willing to take advantage when agents are not around. Clubs comprise some cunning people; remember, most are owned by millionaires. And those are people who have made large sums of money by being shrewd in business. As I said, some clubs are taking advantage of young players. When I look at some players and know what they're getting, I think it's outrageous. There is absolutely no doubt some clubs are aware of the financial circumstances in which they are trading. They can and do exploit young guys without agents. What clubs want is a brilliant, outstanding player who has no comprehension of his own value and will hardly cost them a penny. They want to sign him on a five-year deal and save themselves a fortune. The kid is vulnerable and they seek to exploit him.

'That means there will always be a need for people like me. I'm just getting a much better deal for the player, that's all. I can understand the clubs don't like that but it's the reality of a professional sport. There's nothing illegal in what we're doing.

'But, having said that, many agents only want to represent the superstars because that is where they know they will earn the big money. They're not really interested in helping a lock forward who isn't an international, isn't going to be one but needs help to get as good a deal as he can from a club.'

But does Burton believe salaries for the top players will continue to rise? 'Yes, undoubtedly. The owners will put more money in to attract the leading star names of the game to their particular club. Salaries for the best players will be like houses. Some years ago, people who were told their house was worth £3800 dreamed it might one day go up to £4000. Now look at today's values. It's the same with players' wages.

'The top players will always get the big money. And those sums will rise steadily, they're bound to. The trouble is players get publicity and people on the outside think all of them get that sort of money. But they don't.

'The people who run clubs now will continue to put money in because they are thinking in a few years' time they may get a share of the Six Nations Championship monies. They believe that may go into a pool and they could get a lot.

'As for the agent, it is his job to get the best possible deal for his client. And that means finding not just any club anywhere and saying to the player, "Get in there, sign the contract and don't bother me again for three years." It's about finding the best club, the right club for a particular player and then making sure the terms suit that person. Of course, the club must be happy too. Then, it's a two-way relationship and there is a chance of it becoming a real success.'

But what of the rugby situation in general? 'You would have to say it is pretty good at the moment. You and I remember the days when we had beer kitties and all had to pay match fees, which was of course the players' contribution to the general running of the club. Inevitably, the professional game has brought in a different set of values and new people. So you will always get differences of opinion between the old tub-thumping amateurs of the past, now likely to be members of the so-called Reform Group in England, and the proper professionals. But I believe rugby is a broad church – I see no reason why both cannot survive and thrive in the same sport.

'So much has changed and we have to accept that. Now we have the first waves of young professionals coming along and saying, "What are my prospects?" When it first went professional, no one was ready for it. I remember Ian Smith, the Gloucester and Scotland flank forward, coming to see me and saying, "I haven't got a clue what I am worth." No one else had, either. But things have moved on rapidly since then, it's now so different.'

Mike Burton has around ninety rugby players on his books and his view is very different from a few years ago. He thinks others have changed a lot, too.

'I no longer have the image of that old-fashioned RFU in my mind. To be honest, I have a high regard for what Twickenham has achieved in a very short number of years. For example, in the early 1990s during a recession, they rebuilt Twickenham for £75 million. The same goes for the Welsh Rugby Union who put up the Millennium Stadium, on time and for £126 million.

'It's all right making jokes about the old blazers and "old farts" as Carling called them. But those days have gone. Consider what happened in 2001–2002 with the supposed rebuilding of Wembley Stadium and the mess that got into with estimated costs ballooning to £660 million. The FA then pulled back from the brink and said they couldn't afford it and the Government refused to bail them out. So you have to say what the RFU and the WRU achieved was a remarkable testimony to their judgement.'

I must admit when I realised Burto had uttered those words, I began to think the old boy had gone soft in his head. Probably too many rum punches as opposed to just punches, while leading assorted groups of sports fans around the globe. But when you sit down and think about it, he is almost certainly correct.

And there was more. 'And then all those hospitality boxes at the new Twickenham were sold to corporate business. Years ago, RFU senior officials confronted me and told me that corporate hospitality was a dreadful thing. Now they have adopted all the things I do and did for several years.

'Look at rugby in general. All the major stadia in the northern hemisphere have been rebuilt, with the exception of Lansdowne Road, Dublin. Even there, Ireland should have a new home in three or four years' time. Look at Murrayfield, Twickenham, Cardiff, Paris – superb new stadia. Corporate hospitality is now an integral part of the game. That is how it should be because the club game does not drive revenue streams – the international game does and always will do. You need to maximise your earnings potential where the demand is at its height.

'Clubs must be funded by the Union in whichever country we're talking about. Clubs need a share of the international revenue, that is where the only serious money is in this game. At the moment, you have a situation where some players in a team are earning £150,000 a year and their clubs are getting gates of around 3000. They're getting crowds like Third Division football clubs. Now you don't need to be an economic guru to see that can't continue.

'Unions must sensibly allocate funds to their top clubs and also cater for the rest of the game. The people at the grassroots are not lunatics: they understand the dangers of the situation. The fact is each national Union should own all the competitions and look after every section in the game. It is the same in every country, or at least it should be.

'The RFU, the WRU and the SRU are big brand names. They should pay the players and look after the development of the teams at all age levels. We don't want to lose our club set-up and if we leave it to the clubs most will go bust. But that won't happen if the Union fund them from a central pot, as the RFU are doing with the English clubs.

'It's different in soccer and always will be. In English soccer's Premiership, clubs generate so much money themselves that some players get £40,000 to £60,000 a week or even more. Therefore, they don't need the financial support of the Football Association. In rugby union, clubs need the support of the governing body in their respective countries because the international game makes the money. And some regard has to be paid to the smaller clubs which I believe the RFU is now doing.

'The old game has gone, we have to accept that. It was great and it was glorious but it's gone, finished. What has come in its place may not suit everyone but it is here, reality. We must accept it. But that doesn't mean we overlook and forget the grassroots clubs, not at all. Because they too can have a place in the modern game of the future. That is why I don't think anyone should be too downhearted about rugby today.

'The fact is, the amateur game will continue to thrive as long as the RFU, the WRU and all the national Unions support it and it is not ignored. That is why I thought it was an important point the Reform Group made at an Extraordinary General Meeting of the RFU in spring 2001. It was essential the people running the sport realised there is another sport out there and it has to be cared for, just like the professional version.'

But equally, there can be no denying that much of the interim period from amateurism to professionalism has been a long painful process. There have been casualties, including once-esteemed clubs, especially in England such as Richmond and London Scottish. In Wales, it has perhaps not been as dramatic because no major club has actually folded thus far, although of course Cardiff and Swansea played one season *out* of the Welsh competition, preferring fixtures against the English Premiership clubs.

'It has been a painful time, that's undeniable,' acknowledged Burton. 'Even with the half-year separation they had in tennis when Wimbledon initially banned professionals and insisted amateurism would be preserved, the eventual transformation from amateur to professional in that sport was much less painful than in rugby union. But the factions in rugby union are wider and more varied; in tennis, you have a lot of Wimbledon fans but not many tennis fans. But in rugby union thousands of regular supporters turn out everywhere and they all want their say.

'Now, I think a more hard-hearted professional attitude will continue to emerge. It will have to. You can see the need for greater professionalism when you remember that twelve senior English clubs recently got together to try and deny anyone else promotion and therefore access to their privileged world. That was a joke. Even in English Premiership soccer where millions of pounds are involved in businesses, three clubs are relegated each year. Yet the English Premiership rugby clubs tried to seal themselves off from such a harsh reality for years to come. That sort of action, that pulling up of the drawbridge, could not be allowed and never can be. If the top clubs ring-fence themselves, that would be disastrous. It would be even more dangerous if they held power in deciding who would join them.'

Something else which needs careful attention is the question of how to limit the number of fixtures. I have always been a great believer in the theory that a good horse only has a certain number of races in it. It is the same for rugby players: it is not only the physical demands but the mental aspect of continually having to play at the highest level. Whereas I admire and wonder at times at the physical fitness of the modern player, the human body has not evolved to Superman yet.

Therefore, I think the answer is a carefully laid out, structured season that primarily benefits the players who can produce consistently high performances. That is of paramount importance. That, in turn, would help promote the commercial side of the game. You would derive commercial benefits by the regular and increasing attendance of the public. But one thing is essential – a common policy among all nations and all parties. And that is why we have not yet been able to organise it. Because, by the very nature of life, one thing is never missing – self interest.

Our fundamental problem in the northern hemisphere, I believe, is still the fact that we have all these clubs to satisfy. The southern hemisphere doesn't have this difficulty. For example, if you reduced the Celtic and English Leagues to eight teams each it would mean fourteen League games in total for a season. With ten teams, it would give you eighteen matches. That is probably about right given that the top players then have to play Heineken European Cup games, matches in a domestic Cup and then anything up to eight internationals from October/November to April.

As it stands, the clubs in both England and Wales don't attract 20,000 people to every home match so they need more matches to bring in around 7000 fans each time. There is only one other solution – the Union funds the clubs and makes up the difference. That isn't likely in every case in every country so there isn't any easy answer. And even when you find one country getting it right, another Union says, 'That won't suit us'! In England, the RFU agreed to do this in July 2001 but, for example, the Welsh Rugby Union were continuing to resist the idea in early summer 2002.

Yet Mike believed that we had nearly got it right in Wales where several of the leading clubs are centrally funded by the Welsh Rugby Union. At least, that was his view before the events of 7 April 2002, when, at an EGM, the Welsh clubs threw out the Union's recommendation that the number of top clubs be cut from nine to six. Mike believes the WRU are putting too much money into the teams below the top and nothing comes out of it. He may well be right. And we should not forget the lack of progress and decisive leadership by the WRU even after seven years of professionalism has caused untold difficulties for those involved at the top level of the game in Wales.

In England, he thinks there should be two groups of eight in the Premiership. 'I think there will be quite soon because several rugby league clubs want to set up a rugby union side and join the top clubs. Given that scenario, England has the potential to have the best competition in the world. I'd also like to see set up some sort of franchise in Cornwall, an area which loves its rugby. I also think great clubs of the past with a long rugby tradition, the likes of Coventry, Moseley and Orrell should be assisted and Richmond and London Scottish re-established as top clubs. Coventry were a fantastic team in my day and central funding would be the answer. I believe we have to take account of tradition because we don't want to lose those hotbeds of rugby like Coventry and Cornwall.'

Burton foresees more clashes ahead and some casualties, but feels it is all part of the ongoing process of turning an amateur game into a professional one. I suppose he is correct, sad as it has been to see clubs like Richmond and London Scottish being taken over by London Irish. But what worries me is the type of young person we shall have coming into the game of the future.

Yet Burton remains generally confident and upbeat. He thinks the in-fighting within rugby union has been inevitable and will settle down within the next two years. It had been a thoroughly painful process, he said, and because of the acrimony, some had fallen by the wayside. But he saw it as an encouraging sign that the IRB, who are a safety net because of their powers of leadership, were now a more assertive organisation than when the Board consisted of just eight countries. Today, 78 countries hold membership of the IRB. He believed that, under the chairmanship of Vernon Pugh, they were starting to give the proper global leadership the game needed.

One area of the rugby-playing world that almost certainly has been neglected is the South Sea islands and those marvellous rugby nations of Fiji, Tonga and Western Samoa. All three have suffered enormously by the loss of so many of their finest players to Australia and New Zealand, a southerly migration which echoed the footsteps of their predecessors long years ago.

Now, however, the IRB have brought in regulations which will tighten the rules of qualification for another country. Burton thought it was long overdue: 'I thoroughly agree with the plans to tighten up on these rules. I've said for years that if Western Samoa, Fiji and Tonga were off the Gower Peninsula, Wales would be the greatest rugby nation in the world.'

Now, he thinks we will see the emergence of Fiji, Tonga and Western Samoa in their own right as international teams, which has not been possible while New Zealand and Australia have been able to claim their best players through some ancient birthright. Once those islands get a professional base to their game they will be a world force.

'But again, they won't make great money out of their domestic scene. So international rugby and the money it makes must fund them. The international Unions must think about the welfare of the game.'

I broadly agree with those views. But it's also possible to be a mite cynical, especially when you recall instances such as Frank Bunce, that marvellous centre three-quarter, representing Western Samoa in one World Cup but New Zealand in another. As for that outstanding No. 8, Willie Offahengaue, he didn't seem able to make up his mind whether being born in Tonga, educated in New Zealand (he played for New Zealand Schools) and then travelling to Australia when his New Zealand visa ran out, qualified him for the first, second or third country.

As for the issue of qualifying for a country through your grandparents, it took a New Zealander to bring it to a head in Wales and some loopholes that were being exploited are now being tightened to stop any further abuse. We have to welcome that.

We were all questioning these strange qualifications which enabled Tongans to represent Australia and All Blacks to wear the red jersey of Wales. Maybe the solution is to go back to phase one – i.e. if your parents were born in a country or if you were born there. Just those two qualifications, nothing else. I don't believe that the grandparent thing is relevant any more, it's too open to abuse. Who can check whether your grandfather was born in Cardiff or Gloucester or whether your grandmother once changed trains at Crewe?

I accept a youngster can still have a very strong tie to a country by his mother or father and that is fair enough. But the whole episode got out of hand with people energetically trying to find some connection to their past, however tenuous, to qualify for a certain country.

As for the South Sea island nations, like any small nation they need to utilise every possible resource and clearly they can't do that if most of their best players go off to New Zealand or Australia.

Of course, we only thought of this idea of representing a different country in the professional age. When players were amateur, they often played their rugby in another country, yet they never *represented* that country. Cliff Morgan, one of Wales's greatest outside halves, played his club rugby in Dublin at one time but he didn't turn out for Ireland claiming qualification through his grandmother! Barry Nelmes was an English prop who played for Cardiff for many years, but he retained England as his national team. Wilson Lauder, the Scot, lived in Neath and played club rugby for them for years but represented Scotland. No one ever thought otherwise.

But what has come about are greater opportunities of finance through the professional game. Players have tried to take advantage of that. Maybe the prospect of international players threatening to go on strike goes against every tradition of the game, as we knew it. But people should look at the whole context rather than just the effect. It is essential that people understand the confusions and frustrations players have felt due to the lack of direction within the game. Players have been left to form their own opinions as to what professionalism means.

The England team threatened to go on strike during the season 2000–2001 principally because the RFU had taken so long to resolve an issue concerning intellectual property rights for the players. They had prevaricated endlessly, frustrating the players and, allegedly, taking advantage of their goodwill and the common perception that they would never force the matter to a head. In the end, the players became so fed up that they did and the RFU had to resolve it quickly. Which, of course, they did.

I strongly believe most players are just not interested in politics. They want only to train and play. But they feel the frustrations everyone else in the game has felt. The issue regarding the England players was about their futures and you cannot blame young sportsmen for expressing concern at that. Frankly, it was a sad indictment of the authorities that these young men had to resort to threats to get the issues resolved. And I am sure that decision was not one they took lightly.

Much the same happened with the Welsh international squad during the 2001–2002 season. Indeed, just a week before the match with England at Twickenham in the Six Nations Championship, there was a real possibility that the top Welsh players would refuse to take part. The players took that drastic step, not because they just wanted more money or some other material reward from the WRU but because they, like the clubs, had become utterly frustrated and sick of the constant delays by the Union in implementing a properly run, well-administered structure for the benefit of the professional game in Wales. They cared for the future of the game in Wales to such an extent that they knew painful decisions had to be taken by the Union for the good of the game. They believed the number of leading clubs should be reduced so as to create an elite in club rugby for the benefit of the international game. Yet the Union continued to sit on the fence, even after a working party the WRU themselves had set up to investigate the matter, reported back with clear recommendations. Trouble was, the Union didn't like those recommendations and therefore prevaricated, calling an EGM and allowing the large number of junior clubs to veto the proposition that the number of senior clubs in Wales should be reduced to six: Llanelli, Cardiff, Swansea, Newport, Bridgend and Pontypridd.

But rugby union is not just about Australia, New Zealand, Wales, England, Italy etc. In the southern hemisphere, it's not just about famous provincial sides like Auckland and Queensland and Natal's Coastal Sharks. Nor is it solely in the northern hemisphere about clubs like Cardiff and Leicester, Llanelli and Bath, Stade Toulouse and Cork Constitution, Hawick and Benetton Treviso. What it is also about is the Bedwas' second XV in Wales, the Old Grammarians team in England and the many thousands who play the game solely for the love of it, the friendship it creates and the fun it provides.

I witnessed this level of the sport when I travelled recently to Nassau in the Bahamas. Not a traditional rugby haven, you might think. I went to speak at a dinner of the Buccaneers rugby club of Nassau and there I found the same spirit and healthy attitude to the game that you can see in many parts of the globe.

There was a celebration game between the Bahamas and the Rest of the World, and that was interesting and fun to watch. It was nice to see young Bahamian sportsmen, a generation of young black players coming up through the ranks and experiencing what rugby has to offer. These young men were not concerned about contractual problems or other associated difficulties facing the professional game back in Cardiff, London, Paris or Auckland. They were there simply to enjoy rugby.

The fact is, there are two different games now. But we should never forget or ignore those who play at the lower level simply because we are preoccupied by events concerning the professionals. The amateur game will continue to need management and finance from central funding to ensure the game grows. So you require a structure that encourages the amateur game to grow, promotes competition and the opportunity to reach higher echelons of the sport.

I believe we can get too wrapped up with this professional thing. That is why Burto is right when he says the amateur game will continue to thrive – as long as the national Unions support it, provide financial assistance and, above all else, don't ignore it. I agree.

But what about that dreaded subject, tickets? What has the cagey old operator, Mike Burton, got to say on that topic? Hasn't he been responsible for driving prices higher for ordinary rugby fans who have been unable to get tickets at face value? Hasn't he profited hugely at the expense of the game in general, but particularly in England, and especially the RFU?

Burton chuckles. 'I told the Rugby Union years ago I could make them lots of money. Even when I was still playing, I was hiring a London bus or two to take corporate clients with tickets I had acquired. The buses sat in the north car park at Twickenham. The committee men at Twickenham just complained about Mike Burton having all those tickets. They couldn't do anything about it but they kept complaining and didn't take advantage of the opportunities themselves. Even though I offered to help them.

'In the twenty-three years since I started getting involved in this business, I estimate I could have made the RFU £60–£70 million if I had been operating on their behalf. They could have done it simply by allocating enough tickets for that sector of the market. They lost so much money. There will always be that market, that corporate sector. And as long as it doesn't get out of balance I see no problem.

'People today want to park somewhere near the ground, arrive early, have a nice four-course lunch with a glass or two of wine and then have a good seat for the match. People also want a replay facility in the ground. They want to have a referee link as well so they can hear the decisions being made. All this has come from the USA. We are providing that facility.'

The RFU are starting to cater for these people. But they are twenty-five years behind the times in terms of need, according to shrewd old Burto. They had missed a glorious opportunity for so long, he said. 'The merchandising is a valuable source of income now but just think what it could have been for those last years. Rugby now, whether we like it or not, is about money. TV money is mega money, sponsorship deals are big money too. Corporate hospitality is big. Sums from gate receipts alone which used to be the backbone of all the Unions, are now fading almost into insignificance.

'It's no good people talking of black markets and illegal tickets. Because the fact is, the governing bodies have taken the black market out of the game by the extraordinary prices they have charged for tickets in the modern game. At the 1999 World Cup, the World Cup committee charged £150 for tickets for the final and £85 for tickets for the semi-final. Those were black market ticket prices.'

So what of the game in general, from the agent's point of view? As our conversation came to its conclusion, I was greatly encouraged to hear Burto so upbeat and positive about rugby and its future. He thinks the game is better now than it's ever been due to professionalism and the ball skills in the modern game were far superior. It was so much faster, it left you breathless just watching. 'We thought we were operating at a peak. But the way the game has moved on, the progress it has made since our day has been extraordinary.'

Well, my retort to that is part agreement, part disagreement. Generally speaking, lots of skills have been improved but a lot have been lost. Every generation has skills and different standards and requirements. Before I started playing, for example, full-backs were skilful if they never flinched under the high ball and were capable of rifling the ball back into touch with either foot. Then, one of the great law changes came in, forbidding direct kicking into touch when outside your own 25. After that, the skills of the full-back changed to embrace running rugby. We saw how J.P.R. Williams transformed the skills of the full-back to the new requirements of that generation. There were other great runners from full-back too like Serge Blanco and Andy Irvine.

The modern game now requires great handling skills under intense pressure and especially at close quarters. Players must have the ability to absorb shock, to take the heavy hit while distributing and recycling the ball.

On the other hand, I don't believe there is greater skill in the game now. Players years ago had greater dexterity and qualities of improvisation. Preparation now is all whereas years ago one of the great skills was reading of the game and improvising. There was greater flexibility in the game then. For instance, what was more skilful than jumping in the line-out against Frik du Preez of South Africa, a man who was no giant yet was one of the finest and most consistent of ball winners in that facet of the game? To compete with Frik, you had to overcome opponents who would stand on your feet, hold you down with their arms or grab your testicles as you jumped up. Yet somehow players still competed and distributed good quality possession to their scrum half. Delme Thomas of Llanelli and Wales was a classic line-out man of his time and, after that, Bob Norster of Cardiff and Wales and Wade Dooley of Preston Grasshoppers and England. All three men represented the British Lions and were superb operators at the line-out.

By contrast, today you can admire the athletic-looking lifting in the line-out as tall men reach once unimagined heights. Oh, I should confess, that is speaking very much tongue in cheek. I have general admiration for some of the ball-handling skills of the big forwards in the modern game, but you wouldn't say the passing in the backs is more skilful than it was when people like Mike Gibson and Gerald Davies were playing.

I am not talking just about the 1970s either but even further back than that. Cliff Morgan's era, for example. And in the 1970s, it wasn't just Welshmen who had skills to offer. Someone like the Scot Andy Irvine was a superb footballer and another was Bob Taylor of Northampton, England and the 1968 British Lions. Bob was a super ball handler. Then you had that great French back row of Rives, Bastiat and Skrela. And let's not forget other Scots like John Rutherford and Jim Renwick. So I baulk at the suggestion that it's a lot more skilful today. Just different.

Burto's response was typically challenging. And interesting.

'But it has changed. I go back to when I played international rugby. I faced Wales four times and they were a fantastic team, they played with fire and heart. They talked of the *hywl*, the passion, and that is what it was. Four or five of their players were the best in the world. When I saw Wales play in this last season's Six Nations Championship, their team still had fire and heart. But England? They were dispassionate about it. I looked at that and realised how much of a gear England have gone up. Now, the two genuine world powers in terms of rugby are Australia and England.

'The French are like the Welsh; they too play with their hearts, with fire. They play with passion. But to be clinical as the modern England side is, you have to remove that passion to a certain extent. Because it alone is not enough. Opponents expect passion but do not fear it. Professionalism has brought all this about.

'I don't want to see countries like Wales and Scotland fall by the wayside. Their demise would suit no one, England included. Wales have had fantastic players and great characters. Some of the guys I played against were geniuses. Maybe there are few of those left today but there is still some ability. But they're going to have to work hard at it to bring it out today and really develop it for the international stage. Because it has been accounted for in the modern game. Talent is covered all the time. Look at a player like Brian O'Driscoll – he is closely marked the whole match. Opposing teams sit down and work out how they will play him. There is always someone to put that tackle in, to frustrate him.'

As for Scotland, they too are struggling in the modern era with a shortage of true international-class players. They did scrape past Wales in one of the last matches of the 2002 Six Nations Championship, but in truth there was very little to choose between two poor teams. And then Scotland lost to Canada in a Test match on their 2002 summer tour.

From my point of view, I think a lot of things are going to change very quickly in rugby. Certainly from a Welsh perspective. If you had been running a normal business, you would have been bankrupt before coming to the market. But financiers' tolerance for sporting involvement that defies logic has meant rugby has been able to survive in my country.

The speed at which the game left its old amateur status for the new professional era has, as we all know, led to huge problems, especially concerning finances, that are only slowly being eradicated. But you have a distinct feeling that there is now a realisation that rugby in the modern era requires a far more professional outlook to manage its portfolio and its future. People are beginning, some reluctantly, some through logic, to agree that the message is now louder and clearer than ever. If you do not have a commercial approach and attitude, the game could be in serious trouble. Clubs must run a proper business with efficient, motivated and committed staff. They must be accountable to their members and investors. There must be a proper business plan with appropriate targets for the future.

Happily, the IRB have brought a more professional approach to the management of the game in recent times and that has undoubtedly helped. Yet I feel the game needs an overview, somebody to say, 'That's not working, let's do something else.'

Yes, generally the game *is* better than it used to be, although some of it I don't like. I think we should take stock of what we have got and where we are going. I don't want to go away from this concept of a game for all people, a game for big and small, wide and thin. There are concerns in that department.

I accept it is not the same game I knew as a player. We hoped it wouldn't change but deep down we felt it would. Perhaps the biggest thing that has suffered was that camaraderie and friendship, especially between teams. The hard abrasive physical confrontation used to be washed away in the clubhouse in the evening after the game. Even at international level, we had opportunities to spend time together with our opponents. Maybe the Lions tour every four years is the only remaining opportunity players from different countries will have to get to know one another. But even those tours are so much shorter that they perhaps won't offer the players the same opportunities to create friendships as we had on our sixteen-week tours.

As with all things, there is good and bad in this new game. But if you take another aspect of professionalism, isn't it the case that any sport that has money at its core eventually loses all its old traditions and ways? Isn't it true that money eventually corrupts everything?

Mike Burton was brutally honest. 'Yes, it does. I had a little scrum half who came to me. He'd negotiated a £12,000 deal with a club and thought that was good. But we doubled that, negotiated an extra £5000 for a successful season and number of matches played and we persuaded the club to give him a car, too. But the boy can play so I feel no guilt.

'When these guys go on the field, I never cease to have respect for them. It makes a tremendous statement about them when they cross that line, it's like the professional boxer stepping into the ring.

'The truth is, everybody wants the best players so the price of those players will go up. I'm not driving up the values or prices of players – the clubs can say no and some do. But those clubs that really want the best players know they will have to pay the price. It's as simple as that. The agent will always be criticised because very few stand up and protect themselves. But it's the players that keep me in business. I am not driving up fees, I am getting a competitive salary for a good player. It's the player's reputation that earns him a good contract.'

Burto reckons he makes as many mistakes as the coaches and managers of teams. He tells the story that when Steve Borthwick, the young Bath second-row forward, went to see him, he told him to go away and learn the game for a couple of years before bothering him again. Of course, Borthwick is now an England international and is regarded as one of the best young lock forwards in British rugby. Oh, and it won't surprise you to know that Mike Burton is not his agent. 'I messed up on that one,' said Burto, somewhat ruefully.

CHAPTER 4

The Club Benefactors

What has been the great pity of this long, painful dispute between the Unions and clubs in the northern hemisphere is that people like Peter Thomas, the Cardiff chairman, and Nigel Wray, owner of Saracens, who only ever wanted to assist their clubs, have been painted by some as the bêtes noires of the game. It has suited those in administration to blame owners or club backers like Thomas and Wray for the ills the game stumbled into once professionalism was legalised. It is a regret to all of us that there has been such conflict in this field. Given harmony, I believe that both clubs and countries could have been hugely successful long ago.

Even in February 2002, when Thomas, the chief benefactor behind Cardiff rugby club, and myself saw Vernon Pugh, the IRB chairman, at the Ireland–Wales Six Nations Championship match in Dublin, I expressed my frustration that the pair of them, both hugely successful businessmen in their different fields, could not have worked together for the good of rugby in Wales. Peter agreed with me.

Let me make it perfectly clear where I stand in this debate. I admire Peter Thomas for his business acumen and his love of rugby football and the Cardiff club. Some in Wales have tried to claim that Thomas has wanted to steal the Cardiff club, whatever that may mean. That, I might say, has been one of the less offensive claims made against him and others in a dispute that has been long and bitter. But Peter Thomas and many like him are no ogres.

I regret especially that the WRU found it necessary to take what many regarded as such an intransigent line in dealings with the clubs. The Welsh clubs were let down by the WRU and perhaps Vernon

67

could have done more to achieve a breakthrough, for the benefit of both sides. Had there been a positive spirit in the air, I firmly believe many of the difficulties would have been overcome. Alas, no spirit of compromise was ever very apparent. Vernon wanted the leading Welsh clubs to sign a ten-year agreement with the WRU, so that the Union would have a controlling interest in the clubs. Cardiff and Swansea refused to accept such an absurdly lengthy commitment. We didn't want to tie ourselves to the Union because we did not believe that the WRU was an organisation capable of making good, economically sound business decisions for the benefit of the clubs as well as the Union. The WRU had their agenda, which was right and proper, but inevitably the clubs would have another. We couldn't see how they could operate on both sides of the fence.

It is my belief we have been proved correct in our opinions because here we are years later and the game in Wales run by the WRU is still in a mess. They are still not making the decisions which the situation cries out for such as reducing the number of top professional clubs and establishing a proper professional structure for the top end of the game. If we had signed, we would now be in an even worse state than we are. I think Vernon Pugh was wrong to take the hard line he adopted on this topic. Because I am also certain that Vernon had the ability to hold the whole thing together and take it forward to a common solution, had he been prepared to be more flexible. He was and is a good administrator and it was a pity he wasn't around long enough at the WRU and wasn't willing to wait longer to find a way out of the difficulties. He, perhaps more than anyone else, was best qualified to do that with his experience and considerable intellect. It was to no one's benefit that the WRU and a couple of its leading clubs, Swansea and Cardiff, had to go to the courts because a domestic dispute could not be resolved by negotiation. To this day, I and many other people in Wales regret that.

Why did it ever get to court? Quite simply, Cardiff and Swansea refused to sign those ten-year agreements with the Welsh Rugby Union. Their retort was to threaten to throw us out of the Union. The clubs' only recourse was to go to court, claiming alleged restraint of trade. The Union wanted to tie them in for ten years even though the TV contract they had negotiated lasted only half that.

Cardiff were in the fortunate position that they had been able to go to their members and raise about £3.5 million to help us through those difficult times. So we were able to face up to the Union's repeated demand for a golden share in our club. When we stood firm, that demand was retracted and exchanged for the equally impossible demand that we sign up to the Union for ten years.

Eventually, sense prevailed and both parties settled out of court but alas, only after much of the £3.5 million had been spent on legal fees rather than on developing the structures of the game. Anyway, Cardiff and Swansea returned to the fold on the basis of certain understandings proposed by the Union one of which, it was reported, was that they would push for a British League. But that, of course, has not materialised.

Perhaps it is interesting now to speculate what might have happened had we not decided to go back to the Welsh Union, and had the RFU not come to a general agreement with the English clubs. Perhaps there would have developed a cracking, independently financed and run, Anglo-Welsh competition with a strong English West Country/Wales element with regular fixtures between clubs like Gloucester, Llanelli, Bristol, Swansea, Newport, Cardiff, Bath, Pontypridd, Bridgend and perhaps Worcester.

But what of the owners? Well, I should lay my cards clearly on the table here. I have known Peter Thomas almost since I was a boy, which straightaway disproves the theory that he is just an outsider, a businessman aiming to extract money from the newly professionalised game. Some hope of that! But let me tell you a little story about Peter Thomas and myself.

Looking back, I suppose it was the sort of thing they'd seen countless times up in the Welsh valleys. Young whippersnapper of a player turns up and the locals take one look and say, 'Well, don't like the look of 'im' or 'He's too small, mun – those big buggers'll 'ave 'im for breakfast.' Perhaps, too, some in the kid's own team don't know what he's like and wonder about him. 'Aye, I'll say,' laughed Peter Thomas when we met up to talk rugby and discuss times, old and new, together. 'I'll never forget your face when you fed the scrum in that match at the Resolven club on the outskirts of the Neath valley. Remember that?'

I have to say, well I might. It was the first game I ever played with him, and we were in an Invitation XV which played the Resolven side to open their clubhouse. Peter, who is about five years older than me, was a hooker and he played on occasions for the Cardiff first team. It was around 1966 and a very young G. Edwards was feeding the scrum in this particular match. Thomas, who was quite tall for a hooker, remembers almost kicking the ball out of my hands – he flicked it. I jumped back in surprise and Thomas told me long after, he thought to himself, 'What have we got here? This frail boy won't last five minutes in Welsh rugby.' Keith Bradshaw, the Bridgend centre who won nine Welsh caps between 1964 and 1966, was playing centre that day. I can't remember it now but apparently I then made a break around the scrum and took off upfield for a try from about 70 yards' range. Peter said later Bradshaw went up to him and said: 'Who the hell is this kid?' Who indeed?

Certainly it wasn't unusual to see Peter Thomas at a match like that. He was a very enthusiastic player and a strong, durable hooker. He has remained a Cardiff rugby man through and through. In fact, Peter and his entire family have been long-standing supporters of Cardiff. To call them supporters doesn't seem adequate. Peter's brother Stan also played for the club; he played anywhere really. In those days, Cardiff had a Rags XV which was the seconds and an Extras which comprised the thirds. Peter also played for Ebbw Vale. Stan went to play for Penarth after the Extras were given up. Even in the amateur days, Stan and Peter were instrumental in supporting the club financially and in offering their expertise. Way back, it was Stan's idea to build hospitality boxes. The family money came from Stan and Peter's dad building up and then selling his pie-making business and in 1971 the boys formed another company, with Mary their sister joining them. That became one of the most successful companies in Wales and they sold out to Grand Met for an amount in excess of £75 million. Now they are both successful businessmen in the world of property and airports. Peter Thomas genuinely loves and supports Cardiff. He has always wanted to see them compete with the best in Europe. In Wales, you have a lot of envy between the haves and have-nots. Peter hasn't put the same sort of money into the club as the English owners because he isn't the sole owner. He isn't even the majority shareholder and I don't imagine he would want to be. He has always respected the traditions of Cardiff rugby club and understands that it is a community with many people wishing to support the club in many different ways.

I went to see him, in his modern office suite overlooking Cardiff

Bay. There, seated at a boardroom table, we traced the source of these painful, protracted difficulties between the senior clubs and the WRU as we discussed his role, his views on what had gone on in the game and where, if appropriate, blame should be laid. But first, he pointed out, it had only been by the introduction of a number of owners that several clubs in the professional game had been able to survive. These clubs, he said, had found themselves in a terrible situation as a result of professionalism. The likes of Mike James at Swansea, Nigel Wray at Saracens, Tony Brown at Newport and Malcolm Pearce at Bristol, to name but a few, had played crucial roles in saving the clubs.

Thomas says that he never wanted to be an owner. 'I just wanted to be part of a very large group of 1000 people who are shareholders in the Cardiff company. Benefactors is perhaps the right word to use. If I was asked to be the sole owner, I would decline because Cardiff is too big a club to pass into just one person's hands. The limited company just runs the club on a financial basis and has responsibility to shareholders. Cardiff Rugby Club is the main thing.'

Thomas says that if Tom Walkinshaw had not put money into Gloucester, the club would not have survived. 'Gloucester would be in Division 2 or 3 now. But in fairness to Tom, like we have done at Cardiff, he has retained the old hierarchy of committee stalwarts. That ensured a proper continuity, it meant those people who were lifelong rugby men and knew the game well retained a role. I regarded that as most important. We at Cardiff still have Dr Jack Matthews, the former international who played for Wales in the centre from 1947 to 1951 and was a Cardiff stalwart, C.D. Williams, lifelong supporter and player for the club and one of its great servants plus two more like him: Bob Newman and Bob Lakin.'

When the question of owners arises, people always say, 'What motivated these people to get involved?' I suppose the answer is that different people had different agendas. There was much mistrust from those early days because suddenly the old guard could see their influence diminishing and new people coming to the fore believing they could run the business better. That caused a lot of suspicion and confusion. Some of these new owners had a long tradition in the game, some didn't.

Personally, I find it hard to understand why anyone who became involved did so for personal financial gain. Those who thought it was a means to making money had to be in cloud cuckoo land. It was very apparent the game would take a long time before it could hope to start rewarding any initial investment. For a start, the Unions wanted to control all the TV rights. The clubs and owners tried to operate their individual businesses within the constraints of a Union-led business. But I didn't envy them because they had to struggle from the very beginning. Peter Thomas said, 'You had this huge element of mistrust created almost overnight and it has taken seven years or more to break that down. It's still not completely broken down although some progress has been made. So much so that I'd say there is now a lot more understanding of the importance of benefactors/owners, call them what you will.

'That mistrust has been the main factor behind the enormous losses Premiership clubs sustained in those years. It was only after six years that some people began to realise how much danger there was in the situation, how much ill-will and trouble. But the pain has to stop now. What is needed everywhere is a management board for the professional game.' Thomas estimates he personally has invested around £3 million so far, as his personal financial stake. But others have made a far bigger commitment. I understand for instance that Nigel Wray, the Saracens owner, is said to have invested £10 million and I feel desperately sorry for him. He has taken Saracens from nowhere to a club with a healthy four- or five-figure gate most weeks. That is no mean achievement. Thomas agreed, saying: 'I don't know anybody who had such desperate luck as Nigel in the season 2000–2001. The Australian centre Tim Horan and that thrilling French three-quarter Thomas Castaignede represented brilliance at its best, players everyone would want to go and watch. Yet they hardly played because of injuries. It must have cost Nigel a fortune.'

Then, Castaignede had to have another operation and missed almost all the 2001–2002 season. But, on the other hand, there have been some bad decisions by the club owners. Most undoubtedly saw rugby as an opportunity in a football sense. They looked at the way Premiership soccer was going in England and thought rugby could be the same. They thought perhaps they could make a financial killing. Not all were like that – some have the game at heart and always have had, and I wouldn't accuse Peter Thomas and certain others of believing he could make money at rugby's expense. Far from it. But some did and they did great damage. But you cannot judge all the owners by the few who were like that. If nothing else, their involvement has given the Unions food for thought. The trouble was the Unions dithered from the start. They were not sure they wanted to go professional by which time the club owners, being businessmen, didn't hang about. They knew that if they didn't sign the best players someone else would. But if the Unions had signed the players at the outset it would have alleviated most of the problems which have dogged the game since 1995. We would have had a different structure. But I suppose the Unions did not have enough money to support a ploy of signing up all the players. It certainly wasn't an option in Wales for the WRU although perhaps it could have been in England for the RFU.

Inevitably, much of my conversation with Peter Thomas concerned Cardiff, Welsh rugby and what had happened there over the years. In England, for sure, there were also problems but somewhat different ones. I felt it essential to discuss these dramatic times with one of the key men in the English club game during this period, Nigel Wray, the owner of Saracens. If you go back to the years before professionalism and remember the name Saracens, you think of a public, council-owned ground in North London where the club used to play. Dogs used to roam freely across the first XV pitch, as was their right because it was council-owned, and you can imagine the state the playing field was in sometimes and what the groundsman had to do to get it ready for matches! Now Saracens play on one of the finest surfaces in Britain, at Watford. They share the ground with Watford Football Club and have excellent facilities with a capacity of around 25,000. More than that, they have had some world-class players and exciting stars of the game wearing their famous black shirt – Philippe Sella, Thomas Castaignede and Alain Penaud from France, Michael Lynagh and Tim Horan from Australia, François Pienaar and Jannie de Beer from South Africa. More than that, they have had all manner of England internationals and British Lions such as Richard Hill, Dan Luger, Kyran Bracken, Danny Grewcock, Tony Diprose, Paul and Richard Wallace (of Ireland), Julian White and a host of others. When a team like Leicester comes visiting, Saracens might attract as many as 15,000 to 20,000 supporters to their all-seater stadium and they entertain them in much comfort. When Cardiff went up there to play them in the Heineken Cup of 2000–2001, I was hugely impressed by the set-up and the way the club was going about its business. Much of that was down to Wray, a man who has made a considerable fortune in property investment. Like Peter Thomas, Nigel Wray's involvement in rugby did not come about just when professionalism started. He had an association way back, in the 1960s and 1970s when he played for the Old Millhillians club in North London. 'We used to play Saracens every year,' he remembers. Wray was in the Old Boys' club's first XV before a damaged knee forced his retirement. He also played at centre for Hampshire in the English County Championship although, as he quickly adds, 'I was never on the winning side.'

Nigel, like Peter, is a true rugby supporter. He flew out to Australia to see the Lions play the Wallabies in June/July 2001 and he encourages his own club, urging it onwards and hoping to see it achieve great deeds. Thus far, the only piece of silverware it has lifted whilst under his command was the 1988 Tetley's Bitter Cup when Saracens thumped 48–18 the weakened XV which their North London rivals Wasps fielded in a wonderful match which was a triumph for the retiring Lynagh and Sella. Since then, life has been tough for Wray and Saracens. So how does Wray now sum up the last six years since the game went open? Given the chaotic administration of the game over here – his words, not mine – he thinks it has made quite remarkable steps. 'First, you have the success of the England team and also the developing presence and power of the Lions, which is now one of the most exciting brand names in the world. Plus you also have the success of the English clubs in Europe where Bath, Northampton and Leicester have all won the European Cup and Harlequins won the European Shield in 2001, followed by Sale in 2002. To my way of thinking, all that is cause for great optimism if we started to run this game properly.'

But does he think rugby should ever have gone professional in the first place?

'Yes, certainly. You can't turn back the tide. How on earth could you have £10 million worth of sponsors' money, TV rights and crowd revenues for one game at Twickenham and give the players nothing? The world doesn't work like that. All right, the Unions might say it was channelled into junior rugby and youth levels, and much undoubtedly was. But ignoring the players' right to financial reward was no longer a tenable position. All the players would have gone to

74

rugby league if union had stayed amateur, or to other countries. Life has to move forward. Furthermore, I cannot see how it would be possible to have a great sport on TV which is tremendous theatre without the players being professional in their attitude. That means things like training all day and spending quality time in preparation.'

But Wray also has a little secret confession to make. 'Had I known what I now know about the whole thing, I would never have become involved. Had I understood the cost of the ticket, I wouldn't have considered it. But having done it, I am pleased to be in because I still consider it a great game with a fine spirit and outstanding people.'

Wray just wishes it had been done differently. As for the cost of his involvement since he first appeared on the scene, he was also frank and to the point. I swallowed hard when I heard to what extent he had been involved. 'Gross about £10 million; net of tax, I would be looking at £6 million loss,' he said cheerfully. 'But having said that, if we can start operating together – i.e. the RFU, the Premiership clubs, the Six Nations Committee – then I think you are going to be quite staggered at the progress this game is going to make as a commercial property in the next five to ten years. It is terrific television, it has a great ethos although it must be made even more exciting in terms of TV presentation.' In May 2002 Wray announced that he was giving up control of the Saracens club to bring in five new board members and investment of more than £3.5 million. Wray released nearly 50 per cent of his shares from his original 96 per cent to extend the club's financial base. Given that Saracens lost around £600,000 last season the move, which broadens the financial burden, probably makes good business sense. Wray remains part of the new board but is no longer the majority shareholder.

Of course, there are plenty of entrepreneurs/businessmen who will not be around to see any possible future fruits of their own investments. Men like Sir John Hall at Newcastle, Ashley Levett at Richmond, Geoff Read at London Irish and there are others. They all played a part but were gone long before any golden fruit was apparent on the tree. But Wray can see a day when that fruit will be ready to pick.

Wray is neither angry nor bitter at the internal wranglings that have taken up so much of the past six years. But what gives him great concern is all the unnecessary pain that everyone has been through in that time. He feels it has been money down the drain rather than cash poured in as an investment to take the sport forward to where it could have been by now. 'I feel an enormous sense of frustration and, if you had been trying to do a business deal in similar circumstances, you would have said forget it long ago. I am not angry with the individuals but I feel that the organisations involved, the Unions, were incapable of coming to a decision, for years.'

There is no doubt we need a sensible agreement. The Unions say international sides must have first call on the players and I support that. It is still of paramount importance that players always play for their country. No one disputes that. But you also need common sense and compromise. So what Nigel is saying is right. In Wales, we have these dual contracts which will help the players. The Unions will pay the clubs so much for the players' release. That is only fair. Because it is not just four or five international matches in a season now, as I said earlier. Wray likens it to having had a lovely car in the garage. Somebody borrows it and goes on borrowing it and each time they bring it back, it's a little bit damaged. But nobody ever pays you for borrowing it. Yet he believes there has to be plenty of money in the pot to share around and create a base for success. I have to say I was somewhat surprised that Wray dismissed words such as anger and bitterness, because in my case, I am angry and bitter purely because I feel it has all been so unnecessary. A bit of common sense would have gone a long way. I don't believe the club owners went into it primarily to make money. They wanted to make their clubs the best in the country. But having put in so much money they wanted a bit of a say in how it was run. But at every turn, whenever they wanted to do something positive, there was always a 'No'. Not a compromise, or let's see. The clubs were by no means always right. They made mistakes but the response to anything coming from the other side of the table was always 'No'. I witnessed that too. I vividly remember one Union official angrily banging his fist down on the table at one set of discussions with the clubs, saying, 'Whatever you come up with, the answer will be no.' With that kind of attitude, it was no surprise compromise was rarely in the air.

The reason was that the administrators felt threatened, they felt the entrepreneurs wanted to run the game. So the Union officials wanted to assert their authority because they feared the clubs would become more powerful than them. But how could you expect these guys to invest their money without having a say in the way the game was run? That was only right and proper, only fair. If you put money into running a business, you are not then told there is another company that will decide how it's run. In Wales, the Union's position was flawed. First, they said now that the game is open go away and make yourselves strong clubs and run them on a business basis. Once we had done that and raised money, then the WRU turned around and said they wanted a 51 per cent share in our company or they would throw us out of the Union. They wanted the golden share.

Then they said we must sign up to the Union for ten years. That was equally ridiculous. Most clubs in Wales could not argue against the Union because by then they were owned by the WRU. Clubs like Llanelli, Neath and Bridgend didn't have two brass farthings to rub together.

To this day, no one will convince me we didn't do a thing which we thought was right and proper for Cardiff at the time.

Would it all have made more sense, I asked Wray, if the Unions had contracted their players? He felt that simply hadn't been possible. 'The average England player is perhaps on £130,000 with win bonuses and appearance money for internationals taking it to £200,000. But for the RFU to have centrally contracted all the players, they would have had to offer more than a three-year contract to everyone. But where would the clubs have been without their best players? Totally unable to offer a high quality product to its supporters. You can only serve one master unless the two parties work together and that didn't happen for too long. But the fact is each side needs the other. For England to be successful, the clubs must succeed by playing good rugby, hiring good coaches and quality players around whom the England qualified players can play and improve. For the clubs to be successful, they need a successful England team. England is the shop window and will get the kids playing. I think we began to see the start of that process during 2001.

'England is a fantastic property yet we shouldn't forget the England team is watched by largely the same 70,000 people every time they play. Debenture holders, sponsors and others have automatic places at England matches so it is the clubs who must attract the new audiences to the game, provide the forum in which new people can come and see rugby and offer entry at affordable prices. Those new people could never get to see England because they wouldn't get tickets often enough, if ever. Remember it is the clubs who are also doing a lot to entice this new audience by going out into the schools. If you watch good club rugby today in England, you see the international stars and that option must always be there to attract the new generation of support. That is the only way the game can expand.'

It seems that in England they have at last found a way for the Union and the clubs to work together. But it took a long time to come to a sensible solution. In Wales, the Cardiff club launched something called 'Capital Rugby' which involved us going into over a hundred schools in the Cardiff area and the Vale of Glamorgan. I am the Chairman of that organisation and we have coaches and former players going into these schools to help raise awareness and develop interest and skills. Now, the WRU have come on board to help instead of them doing it themselves. There is no question that both Union and clubs need to work together.

I wondered how much Wray estimated the English owners had put collectively into rugby union since their involvement began. He thought the figure would be between £100 and £150 million. A lot of money. But he added, 'Sir John Hall was right five years ago when he said this lot will never come to an agreement so let's have a dust-up now and get it over with. We should have done that. We would have sorted something out and proceeded far earlier than was the case.'

For me, there are two thoughts here. You can try and get on with people and work together to find a compromise or seek confrontation. We in Wales chose the former but it was very difficult.

In Wales, we had another difficulty because you need people to stick together so that you have strength in unity. But not every club came from the same position so that was never going to be viable for us. All the Welsh Premier clubs were saying to us at Cardiff, 'We are right behind you' but, when push came to shove, it was only Cardiff and Swansea who did what they said they'd do and walked away from the Union. Then, when we did that and opted out of

Welsh League rugby by playing a season of friendlies against the English clubs, the other Welsh clubs said we had let them down. Yet they had said all along 'Take us with you.' I think a lot of other clubs wanted to jump away from the WRU but they lacked the resources to go through with it. But despite all this, Nigel Wray remains positive and insists there is still time to make this game really great in a structured, financial way. But for that to happen, he adds, the RFU and the clubs must now work together positively and the WRU must work with the Welsh clubs etc. Going forward together was the only way.

What does he say to those who point out that no one forced the owners to put all this money into rugby? In a business environment, wasn't their loss their concern?

He considered that for a moment and then admitted people were entitled to their views. Yes, he said, it was a business and you accepted the risk factor. But did you as a businessman accept deliberate, wilful obstruction of your aims and ambitions by a third party? Was that fair and reasonable, he asked? Wray knows the reality of the situation as well as anyone. Did not certain business-men get involved purely because they thought they could create the Manchester United of the rugby world? 'Well arguably, that is what we are all trying to achieve, to create a fantastic rugby team for the future. But I think to be fair nobody foresaw the degree of loss. Today, things are much more rational than they were six years ago. I do not expect to make a fortune out of rugby but I do want to create a Saracens club that people can be really proud of and one which, hopefully, tens of thousands of people come regularly to watch. I want to have the club standing on its own feet financially. I don't expect it to start making considerable sums of money but I would love to see it make a little so that it could start re-investing more in academies and community officers who go out to even more schools in the area. We do those things to a certain degree already but there is plenty of scope for improvement and extension of those policies. The academies which have now been set up in most major centres of England are designed to streamline the process of youth selection, to fast-track the best prospects and to work hard in enhancing levels of skill, fitness and tactical awareness.'

Wray went on, 'Financially, I don't mind the club making a reasonable loss: £200,000 to £300,000 per annum loss is bearable.

But the degree of losses thus far have not been reasonable. Sure, Saracens could cut its losses quite dramatically overnight by doing things like stopping the academies and community work. But that would be a shame.'

Yet, despite the problems, Wray does believe rugby will be a great deal bigger than anyone concedes; the Lions of 2001 were the first signs of that happening. One of the arguments against the club owners is that they paid far too much to the players. We said earlier that deciding payments was difficult because no one knew what anyone was really worth. But does Wray accept that several players were overpaid? Was his club guilty of making that mistake?

'If you look at any sport anywhere, players in your terms and mine are always overpaid. Look at football and the trends we have seen there. Roy Keane was said to have negotiated a deal worth £54,000 a week but by the end of the 2001–2002 season, David Beckham's advisers had achieved a new deal for him at Manchester United worth around £90,000 a week. Keane must have thought he had underestimated his worth!

'Rugby players deserve to be very well paid. It is a short-term profession and is highly demanding physically. You are quite likely to get injured and, even if you do well in a rugby sense and earn a salary commensurate for a top player, by the time you reach thirty-two, you will probably have to stop playing professionally. Then you have the rest of your life to live and you are ten to twelve years behind your contemporaries in terms of a job. It is a precarious short-term existence and you need to be well paid. Therefore, players arc entitled to get what they earn.'

I think it's natural players will always hang out for the most money and, in general, I agree that they should be very well paid. However, things have almost escalated out of control in professional football, but TV money is paying for that. But for rugby players there is no real yardstick. We in the northern hemisphere could only go by what the Unions were prepared to pay players in the southern hemisphere. We didn't know what a player was worth. But he was only worth what the game could sustain and that remains the case.

Without the owners coming in, I suppose the players in Wales would have been on about £20,000 to £25,000 a year. The top English players would probably have got around £35,000 to

£40,000. But Nigel brought in a player like François Pienaar and he wouldn't have come cheaply. Other people got to hear what a guy like that was on and, before you knew it, the whole thing was escalating, more than the going rate was paid for the good players. Therefore, the ordinary players were being paid a lot more than they were worth and the whole thing spiralled. But that is being wise after the event.

I raised Peter Thomas's view that a lot of the pain would have been avoided without what he called the obstinacy of the Unions and the dictatorial manner of some officials which had cost the game three years in its development process. Did Wray agree with that?

Wray felt that it came down to this. 'Why should a company, with a structure influenced by however many people all of whom want their free tickets and want to defend their corner, feel comfortable when this kind of major change and challenge comes along? It is not a body that can make proper decisions quickly. Peter Thomas obviously has more experience of dealing with the Welsh Rugby Union than me. I don't know about them specifically but, yes, in any amateur-based body, there are people who would resent any loss of power or control and would therefore obstruct the growth of professionalism where they didn't control it. Without a doubt that has gone on and it has been holding the game back. It just reminds me what could be achieved if we organised the sport differently.

'The owners are definitely not blameless. We have made stupid decisions and have been blind to certain things. In the beginning, we completely underestimated the level of investment required and the scale of the losses. We could have held back the investment and limited any loss if we had made a more thorough analysis rather than saying, "It's a great game, let's get on with it." You can't improve spectator facilities, invest in the schools and do community things like that unless you have the money to afford it. Money is the oxygen that lets the whole game breathe. As owners, we got a lot of things wrong. I didn't go into the game to be as involved as I have been. I intended others should get on with it on my behalf. But suddenly I realised I couldn't just leave people to get on with it. Now, I wish I had taken that attitude and realised that earlier than I did. Because that mistake cost us a considerable amount of money. In a weird way, I feel that the love of the game felt by most owners blinded them to reality for a period of time and that brought them a greater loss than was necessary.'

Wray believes there are still too many people in rugby union clinging to little pockets of power simply for their own benefit. 'I am not knocking the individual Unions but any organisation such as theirs run in that way is like that. One person drives a proper company and he needs two or three people around him whom he trusts and whom he can listen to, to help. So we are talking about no more than three or four people to run the entire show. If you need more than that it gets unwieldy.

'Rugby has to free itself from these people who cling to the Unions. In fairness to the Rugby Football Union, I think they are trying to sort out this problem and they have taken some steps by appointing a chief executive and greatly reducing the number of committees.'

I agree with Nigel Wray on this. I don't think there is any question that there are still too many people hanging on to roles in the Unions for their own benefit. I doubt the game will ever get rid of all those people, but at least the Unions are acknowledging and realising that you have got to have an executive with proper executive powers to run the professional game. That means people other than those amateurs who still cling on. The game requires that, it is moving on so quickly.

Where, I asked Wray, do you see rugby being in five years' time? He did not hesitate. 'I think the phenomenal growth of this game in the next five years will shock us. I mean right around the world, but I do think the two major countries of the northern hemisphere, England and France, will see the greatest growth because they have the greatest populations. I also think some of the smaller countries like Scotland, Wales and Ireland may start to get left behind. Inevitably, England and France will move ahead because of their population masses, because of the marketing potential in those countries and because sponsors will be attracted mostly to them. That is not to say Ireland, Scotland and Wales will be incapable from time to time of delivering a hefty kick in the shins to the national teams of England and France in the Six Nations Championship because they clearly have done and will again.

'But maybe an elite club of world rugby will start to emerge and England and France would have to be part of that. Don't get me wrong, the Six Nations is quite a property and England and France will have to play a quality side in it, otherwise it would destroy the commercial property if those countries paraded second teams. Besides, the average supporter still wants to see Six Nations matches. But maybe the winner and runner-up in the Six Nations will start to compete in the Tri-Nations competition of the southern hemisphere later in the year . . . that sort of situation could come about. That is another reason why the clubs have to be tied in with their Unions because that situation would mean more matches, which means more pressure on the clubs. That is OK if everyone is tied into the same goal.'

What Nigel was saying was that the whole concept of rugby was changing and we have got to acknowledge that, but I should declare my hand here and say that I am a big traditionalist.

Of course, by the time the 2001 British Lions returned to the northern hemisphere, things had begun to change significantly in the game back home. Suddenly, after years of discord in English club rugby, peace broke out early in the new 2001–2002 season, with the RFU and their senior clubs signing a long-term agreement to work together. The English Premiership clubs were assured the very considerable sum of £1.8 million each per season, said to be rising to £2.3 million at a future date. The feeling was that they all ought to be able to make their businesses pay with that kind of financial assistance from the top. Alas, there was nowhere near such a happy outcome in Wales where the whole season up to summer 2002 was spent arguing about the best format with which to take the game forward. By contrast, the situation was much calmer in Scotland and Ireland. The Scottish Rugby Union had created two regional squads based in Glasgow and Edinburgh, with a third, the Borders, scheduled for the 2002–2003 season. In Ireland, the provincial system was working well with three of their provincial sides, Munster, Ulster and Leinster, all proving themselves powers in the Heineken Cup.

What did Nigel Wray make of the agreement as the season 2002–2003 dawned? 'There has now been an enormous improvement, that is undeniable. To me, rugby is now like a new business – you need time to invest in it.

'The situation is certainly more promising than it was but it is still far from perfect. For example, by April 2002, the bottom four clubs in the Premiership were Saracens, Bath, Harlequins and Leeds. Bath had won the Heineken European Cup within the last four years, Harlequins were European Shield winners in 2001 and I like to think Saracens have contributed to the growing aura and quality of Premiership rugby. Leeds were the new boys, making a brave attempt to defy relegation in their first season up in the Premiership. And, to be fair to them, they had invested some not inconsiderable sums in signing players like the South African internationals Braam van Straaten and Japie Mulder.

'The thought of those clubs being relegated was absolutely absurd. Bath themselves accept their own ground is fairly inadequate yet how could they go to the bank and ask for funds to relocate or rebuild if they were threatened with relegation? The bank would obviously say no. OK, in the end none were relegated because Rotherham could not match the criteria required to come up. But relegation, if it continues to exist, means effectively you have a one-year lease on your position in the Premiership. To use the home analogy, would people put a new kitchen into their house with only one year left on their lease? I don't think they'd even consider it.

'Therefore, I believe that you cannot expect clubs to invest in their future if the relegation axe hovers. Relegation doesn't make any sense at all. The Premiership clubs have spent five years and £150 million investing. Why should they be kicked out and replaced by a club that has spent virtually nothing and simply doesn't have the facilities for the top flight?

'That doesn't mean promotion should be stopped. The Premiership should expand to accommodate clubs who want to come up and can prove they have the proper facilities required for this level and a sound marketing structure. Remember, the most successful sports nations on earth are the USA and Australia and their major sports don't have relegation.

'Another factor is that relegation could destroy whole regions. Supposing Harlequins did go down, followed by London Irish and then Saracens the season after that? There wouldn't be a single Premiership club left in London. Would that make sense? After all, it could happen, why not? Similarly, if Leeds, Newcastle or Sale went down, there wouldn't be a single Premiership club in the north east or north west. You can't have that.'

I pointed out that you still have relegation in the English football Premiership. And perhaps older readers can remember the time when Manchester United themselves were relegated from the old first division, and spent the following season 1974–1975 in the second division. But Wray retorted, 'All relegation has done in football is create a situation in which all the sides at the bottom and the top are spending way beyond their means to avoid the hangman's noose of relegation. They're all desperate to have more of the gravy and will do anything to keep in there, even if it means financial irresponsibility. No, to me, relegation is one of the things that is still wrong with Premiership rugby.'

But not the only thing? 'No, the structure of the season is still a walking disaster. When you have a situation whereby Leicester, the English champions and the champions of Europe go to Leeds, a newly promoted club, for a League match and get thrashed 37–16, there is something seriously wrong. Of course, the reason for that was that the Premiership clubs were forced to play League matches on the weekend of international matches in Ireland, England, Scotland, Wales and France. That is absurd.

'Leicester were without eleven first-choice players at Leeds. A similar situation affected Bath earlier in the season, a factor which had much to do with them slipping to the bottom of the Premiership table. It is a nonsense to ask clubs to play at such times. Last year, we at Saracens lost eight players when internationals were taking place. It eventually helped cost us a place in the Heineken Cup for this season, and the financial loss of that was very considerable. What it also means, as Leicester's rugby director Dean Richards rightly pointed out, is that those clubs who develop English players are penalised. A club like Gloucester which had many overseas players, benefited from this state of affairs and no one can tell me that's right.'

In Australia, said Wray, they play the season in proper segments. They weren't playing Super 12 matches at the same time as internationals. Also, he added, Australia, New Zealand and South Africa were allowed to wander into our domestic season and destroy it. Yet British, Irish and French touring sides only went down to the southern hemisphere to play when it suited the host countries. I have to say I agree with him.

Wray thinks that until we get a globally aligned season we will continue to have these problems. He feels the current Six Nations season is a nonsense, with players going from this competition to another, such as the English or Welsh Premiership or Cup. Either the players are injured and absent from many of those club games squeezed in between internationals or they're a shadow of their true selves. And who, Wray asked, wants to watch teams playing without their best players?

England's clubs certainly don't seem to have anywhere near an ideal season. For example, on Boxing Day 2001, there wasn't a single Premiership match scheduled. This, as Wray said, at a time in the holiday when everyone is bored stiff and longs to get out and watch some top-class sport. Footballers play over the Christmas and Easter holiday periods; rugby players should, too. Nigel Wray called the fixture lists 'hopeless', further evidence, he claimed, that everything was far from satisfactorily concluded in English rugby. The same is true in Wales, where we had a five-week spell in autumn 2001 without a home fixture and another one of equal length in February–March 2002. Then, at the end of the season, Cardiff were faced with a cluster of matches with some midweek to complete the programme. What a way to try and run a business – with your premises closed down for five weeks on the trot.

Stretching the Heineken Cup out over the course of eight months was equally ludicrous. 'Like going to watch a film, *Gunfight at the OK Corral*, and halfway through, another completely different film comes on. The first film then returns for a bit but then goes off again and doesn't come back for some months. Ridiculous,' said Wray. But he does believe these problems will be resolved. He detected far greater realism among those in authority, and felt much more confident that decisive strides had been and would continue to be made in a forward direction. Hopefully, he added with a smile, without a couple of strides backwards every time someone moved forward.

Finally, then, what of Nigel Wray himself? Will he still be a part of rugby in five or ten years' time? He certainly hopes so, although he adds a small caveat. 'I certainly wouldn't want to be part of it if we still have the frustration of people pulling in different directions. But if we are all pulling in the same way, then I suspect it is going to be a fantastically exciting vehicle to be on and one which could banish most of the memories of the last few, painful years.'

CHAPTER 5

Structure and Administration

'I told the northern hemisphere Unions the simple truth. I said, "We are asking too much of the players. The present position is totally hypocritical. It is too late to turn the clock back and wrong to try to do so. If we don't pay players, you will all become irrelevant because someone else will take over the game. It will be hijacked." I also expressed my view that the present situation was unsustainable and no good for anyone.'

No single issue has dominated the topic of rugby union in the way that professionalism has these last six years. And no single personality played a more key role in the transformation of the game from amateurism to professionalism than Vernon Pugh, Chairman of the IRB. Since 1995 when the game was famously declared 'open', there had probably been more rancour, more dissent, more argument, more unease and more change than at any time in the previous hundred years of the game's existence. Because rugby union had always been strictly amateur and committed to this principle throughout its existence. Nothing, it had seemed, would deflect the game from that chosen course.

There are, of course, still plenty of critics who remain defiant and, in some cases very angry, that the IRB sanctioned professionalism at that famous gathering they held in Paris in August 1995. Those people say that it could have been prevented, certainly delayed and that the game has been the poorer ever since.

My view is quite clear on this. I will have no truck with the view that the status quo should have remained. First, because it was dishonest: money was pouring into the game from the sponsors' pockets, and it was financing improved facilities and new stadia right down to more plush seats and rooms for the committees. The Rugby Football Union, it is said, even had an extensive wine cellar built at Twickenham and stocked with some outstanding premier crus for the use of the committee and their guests. Very nice, too.

But, while all this was going on, the players whose skills and efforts were responsible for this explosion in the commercial attraction of the sport were being denied time and again by the game's authorities. Reasonable, indeed often very practical, requests made by the players were constantly being knocked back. For example, that of players getting time off to go on Lions tours was a burning issue. It became increasingly difficult to expect an employer to go on paying a player's salary while he was away on a tour which could last for up to thirteen weeks. That seemed outrageous with the respective Home Unions earning millions from commercial support. The request was made by several players that their Union should pay all or indeed some of their salary to assist their employer during the time of their absence. But there was always this wall. 'No, a thousand times no' seemed to sum up their response.

I believe that had the authorities shown greater vision in those days, and agreed certain requests such as that one, perhaps the pressure to make the game open might not have developed so powerfully. As it was, however, it became inevitable that the players who are the ones everybody comes to see, should receive proper financial recompense for their skills and efforts. The old game was living a lie – calling itself amateur but welcoming millions of pounds into the respective Unions' coffers, without offering a penny, legally, to the players who were making it all possible.

The second reason I will have no truck with those who berate professionalism is that I don't believe it is a bad thing for rugby. What we now have is fair in that the best players in their respective countries are well paid. The harder they train, the more professional they are in their attitude, the greater the potential rewards available to them. Is that not a better, fairer system?

Thus, said Vernon Pugh when he sat down with members of the northern hemisphere rugby unions, rugby men representing countries like Ireland, England, Wales, Scotland, Italy and France, he

The health of junior rugby is fundamental to the prosperity of the game as a whole. Here one of the Stow-on-the-Wold club sides is in action at their home in the heart of the Cotswolds.

How the stars can help youngsters: The Avon Under-11s photographed with several players from the nearby Bath club after a special training session.
Back row from left: Avon Under-11s coach Chris Hobbs, ex-Bath coach Jon Callard, England lock Danny Grewcock, USA international Dan Lyle and England full-back Matt Perry.

Inga Tuigamala, whose £1 million contract at Newcastle led to a pay explosion in the English game.

Pieter Muller, the South African, who has been a great role model for the Cardiff youngsters like fellow centre Jamie Robinson *(left)*.

What protection for a scrum half! The outstanding 1974 British Lions forward pack, with Bobby Windsor *(left)*, serve me possession on a plate during one of the Tests.

Hard-working IRB chairman Vernon Pugh hands out the medals at a World Cup Sevens final in Argentina. No prizes for guessing the identity of man-mountain No. 1!

By no means all is sweetness and light in the English club game, a point emphasised by overseas stars Jason Little (Bristol and Australia) and *(left)* Ian Jones (Wasps and New Zealand).

DAVE ROGERS/GETTY IMAGES

Jason Robinson, in my view, is one of the most exciting players in the world today. Here, he slips past the bemused French defence to score a try in Paris during the 2002 Six Nations Championship. But England lost and saw France go on to the coveted Grand Slam.

MARK DADSWELL/ALLSPORT

DAVE ROGERS/ALLSPORT

The old game of rugby union was never the same once media tycoon Rupert Murdoch had invested £500 million plus on southern hemisphere rugby, back in 1995.

Gareth Davies, the former Cardiff chief executive, who expressed some strong views in our meeting to discuss the media's role in the modern game.

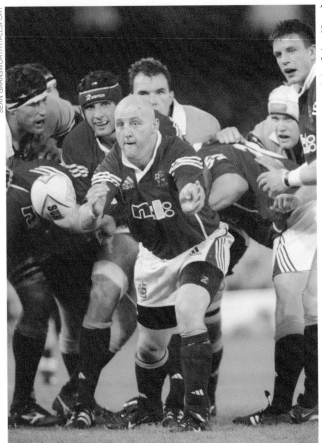

They say 20,000 fans followed the Lions to Australia in 2001. These two pals certainly had a great time.

The outstanding Keith Wood, a player who is able to do most things on the rugby field.

Brian O'Driscoll, Ireland's champion three-quarter, seen shooting through a gap like a startled hare during the Lions Test series against the Wallabies.

A man alone? Lions 2001 coach Graham Henry, who suffered the double disappointment of seeing the Lions lose the series and then losing his job as Welsh national coach a few months later.

Now these boys could play a bit in their time – with me, from left, Michael Lynagh and David Campese (Australia), Barry John (Wales) and Sean Fitzpatrick (New Zealand) at a Hall of Fame dinner, London, November 2001.

One for the future. Iestyn Harris (Cardiff and Wales) still has much to learn about the union game after his move from rugby league. But, as he shows here on his debut against Argentina in 2001, he has the style to succeed.

had a message for them which he knew would be unpalatable in the extreme. That message comprised the first sentences of this chapter and nothing you will read from here on can have a greater impact, in my opinion. It is worth repeating again. Pugh said, 'I told the northern hemisphere unions the simple truth. I said, "If we don't pay players, you will all become irrelevant because someone else will take over the game. It will be hijacked." I also told them the present situation was hypocritical and no good for anyone.'

Ever since rugby union was declared 'open', Vernon Pugh has been painted in all shades of colour. Some have just wanted to throw the paint at him! The Chairman of the International Rugby Board, Vernon is a barrister who practises from Gray's Inn, London, a Bencher at Lincoln's Inn and a Crown Court Recorder. He has held many distinguished positions in the game. He first joined the Welsh Rugby Union board in 1993 as chairman and fulfilled that role until 1997. He is a member and past chairman of the Five Nations Committee and the Committee of the Home Unions and a former director of European Cup Ltd. He is chairman of Rugby World Cup Ltd and became the first elected chairman of the IRB in 1996, and was also chairman in 1994 after joining the previous year. In 1995, he chaired the Board's former Amateurism Committee which brought the game into the professional era. Given that little 'list of honours' his first remark when we met surprised me. 'I had never sat on a committee in my life before 1993 and had a normal player's view of committees.' (Which is to say, not very much.) 'I found sitting on those committees fascinating.'

But in a very short space of time, Vernon Pugh became one of the key figures in the game and arguably *the* main figure in the transformation from amateur to open.

You cannot pretend you are examining all aspects of our game at the start of this twenty-first century unless you sit down and discuss them with Vernon Pugh. So I went along to Vernon's chambers in Cardiff city centre and discussed a wide range of topics with him. Mind you, I was lucky to catch up with him. He had just flown in from the IRB headquarters in Dublin that lunchtime. He was off to London later that afternoon as part of his barrister's work and the next day he was flying to Prague on rugby business. The life of the IRB chairman is a very busy one.

We sat surrounded by shelves of neatly stacked legal books,

doubtless recounting tales of courtroom battles long ago. Talking of vigorous verbal debates, first I asked him whether he had ever regretted the Board's decision to make the game open in 1995? No, he said firmly, not once had he thought it should never have happened. He felt that it was inevitable and good for the game. The good thing was that the sport had been professionalised within the confines of a game we still recognise for what it is. Had it not been at least relatively controlled and regulated, the outcome could have been quite different from what we know at the moment. Did he mean people would have taken it out of the control of the Unions? 'What I mean is the control of what I might call the people who cared for the sport – "rugby people". Administrators, players, long-time supporters . . . people who have known and loved the game all their lives. What has resulted has not been a hybrid game.'

But did Pugh and his colleagues have any choice at that Paris meeting? Could they have turned their backs on professionalism and insisted the game remain amateur?

'If the IRB had put its head in the sand and said it is staying an amateur game, we would have had a professional game controlled by interests outside the sport such as entrepreneurs and broadcasters. They would have looked at the possibility of a TV product and put some new laws into the game. What we would have ended up with would have been a hijacked, hybrid version of rugby union and rugby league. It would have been delivered for a global audience, similar to the sort of thing we had seen in cricket years before with Kerry Packer. Certainly it would have been a very different sort of game.'

Introducing professionalism, as I have said, is not where I take issue. In my view it was inevitable that professionalism came, but I don't believe it was inevitable that professionalism should happen the way it did. Did Pugh agree? Broadly speaking, he did.

What I continue to lament was the way it was introduced, the almost haphazard method in which it was created and then left to take care of itself in some countries, often without any guidance from those in authority. Might not rugby in most countries have expected better guardianship of the game and a greater vision from those charged with its care and future good health?

The background to it all was that a combination of factors which occurred about the same time around 1995 had made for a very turbulent period. When Pugh first joined the WRU in 1993, two years before the vote to take the game open, he says he encountered a game of two factions. Within Europe and the Home Unions – i.e. England, Wales, Scotland and Ireland – the fight was on to retain what was seen as fundamental to the game, namely amateurism. At the same time he, like everyone else, found that France was virtually professional because most of their players were, in everything but name, being paid to play. South Africa, he said, were certainly professional. New Zealand and Australia were operating within the rules but they could almost be classed professional through the use of trust funds and giving their players other opportunities not available to northern hemisphere players. There was, he said, a big divide and they were talking about a different game. He says he could see there was going to be a collision.

'I was also involved in the TV contracts for the WRU and knew that we were on the verge of an explosion in the value of the sport. We were asking for five times what we had received three years before. You could see and feel this huge explosion of values that was taking place. I felt that South Africa and Australia had got it broadly right because they knew that if you required a professional standard of play and a global game, then they had to accept the realities. If you want top quality performances, it means a huge commitment on the part of the players which was only possible if they were paid to do it. We had to manage, charge and accommodate the situation without the two hemispheres splitting which was a very live possibility.'

The big, burly Australian administrator Leo Williams was the key man running the southern hemisphere and Pugh was in constant contact with him. But what could Pugh do about the opposition among the Unions in the British Isles and Ireland? 'Besides the payment issue, it was also clear that there was already a gap between the playing strengths of the northern and southern hemisphere countries. Had we in the north delayed professionalism, that gap would have got bigger and bigger and would have taken perhaps many, many years to close. It was clear that better and more regular competition was essential for the northern hemisphere players. In late 1994 I raised the possibility of a European Cup and that initially received a very hostile reaction. It was said we couldn't do it. Wales and France were pushing for it but the other Unions didn't want to know. By mid 1995 things were starting to turn and there was talk of starting in 1996 or 1997. I knew this would be too late. What persuaded people to face reality and act quickly was the World Cup in 1995, the threat of the WRC breakaway and the Murdoch deal with the southern hemisphere nations. That was critical over the timing issue.'

Pugh said that many players were open and frank about what they had been offered by the people attempting to set up WRC, the breakaway world game plan which would have paid players openly and hijacked the sport. 'Ross Turnbull seemed to be running it and my original information in early 1995 was they had signed about 100–150 top players. Imagine my shock when I found out they had apparently signed over 400. Included among them were said to be various national captains. This was a very serious threat to the structure of the entire sport. What stopped it eventually were the actions of Louis Luyt, the South African rugby supremo, who persuaded key players to stay on, and the alternative deal negotiated by the southern hemisphere Unions with News Corporation. We had good information about all this and it turned almost all the waverers who were dithering on professionalism.'

So when the northern hemisphere Unions met in Paris, there was a report on the table which said bluntly there was no choice. The game had to become open. In Pugh's estimation, had it not happened, it would have been more dangerous than what had happened in cricket with the Packer circus. There would have been an adverse reaction from the News Corporation Group (owned by Rupert Murdoch) and therefore, Pugh believes, there would have been two groups fighting for the soul of the game. He said it was similar with the clubs. Had they taken over the running of the game in England and Wales, you would have had them forming a separate organisation and ending up having the same problems as the Unions. It all came down to how professionalism was introduced, that was what mattered.

'I had chaired a working group of the IRB that presented a report in February/March 1995 stating that an open game was inevitable, beneficial and overdue. We knew that would meet with strong resistance but the reaction was, in fact, thoughtful and reasonably objective. The next stage was a follow-up report to the IRB's October meeting. That would have recommended a firm decision of intent to make the game open; provided a date for its introduction sometime in 1996 and established a new set of guidelines and regulations to provide the framework for having a sport where the very best players would be paid for their services. As it turned out, the events surrounding the WRC Challenge, the News Corporation deal with the SANZAR Unions and the interest being shown by News Corporation in the form of Sky in the UK, totally demolished the planned strategy. I spent my summer break writing a revised report to the IRB, stating that immediate action was essential and that we should hold a special meeting in August 1995. That meeting was historic and very enlightening. A lot of home truths were aired and the difficult decision was faced up to – very few Unions voted against the motion. We had to declare the game open and ride some difficult horses for a number of years. We knew it would be short-term pain but for long-term gain. We had no choice – had we tried to postpone it in the environment that prevailed at that time, others would have dived in and taken full advantage. However, the danger for any form of controlled transition came when the RFU then tried to pretend for a year it had not happened and postponed action.'

England, as the original home of the game, held a key position. Unions around the world looked to see whether the RFU would give a lead, provide guidance on how to resolve these complex problems. But the world looked in vain for leadership from England. They hesitated, did not sign up their international players, did not chart a clear course through the minefield but allowed outside factions to come in and battle for territory. Pugh explained. 'Given that England was the centre of the commercial market in the UK, and given that the RFU was recognised as the leader of the game historically, people expected guidance. Like everyone else, I always regarded people like Dudley Wood as fine figures. But Dudley had gone into retirement and when what was perceived to be the senior Union was left with no clear perception of the change or a vision for the future, it did not grasp the nettle, and that caused a huge amount of confusion and uncertainty.'

Worse still, according to Pugh, it left a vacuum that allowed in some people who, he feared, did not have rugby interests in their heart. 'If there had been an immediate interaction between all the clubs and Unions in that year, we could have saved ourselves and the game so much strife. But people built up entrenched positions that made it hard to achieve unity. The trouble was none of the Unions apart from France knew how to go about paying players and creating a form of professionalism. There was a widespread reluctance to deal with the issues as they were. That was why professionalism took so long to resolve. It has taken several years in most Unions in Europe, but I believe we are almost there now. At last, we seem to have got a pretty good accord between the top clubs and the Unions on a well-regulated provincial or district structure.'

But between the strife and the unity lay long years of agonised debate, non-stop friction and the falling out of many old friends. I was appalled to see a great many people drift away from rugby, dismayed at the rows and public spats which were threatening to tear the old game apart. Why had there been so smooth a transition in the southern hemisphere by comparison with the difficulties encountered in the rugby-playing world north of the equator? For a start, Pugh pointed to the fact that the southern hemisphere Unions had the benefit of a $555 million broadcast contract overnight. That made a big difference. The means were available to put in place a Union-regulated structure, made easier by the absence of a historically strong club game. Conversely, in the northern hemisphere, the unions were in the middle of TV negotiations. The desire to achieve as much money as possible sometimes clouded their good sense in realising it was what you did with the money that mattered more than how you achieved it, he said.

People's desire to achieve money . . . I doubt whether I have ever heard a more pertinent phrase. Because the fact was, almost overnight, everyone in the game was talking about nothing else. I viewed as ridiculous a situation whereby ordinary players not good enough to lace the boots of the best, demanded telephone-number-sized salaries.

Perhaps it was best summed up when one London club rang a player in the north and asked if he would like to join them. 'How much?' was the response. A fee was mentioned and the player is said to have replied: 'Yes, and what else?' A car was mentioned and the player replied, 'Well one car isn't good enough. So-and-so club has already offered me two.' The London club coach hastily decided he'd probably be better off playing with fourteen players than having this guy in his team. Rightly so, too.

There is no doubt it was certainly a rough ride on difficult horses. But the trouble was that people didn't understand what professionalism meant and that caused a fundamental problem in the lower echelons of the game for years to come. Might not that have been done differently? I asked Pugh.

It was something he had often thought about before and after Paris 1995. 'I now believe that the actual decision should have been qualified in some way, if only to initially limit payment to specified categories. However, I am still inclined to the view that it was cleaner to do it the way we did it. But there were some unexpected results. By saying the game was professional, people at every level assumed that it was compulsory and that they had to be professional. Instead of understanding that it was meant to address the problem at the elite level, it went so deep that even those of modest abilities thought they should be paid. If we had the opportunity of doing it again, I would suggest introducing qualified professionalism, whereby it only applied to international squads, for twelve months. Had we done that, it would have sent a clear signal as to what professionalism meant. However, the change in the game was a collective decision from a group of very experienced people – steeped in rugby and knowledgeable about the wider business world. This was very important – it ensured that most of those quality people, much as they may have disliked the change, stayed within the game and ensured a continuity and stability of responsible decision-making as the change worked its way through and the sport entered a new era.'

I am sure Vernon is right in saying the Unions should have made it clear that below first division, the game should remain amateur. Was that now a possibility? Pugh thought so, but what worries me is that it will surely take a lot of unravelling to create the right structure whereby most of the game does revert to amateurism. But Pugh says the other surprise to him when professionalism arrived was just how hopeless business people were at running a rugby business. 'Once they got involved in the sport they threw all business sense out of the window. What has been shown in recent years is that business people get involved because they let the sport rule their heads and not the business aspect. They should have managed professional rugby in a much more sensible way. They were the first to criticise the existing administrators but the evidence of how they managed the sports business has not been encouraging. I thought it would have been good for rugby to have quality business people involved but many of the early experiences showed otherwise – and it is very interesting to see now who is left – almost all of them are rugby people.'

I half agree with that but no more. Yes, such criticism can be applied to some, but by no means all the businessmen who became involved. I think what clouded the issue was that there was a misconception of what the game was worth. Some people thought of it as a Premiership soccer-type investment. Everybody worked from the top down, in terms of value of players. It ran away with everybody and made no sense. But everyone was by then on the conveyor belt. Pugh agreed with me. He felt that in that open market-place, market imperatives were ignored and people paid far more than they could afford. Of course, we had seen this in soccer and now it was happening in rugby. 'I thought the business sense of those coming into the sport meant they would have handled it better. It didn't happen in the southern hemisphere although without the club structure they didn't face the same difficulties,' he said.

But if the first half dozen or so years of professionalism in this part of the world have been fraught with difficulties, then you have to say there has been one delightful aspect of it. The arrival and rapid growth in popularity of the European Cup, which has enjoyed the sponsor support of Heineken, has been a wonderful boost for the game in the northern hemisphere. This was a magnificent concept and even now, so comparatively early in its life, it has forged an unmistakable attraction for players and spectators alike. I dare say the odd administrator hasn't been too dismayed to find himself on a plane to the south of France or the west of Ireland in his various capacities as a northern hemisphere rugby administrator. Very quickly, we saw the great benefit of this tournament. It began in the autumn of 1995, with representatives only from France, Italy, Wales and Ireland. There were four pools of just three clubs, clearly an event very much in its infancy. Nevertheless, there was a great sense of occasion at Cardiff Arms Park when Cardiff and Toulouse lined up for the final, a match which, sadly from my point of view, the Frenchmen won by 21–18 after extra time. A crowd of 21,800 watched the final. The following year, the English and Scottish sides came in and the final, again in Cardiff, was between Leicester and Brive. Again, the Frenchmen emerged 28–9 winners but the crowd had almost doubled in just twelve months, to 41,664. The competition was on the march. In 1997–1998, an English club, Bath, broke the French monopoly of the splendid Cup, by bravely toppling French opponents Brive in the final at Bordeaux. A crowd of 36,500 saw the Bath full-back Jon Callard earn immortality within the proud West Country club by scoring all his side's points, including a late penalty goal which snatched the trophy from Brive's grasp. The many Bath supporters in the crowd went wild with delight. A few months later, one lady supporter struck up a conversation with Callard back at the club's ground in the Georgian city after a home game in the English League. She told an amused Callard, 'We had a marvellous time over in Bordeaux. But what about you, were you there?' Alas, for Callard and Bath, the good times did not continue. By springtime 2002, Callard had left as coach of the club and Bath were struggling to avoid relegation from the Premiership. Brive, incidentally, were by then wallowing in the second division of French rugby.

The following year, it was the turn of the Irish province Ulster, always a strong, proud rugby-playing people, to lift the trophy after a 21–6 win over French club Colomiers at Lansdowne Road. The match lured around 50,000 Northern Irish rugby men south of the border to follow their province and a week later at an official lunch, Ulster coach Harry Williams brought the house down by saying, 'We emptied the north of Ireland of more Ulstermen than Gerry Adams could ever have dreamed of.'

By the time the 1999–2000 competition was played, a total of twenty-four teams were involved, the best from England, Wales, France, Scotland, Ireland and Italy. It seemed for a long time as though Munster would keep the trophy in Ireland, especially after a wonderful 31–25 victory over the French champions Stade Français at the Stade Lescure, Bordeaux, in the semi-finals. But Northampton pipped them 9–8 in the final, Munster's fly half Ronan O'Gara missing a late opportunity to win the Cup with a penalty goal. But perhaps the best news of all was the attendance for that final – 68,441 at Twickenham. And twelve months later, at the Parc des Princes, Leicester kept the trophy in England by overcoming Stade Français 34–30 in a tense, exciting final. Once again, the venue for the final had been sold out, with 47,500 crammed into the famous old Paris stadium. It was a great testimony to the growing appeal of the event, a fact confirmed when Leicester retained the trophy in May 2002 by beating Munster before 75,000 people at Cardiff's Millennium Stadium.

But it wasn't just for the finals that the supporters travelled. Munster arrived in Newport for a night match in their group and hundreds of their followers made for a noisy, happy group supporting their team. And when the draw was made for the first group matches of the 2001–2002 event, Bath supporters were said to be booking their trips down to the south of France in late September at a rate of knots, for the match with the exciting Biarritz side. Among others journeying into France that 2001–2002 season were the supporters of Munster, who saw their team beat French club Castres in the Heineken Cup semi-final at Beziers.

For Vernon Pugh, such a success story came as no surprise but, yet, as a matter of huge personal satisfaction. 'We created the European Cup after much arguing but I knew that it would be very valuable. I thought it would become a European League in time, perhaps thirty-two strong. The disputes over Europe command almost as much time as the IRB – but it has worked. In due course, I sense the northern hemisphere countries will play the majority of their seasons as a European-focused event. Europe is such a small place but with high diversity; it is easy to travel and interest is European-wide now. Having only six Saturdays for European fixtures, which was the case at the start of the 2001–2002 season, does not take full advantage of the competition. There should be a minimum of twelve Saturdays followed by the knock-out stage. Europe is certainly the future at the top level, not domestic leagues.'

For a while in the early months of 2001, we thought there would be an extension to the European Cup. Many countries were actively discussing the idea of boosting the participating numbers but then France and England said they didn't want to increase it. Speaking personally, that disappointed me. Pugh called it 'self interest' but said, 'At the end of the day, the overall general interest usually wins through. It nearly happened, we nearly had a European League. If it had been finalised, it would have made no commercial sense for people to stay out had we put it together. And you could play it for four months of the year in Europe.

'I never agreed with Graham Henry [the former Welsh national coach], knocking Wales into two or three clubs. It is not the nature of the beast. There will always be at least four strong clubs in Wales. But the lack of common interest and agreed objectives has left us with a club system that is short of the ideal role model for the benefit of all the rugby clubs, players, public and the national interest. In 1995, Tom Kiernan and I told the European Nations they had 48 hours to decide whether to buy into a European Cup or someone else would do it. Three hours' discussion was enough – everyone signed up for the European Cup. But England and Scotland were very reluctant to come into it, although for different reasons. They were tough times, trying to keep hold of the game without losing the soul of the sport to some media mogul or a disparate group of club owners. If one person had owned the world game, it certainly wouldn't have been in the interests of the sport. Yet we very nearly got to that position. We were fortunate that in the first year of the European Cup we had the support of ITV and Heineken and got a very good deal. Then England came in for the second year.'

After that first year, BBC television has covered the tournament, apart from a two-year break when Sky broadcast it, with growing success and enhanced viewing figures. But Pugh revealed something not many of us knew. 'The European Cup was really the key area during the most difficult years of disputes between Unions and the clubs. It really was topsy-turvy, with broadcasting as the key. ITV pulled out after the first year, Heineken also pulled out after only a short spell. Without the revenue, the Unions had no means of persuading the clubs to stay with the competition, as opposed to setting up their own. We had a settled TV deal in France but in the UK, we had to cobble together a regionally based BBC and S4C structure for the second year. Then we negotiated a four-year deal with Sky. The English clubs and two Welsh clubs – Swansea and Cardiff – withdrew in the fourth year of the competition and so did Sky.

'The expectation, if not the plan, was that this would bring down ERC and that a new and different European competition would be formed by the clubs for a very limited and elite group. We survived another year with a patchwork of local TV deals and then negotiated a four-year deal with the BBC. They showed great faith in the concept and the competition, even after things looked very uncertain – a lot of thanks goes to Mike Miller, the then head of sport at BBC.

'And then, after another period of time involving long nights of negotiation and discussion – once more in Paris – we sat down with the clubs and Unions. Tom Kiernan of Ireland who had kept the competition alive for five years, chaired the meeting brilliantly and by 4a.m. we had a deal worked out. That now forms the foundation for the coming together of an agreed and fair basis for the European Cup. The great pity is that if all this had been achieved three to four years before then European and northern hemisphere rugby would have been much further forward than it is now.'

Mention of England's power brought other thoughts into my mind. Although the fact is, France have won three Grand Slams in the last six years while England have won none, there is no doubt that in recent seasons we have begun to see the true power and potential of English rugby. The way they barnstormed through the Six Nations tournament of 2001, thrashing Wales, Scotland, Italy and France before losing by six points to Ireland, was an indication of their growing threat. They would probably have won the Grand Slam before the end of that season, but the foot and mouth crisis in Britain meant their game against Ireland in Dublin was postponed.

When it was eventually played, in October 2001, England were clearly ring rusty, given it was their first game together since the previous spring, some six months earlier. But few could doubt England's potential, especially when they contributed nineteen players to the Lions tour of Australia and still went to North America and won three Tests, one against Canada and two against the USA. I think it was pretty clear that several of those young players England introduced on that North American tour would probably have got into some of the other Six Nations teams first XVs. England, in my view, will always be strong although occasionally one of the other countries will be exceptionally strong and provide them with competition. Pugh concurred. 'Everybody is finding their way of advancing themselves. But if you want a country with a fantastic future, it is England. They have had two stages of real development. One was in the time of Don Rutherford. He made a big difference as technical director and now there is another, with all the central funding from the RFU and also Sport England, the Government-backed organisation promoting sports in England, being put to good use in development terms. England is really strong and can get even better. It will be a permanent rugby power. France, of course, will also stay strong.'

And Vernon has to be right, as regards the French. After all, by April 2002, they were celebrating that third Grand Slam in the last six years and a run of eight successive victories, culminating in the 44–5 win over Ireland in Paris, to complete their winter programme.

But given that situation, what are the portents for the Six Nations Championship, now expanded of course to include Italy? My feeling is that if ever this great tournament were weakened or even lost, then the game in this part of the world would be severely damaged. I see its continued existence as most important, because it continues to provide the soul and passion of the sport. Nothing should be allowed to threaten or undermine that.

And what were the views of the IRB chairman on this topic? Pugh said, 'It's incredibly important, especially when you view it against the longer term background and what you should be trying to achieve for the game. It is unique in sport; you have so many visiting fans travelling as part of the whole event. It is a fantastic sporting occasion. There is still huge interest and it is so good-natured. It is so productive in terms of commercial value. TV audiences are enormous. You still get more people watching Scotland v Ireland on BBC than tune into England v Australia on BSkyB. Above all, it is right for Europe to have its own competition. It would be stupid to destroy something that has been wonderfully successful. Maybe it needs some fine tuning, but as a competition it is essential to European rugby.

'Compare it with the Tri Nations. The great distances there mean that perhaps only a hundred New Zealanders go to South Africa to see the All Blacks play. It is largely a home country event which makes it completely different. The travelling involved certainly exhausts the players; that is another factor there and a problem for those concerned with the structure. The rugby is terrific but the issue of distance makes it quite different to the Six Nations. Certainly, if England and France went to the Tri Nations and expanded that competition, it would totally devalue the Six Nations. In that event I don't think the competition could continue in its present form. A lot of the spirit would go out of it as well as commercial value. It would make very many millions of European rugby fans very unhappy. Not that I believe it will happen. In a wider sense for world rugby, it would concentrate resources at a particular level within five or six Unions. The Rugby World Cup would start to lose its significance. But that is the main source of income for the International Board so that would disappear which would mean little money could be channelled to the poorer rugby-playing nations to develop the game in their countries. I believe any sport has a responsibility to those less well off.'

I have to say there have been plenty of things over which I have disagreed strongly with Vernon Pugh these last few years. But I agree wholeheartedly with his thoughts on this topic. The northern hemisphere nations have a wonderful tournament, a unique event which seems successful every year. They need to retain it and they need to stick together.

As I said a little earlier, Vernon Pugh became the first elected chairman of the IRB in 1996 and he outlined what he had been attempting to do at the international game's headquarters in Dublin. He said his chief task had been to turn rugby into a global game and make the IRB into a proper worldwide governing body. Historically, it made the laws but didn't do much else. Transforming it almost overnight from that sort of body for which people didn't have a lot of respect or time to one with a good *raison d'être* was taking a little time, he conceded. He wants a governing body that has a proper vision, does positive things, carries real authority and is respected throughout the world. The game needs a world-wide governing body of stature. To achieve that, he believes you need finance and a good strong, professional executive staff. Concluding this process would be his number one ambition. If and when the IRB becomes that, it will do the things it needs to do to develop the game worldwide. For example, to ensure the wealth is shared fairly. It is about getting proportionality into it, and also to ensure we look for new revenue sources, and then to provide that development money to the countries where it is most needed. 'We are funding progress and advances in countries all over the world. We're seeing some terrifically interesting results and developments in countries like Russia and Georgia. They are already on a par with Romania. I find that quite exciting. In China, too, athletes are starting to get involved in the sport and then there is America, potentially a huge growth area. Suddenly, rugby will develop a wider spectrum and that is the excitement of what is happening at the moment. There is a fantastic future for this game. But we have to find the right balance between self-centred interests and more widespread and global interests, and also recognise the benefit and duty to the less talented players who also love playing our sport.'

Self-centred interests? Can you ever stop them? Pugh admits every Union will try to get as much money as it can and keep that for itself. He says it's not easy because you look for models as a worldwide governing body, but there isn't one that stands out as the ideal for them to follow. Tennis, soccer, athletics . . . none are like rugby. But he believes rugby has the chance to make something good and something better.

Pugh's only continuing involvement in Welsh rugby is as chairman of the Dragon's Trust, with part responsibility for running school and junior level developments. He regards the Welsh Under-21s scene as a great success story, and he is right to feel contented. Four years ago, there were ten schools in Wales playing regular Saturday rugby. Now, through the Trust nearly a hundred school teams play every Saturday. Two years ago at youth level, there were only 30 teams playing in Wales. Now, it is 146 playing in a structured Saturday Youth League. It showed how many keen youngsters were out there but without the organisation to provide them with opportunities to play rugby. Pugh thinks that, in cyclical terms, Wales will be one of the countries that still produces good teams in the future. He remembers thinking when he joined the WRU in 1993 and saw first hand how things were, that Welsh rugby was finished or so it seemed. He thought to himself, 'My God, I never realised how bad it was.' Sadly, I found in those words something of an echo with the situation in spring 2002. Very nearly ten years later.

Pugh said of the early nineties, 'In playing terms there was no innovation, nothing was happening there. Personally, I had believed that I would commit to three years of involvement, and then leave but that is not what I found. There was a choice – either to get out, having seen what it was really like and realised how bad the situation was, or stay in and try to improve things. I honestly thought it would take fifteen years to change. There were two basic problems. The structure was not suited to running a modern commercial organisation, and there was nothing by way of incentive or attraction to spark off a re-emergence of interest in the game in Wales. I realised that delivering both was more or less impossible. The ten or fifteen years could be spent trying to modernise the administrative structure but even then, that might not be successful. I felt that setting targets, providing highlights and key goals would bring the structure into the modern world. I was wrong. Much was done and I feel proud of what was achieved: Rugby World Cup for Wales as host nation; the Millennium Stadium; the Directorate of Rugby which took the playing side into the performance area with the world's first ever paid national coach; restructuring junior rugby through Dragon's Trust; international club competitions in the European Cup and Shield; a national league for Welsh clubs and huge increases in revenue from marketing and sponsor contracts. All successes, but instead of driving forward organisational change, it simply served, on the back of those successes, to cement in place the existing system.'

Ah, the 1999 World Cup. I was as proud as any Welshman or woman to see the sport's greatest event hosted by my country. So much time and effort went into the planning of it, and so many people did so much to make it a success. But overall, was it successful? Pugh's summary revealed a divide of success and failure. Commercially, financially and organisationally he regarded it as very successful. The IRB got more income than they had planned. It was free of trouble and went off well. But in terms of generating excitement, it fell short for two reasons. 'One was the way the game was being played at that time. Frankly, it was at its worst. The best team but still a defensive-minded team [Australia] that relied on others to make mistakes could and did win it. Secondly, we got it wrong by spreading the tournament to so many countries and, more than that, having too many gaps between the matches. With a better structure, it would have been more successful and been the pinnacle that it should have been. Also, for the pool matches, some Unions didn't put the required effort into it. Scotland unfortunately were the worst in that respect, but it served as a lesson to us all.'

Lessons to be learned? Pugh is intrigued by the notion of a World Cup focused in one country which will now happen, of course, in Australia in 2003. I must say I concur. But is it asking a lot of any

104

one country to put it all on because there are very few rugby stadiums in each country? Wales has only one, Scotland one, Ireland one, England maybe two. Pugh would concur with a degree of sharing the tournament but not, he hopes, to the same extent as in recent times.

In 2007, he speculated, it could be England or France's turn. France might make it a 'continental' World Cup, and maybe they would give a few games to Italy and perhaps also to Spain. From my point of view, I would love to see a World Cup played entirely in France. I think they have a number of fine grounds which they have used for rugby purposes, such as at Lens, Nantes and Lille. Then you have others like Toulouse and Beziers and the two Parisian stadia, Parc des Princes and Stade de France which would obviously stage the final. I suspect half the United Kingdom and Ireland would empty as rugby fans went over there for two or three weeks to watch the games. Transport would be easy, accommodation no problem. In my estimation, France would be a wonderful location, especially down in the south in late September.

Our conversation had ranged across a wide divide. I felt Vernon Pugh had confronted some tough issues honestly and in forthright fashion. He had admitted the IRB had got it wrong in some areas and passed criticism where he felt it appropriate. Where, I asked him, did he feel the game was now, as everyone looked ahead to the early years of the twenty-first century? 'Still in a period of big transition but on the verge of a huge leap forward. On the whole, relations are better across the game; we are relatively stable and people are now more prepared to talk to others. We should remember, it was a massive change, the concept of the game changed overnight, after more than a hundred years of reliance on a basic ethos. It didn't change by opening a door and two or three people walking in; rather, 100,000 people walked in. But I am reasonably content we have come through all that and remain integrally strong and with something to build on. But I still don't think rugby has found the right balance between the business person and the rugby person. Look at the IRB; in my time, of twenty-one people there, fifteen or sixteen are hugely successful in business, some millionaires, highly qualified in their own field. But it is not the right group to be running the game on a day-to-day basis, and we need to build up a strong executive staff, implementing the decisions of the policy makers. I don't think many, if any, Union has got it absolutely right yet, we are still feeling our way. But it will come. Once it does, the opportunities will be fantastic. Because other sports are already saying that rugby union is becoming a huge game.'

Pugh wants to see rugby becoming part of the *world* sporting scene. If it gains entry to the Olympics, he would personally prefer to see it as a 7-a-side game because he thinks it would give more countries a genuine chance to win a medal. But he understands the view that 15-a-side is our premier game. The main thing is, Olympic participation would help the game everywhere. He thinks there would be £20 million per annum income available to help less rich countries simply by achieving Olympic status. Now it is £7 million a year from World Cup revenue. He views rugby as a game that can attract so many. It is cheap to play because the kit is cheap and you only need a flat field.

What, I asked Pugh, had rugby lost above all else, in his opinion? 'Rugby in the community is not as strong as previously. A lot of good people that underpinned the game by giving freely of their time are now disillusioned because they find they are running something quite different to what they grew up with and understood. I think it is important that we reorganise the image as well as the benefits of professionalism, that many understand the game can be played for enjoyment and fun at all levels and where the game is not professional. We need to see more of those people coming back into the game. Development worldwide is another area of concern. If you look at South Africa, their elite level is strong but some other levels have suffered. In New Zealand it is reported that no more than a handful of white schoolboys were said to be playing rugby in Auckland at one stage recently. That is a huge change. On the other hand, participation numbers in Australia have expanded at a great rate. I would say that everywhere, not just in the UK, there is a need to wed rugby back to the community.'

Mention of the Pacific raised another issue in my mind. It is obvious New Zealand and Australia have benefited from having an influx of island players over the years. Pugh felt it was a particularly tricky matter. 'If you take New Zealand as a prime example, looking at the short term a large percentage of the teams are non-whites but they are New Zealand people. There is no doubt New Zealand used Samoa as a breeding ground, Fiji and Tonga to a lesser extent. This was a version of Wales's own so-called "Granny-gate"! But if you go to Auckland, there are more Samoans living there than in the whole of Samoa. We accept things are very difficult back in the islands. So much so that Samoa were unable to turn up and play Ireland in the autumn of 2001 because they just didn't have the money to travel without the IRB intervening to give direct financial assistance. The host countries are reluctant to give a share of the gate or any part of the commercial revenue. The bottom line is that we have huge problems in these islands sustaining them in the changed professional world. But we will never stop a migration movement. There is not the same wealth or opportunity in their islands. The IRB has tried to address this issue by the country rule but the Samoans are saying to us that we made a mistake by introducing legislation for one cap one country. The risk is that players might not accept a Samoan cap because they want to go to New Zealand and they know their future may be better there. What we have to do is develop a long-term plan for these islands which is financially based on good value for the long-term because they are such exciting rugby-playing countries.'

The clock ticked on and Vernon's car to London awaited. Had he enjoyed his involvement in the game these past years, despite all the problems? He thought carefully. 'Yes, it's been exciting and rewarding despite the trauma. I have enjoyed it but at the same time it has exercised all the qualities I have and exposed others I lack. It has been incredibly demanding, a ferocious roller-coaster ride. It was not straightforward to achieve a sea change in the game, but these difficulties were nothing compared to trying to manage the consequences of the changes. It has been difficult to regulate the game, a huge challenge. But I wouldn't have missed it for the world because the opportunities on the positive side have been considerably greater. The worst times have been the domestic times. All the hassle we had within Wales I found hard. Falling out with people I liked and had been on good terms with was very painful. But I hope that is all over – life is too short not to get over it. I must say, if I had not had a job I enjoyed doing and huge support from those close to me and the great friends I have throughout rugby, I would have gone mad. But with a separate and demanding job and the benefit of sharing and listening to some very wise people, I was able to keep a sense of perspective. What has been and continues to be hugely satisfying for me as chairman of the International Board is turning up in countries like Morocco, Chile and Uruguay where people still spend voluntary time setting things up for rugby to prosper. In Chile, for example, there is a strong rugby community. They have carved a ground out of the Andes mountains and have raised half a million pounds themselves to spread the message about the game. They are so proud about it and I share that pride. In Uruguay, they opened a new international ground in Montevideo in July 2001 which is fantastic. They have done so well, and it has been great to see that level of achievement. There is something about this sport. It doesn't matter where you end up, you have similar enjoyable conversations and find a similar camaraderie.'

I agree. To see the enthusiasm of local kids anywhere playing the game and to see the enjoyment they get from it is wonderful. It's fascinating to see the growth of the game. I went to Moscow in 2001 and saw teams from Paris, Warsaw, Vienna and other places competing in a tournament. Their enthusiasm was delightful, infectious.

Perhaps the smile which these newer recruits to the game wear upon their faces is a reminder to us all that, above everything else, rugby is a game which inspires pleasure, creates friendships and offers achievement. There is no doubt that it has been forced to endure a pretty rough journey these past seven years. But as the pain of professionalism at last began to recede, like so many of the modern players' hairlines, the reassuring point was that rugby football was still making people smile, giving them intense pleasure and providing the background for the creation of lifelong friendships.

It is surely only a special sport that could have withstood all that and continued to offer the world such wonderful qualities.

CHAPTER 6

Woe in Wales

In spring 2002, Welsh rugby continued on a downward spiral. The Six Nations Championship had produced more disappointing results with defeats by Ireland, France, England and Scotland. In the immediate aftermath of the heavy loss in Dublin, national coach Graham Henry resigned, to be replaced by another New Zealander, Steve Hansen, formerly a coach with Canterbury Crusaders and New Zealand 'A'. Then the Welsh lost both Test matches on a brief tour to South Africa in June.

A working party was set up under the auspices of Sir Tasker Watkins. It included members of the WRU including the chairman of the WRU General Committee, Glanmor Griffiths, though sadly, three of the WRU officials decided to resign halfway through the deliberations. The commission also included several former players such as D.K. Jones, Gerald Davies and Gwyn Jones. Its recommendations were, chiefly, that a full-time executive board be appointed to run the game at the top level. But that did not mean putting senior members of the WRU committee in executive positions. They should be full-time professional people best suited to do the job. As part of this plan, aimed at improving the fortunes of the national side, it was proposed that the number of leading clubs be cut from nine to eight, with further reductions problematical. But the major clubs' recommendation, to have only six top clubs, was put by the WRU to a vote by the member clubs of the Union and, at an Extraordinary General Meeting of the clubs, was lost by a margin of 325 to 98. Not surprising really, because only those who believed that turkeys would vote for

Christmas would have expected the motion to be carried.

Astonishingly, such was the arrogance and audacity of the Union, that they came out with their own deliberations before their own official report had been published. Basically, they proposed a maximum of eight senior clubs, which of course hardly addressed the issue at all. As for the idea of only six major clubs, the WRU refused to take that decision themselves so, predictably, it was defeated.

As a result of the decision, however, Welsh rugby was plunged deeper into the mire. The so-called 'Gang of Six' – owners of leading clubs Cardiff, Swansea, Llanelli, Bridgend, Newport and Pontypridd – were described as evil people trying to create a ring-fenced elite. Yet all they wanted was the best for Welsh rugby and an environment in which the best could excel and prosper. Surely that scenario would have been of great advantage to the national side?

The players certainly thought so because they then threatened strike action in the weeks leading up to the international against England at Twickenham. To the best of my knowledge, the claims of some people that the clubs forced the players to threaten strike action was quite wrong. As the Welsh captain Scott Quinnell said, 'This isn't for us or our futures. This is for the benefit of the Welsh game in twenty years' time.' What he meant by that was that there had to be a better system implemented for the top level of the game, one in which the best players could be drawn together into a small, elite group of senior clubs.

In the end, the players withdrew their strike threat and played out the rest of the Six Nations season. Some people said that when the WRU decided to put the senior clubs' proposal for reducing major clubs from nine to six to a vote, thereby virtually assuring that the other levels of the game in Wales – i.e. all the junior clubs – would vote against the proposed motion, the players had been fooled and should have gone through with the threat. But I disagree. I don't believe they should have gone ahead with the strike. However, what was very plain was that the whole future of Welsh rugby lay in the Union making some unpalatable decisions.

As regards the elite end of the game, the idea proposed was simply to have an executive body to run the professional game with both Union and clubs having an input. They needed to do this, I believe, to come into the real world. The requirements of the professional club are very different from those of the amateur clubs. You want your best players playing in a professional side, playing against the best. Those players are, generally speaking, all with just half a dozen clubs and that is where the professional game is. These clubs supply all the players for the national side which is where all the costs are. Yet it is the two hundred other clubs who have the bulk of the votes which run the game in general and that cannot be right. The majority of the Union's votes come from the smaller clubs.

The Welsh committee has slowly come to acknowledge that the professional game needs a different standing and a far greater amount of finance if Welsh rugby is to compete at the highest level, whether it be the Heineken Cup, the Six Nations Championship or the World Cup. We have to be mature and realistic about this. Some WRU people said originally, 'Why worry? Let our best players go and play in England if they want to and are interested only in chasing money.' But what sort of attitude was that? They thought they would come back and play for Wales in every international but that wasn't certain. Some said, 'Well, does it matter if they play in England?' My answer was: of course it did. You can't have your best players turning up to play in Wales just a handful of times a year. Where would be the incentive for youngsters to go and watch clubs like Swansea and Cardiff if all the best Welsh internationals who used to be with those clubs were playing in the English League? I don't think the game could survive under those circumstances. It would be only a matter of time before Welsh club rugby petered out. No one would go to watch the clubs. People should remember rugby is simply not the same as soccer. It is much, much smaller.

As Peter Thomas, chairman of Cardiff says, the ambition of every club is to be successful on the field and financially sound off it. That requires good management and housekeeping based on the structure in place. But, he said, under the system we have had in Wales it would not have been possible for the major clubs to compete if they had not had private money. Even so, those with the private capital were both frustrated and increasingly annoyed. Because the senior Welsh clubs were the ones developing and bringing through the talent which would go on to represent the national sides and create money for the Union.

As Thomas said, 'We just wanted parity with the Celts who were receiving £1.6 million for the Scots and Irish provinces. Then, a deal emerged in the English game in summer 2001 under which the clubs in the Premiership received £1.8 million each from the RFU.'

It is a different world in Scotland and Ireland because provincial rugby has taken over in those two countries. The Irish Rugby Football Union (IRFU) run and finance four provincial sides: Connacht, Leinster, Munster and Ulster while in Scotland, the Scottish Rugby Union (SRU) now run the Edinburgh, Glasgow and Borders provincial teams. Some, like the former national coach Graham Henry, continue to call for the establishment of a handful of provincial sides in Welsh rugby. But they clearly do not understand the history and tradition of the game in Wales. The stark fact is there is no tradition nor likely appetite for provincial rugby in Wales. It is the same in England. Clubs are the traditional focus in both countries and are likely to remain so. I see no sense whatsoever in shifting to a provincial set-up. I think it would bring still greater disaster upon the game in Wales.

Hardly surprisingly, the Welsh clubs wanted a slice of the financial cake, like their English counterparts. Because as Thomas said, 'We have been paying for the players and those players go on to fill the national stadia whenever they appear. Why are we wrong to request a slice of that money? Those grounds are filled only because the players are there and those players are being paid by us week in, week out. If you loan out a commodity, you expect some financial recompense. Also, the clubs simply cannot make their businesses run successfully without serious financial assistance from the Union.

'What the clubs in Wales (and England) have said is they only want a percentage of what they are generating through their players. The whole treatment of the clubs has been poor throughout. The TV contract for Welsh domestic rugby coverage was negotiated five years ago with no consultation of the clubs. We were told, "You will be given this amount of money. You will do this and do that for it." But a proportion of that money was given to the lower division clubs even though they were never going to appear on television. The international stage is the arena from which, traditionally, money has always been created for the junior clubs.'

There is another aspect to all this, which is that the revenue clubs are managing simply is not enough to sustain their businesses. And things like constantly chopping and changing the kick-off times for club matches to suit the desires of the TV people have played a large part in keeping people away from games.

Let me give you an example. Over Christmas 2001, Cardiff played Pontypridd at home and the better part of 9500 people turned up to see the game. It was always going to be a 2.30p.m. kick-off because that was the preferred time over the holiday. Soon after that match, Cardiff had another home game, against Glasgow in the Celtic League. The kick-off time was put back on the Saturday afternoon from the preferred 2.30 or 3p.m. kick-off, to 5.30p.m. because television wanted to show the match live. The result? Our crowd was little more than 4000 strong.

Now of course, Cardiff get a percentage of the TV contract fee for that. But in my view, it goes nowhere near truly compensating for the loss of so many supporters at the gate. And then there's another thing. One of the businessmen whom I know well and who'd had a hospitality box at Cardiff, told me one day they would not be renewing it at the end of the season. 'It's just that with so many Saturday evening kick-offs now, Gareth, I can't even get anyone to come along to the box for free hospitality.'

Early in January 2002, there was a similar example at Swansea. A home Heineken Cup match against the attractive English club Bath ought to have meant a bumper crowd at St Helen's. But what happened? TV said it wanted to cover the match live, and so the kick-off was put back to 5.30p.m. The crowd was pitiful, little more than 2000. Swansea might have had some money from the TV deal but, like Cardiff, what had they lost in terms of supporters at the gate? Also, in my experience, going to rugby matches is a habit. Let supporters get out of that habit and you risk losing them. For ever. The point is, people are voting with their feet on the issue of Saturday evening rugby. Yet we have to persist with it because the Union negotiated an agreement with the TV companies on their behalf, without seeking their views. Is it any wonder the leading clubs are disenchanted with their Union?

Thomas insists the Union's approach was all wrong, and, in his opinion, it came down chiefly to one man, the then chairman of the

Welsh Rugby Union and now head of the International Rugby Board, Vernon Pugh.

Thomas said, 'Pugh was in charge of Welsh rugby at the time but I found him inflexible. Consequently, I believe he damaged the game in this part of the world. He took an incredibly tough, uncompromising approach, and though he is a man of great ability, he couldn't delegate. I believe the whole business cost the game three years in terms of finding a compromise, a solution to our difficulties and problems.'

The pity is that someone like Vernon Pugh, a very clever outstanding professional man, *could* have achieved so much more. Pugh is a strong character and it was unfortunate that Peter Thomas and Vernon Pugh were always at loggerheads and it was, sadly, a missed opportunity. They couldn't see each other's point of view and there was no compromise. That was sad because it cost the Union and the clubs a lot of wasted time and effort and caused financial strain as well. Unfortunately, at the end it became acrimonious and descended to differences on a personal level.

But Thomas's criticisms were aimed not only at Pugh. There were others on the Welsh committee, he said, who should shoulder their share of responsibility for the dissent and rancour in the early years of professionalism.

Peter said, 'I have no doubt that when you are appointed to the WRU committee, it is the highlight of your career. Giving that up is not easy and no one suggests those people should give it up. The WRU is the governing body but it is now a commercial game operating in a commercial world and the members of that committee by and large don't understand that. I heard one senior WRU official say: "Thomas will always put his money in." It wasn't said in a nice way. Was I angry? No, just disappointed that they clearly still had not grasped what the game is all about today. It makes me frustrated because you are dealing with people who have only personal ambitions at heart and not the depth of the infrastructure and the future of the game. It is the people's game, it is still our national game in Wales and nothing should be more important, nothing should come before getting the structure right and effective. We take great pride in rugby in Wales; it is the talking-point of most families in Wales, even today, most days a week. We are a nation that reads newspapers back to front because of our love of sport and in particular rugby football. I know that passion is still there, as strong as ever, despite it all.'

I am deeply disturbed that as we reach the summer of 2002, it seems to me that Wales is just about the only major rugby-playing nation of the world which is still failing to come to terms with professionalism. England, Ireland and France have workable structures; the southern hemisphere nations have got their houses in order. Perhaps Scotland is the only other country that has yet to make a formula work well for it although there are signs that it is now happening. That Wales should be one of the last countries to agree a viable professional formula for the game concerns me no end.

Thomas adds, 'I don't accept rugby should never have gone professional, that it wasn't a game suited to professionalism. It is a skilful game, as skilled as any other sport. The people participating, young men and women nowadays, work very hard at their jobs and deserve the rewards they are getting in a professional sense.'

At the end of May 2001, the WRU were saying they wanted to have two warm-up matches for the delayed Six Nations game with Ireland that September and, suddenly, you had four international games before Christmas, another five after Christmas and then a tour. Before you know it, you will have anything up to fifteen internationals in a year and what does that leave for the clubs? Enough is enough.

What you must have in that situation is common sense and the players themselves need to have an input as well. Peter Thomas has done a lot for Cardiff and indeed for Welsh rugby. He has offered much common sense for those prepared to listen. But successful businessmen tend to have strong opinions and because they have stood up to the Unions they have never had the support they deserve. In the eyes of the have-nots, they are the ogres. But let me tell you, if it had not been for the likes of Peter Thomas of Cardiff, Mike James of Swansea, Tony Brown of Newport and a couple of others, I know that Welsh club rugby today would be in an even worse situation.

The satisfaction Peter Thomas gets is seeing Cardiff compete with the best. But we haven't quite achieved that yet nor matched his aims and aspirations.

What of those who thought they might be buying into a club that could become the Manchester United of rugby in the future? Thomas asks what is wrong with that. 'You have always got to have heroes. Clubs like Manchester United have set the standards and pace for others to try and match. That's true whatever the sport. Having heroes is part of life. Although every single rugby club is light-years away from being a Manchester United at the moment, I suspect every one has United's ambition in the way they run their clubs. They are breeding good youngsters for their future teams, they are looking to maximise their activities in the commercial field, they want to utilise their global assets. I know that we at Cardiff have a website on which we market our goods worldwide, selling merchandise where we can and creating a marketing programme. Of course, we are minor compared to Manchester United but why shouldn't we dream, strive to match them and what they have?

'Rugby has a long way to go in professional terms, it is true. For example, one good soccer player in the Premiership is probably earning more than the whole Leicester Tigers rugby squad put together. But why should we not see the £1 million a year contracted rugby player emerging? It will come, that is certain. Perhaps in four or five years' time, maybe sooner. In the meantime, why not have the ambition to raise rugby union to the level of Premiership soccer? There is nothing wrong with ambitions. Rugby union on the world stage is already a tremendous sport. You have great tournaments like the World Cup, the Bledisloe Cup, Super 12, the Heineken European Cup, the Sevens tournaments etc. It is a wonderful formula of entertaining sport. It hasn't been easy for rugby. What you have got to remember is that professionalism was thrust upon the rugby world overnight. There was little thought given to how it could be implemented. If they had said, as of now, a section of the game decided by the Unions will become professional but our recommendation is that the number of clubs embracing professionalism will be governed and controlled by the Unions, then it could have worked without all this pain. But as it was, there was no thought given to it at all. That was where the seeds of all this trouble, these difficulties lay. It was poorly presented, with absolutely no thought or planning involved.'

But Thomas, like myself, would like to think the worst is past. Put it like this, he argues, if there is not an acceptance of the main issues of professional management, distribution of earned income solely to the Premier clubs to give them an opportunity to put their businesses on a firm footing financially so they can make a profit to put back into the game . . . if that doesn't happen, you will have a large number of investors walking away from the game within the next twelve months. Thankfully, he doesn't believe that will happen, though. But what is Thomas's reply to those who say 'We didn't ask you to put all this money into the game'?

'Well, in order for the game to compete at the professional level, the Cardiff Athletic club management team didn't have the human or financial resources to take it forward, so they invited the membership to invest in their company. Over a thousand members did. Without that money, Cardiff would be a second division club today, and you would have provincial rugby in Wales. Because all club rugby would have remained amateur without any support of this kind.'

Some people have short memories in Wales. But we would do well not to forget that, amid professionalism, Llanelli went bust and the WRU bought their ground. Neath also went bust and were bailed out by the WRU. Bridgend were hanging by a thread. It was a real mess. In fact, it was frightening to see it. Our whole infrastructure was floundering. The strength of Welsh rugby in that great era of the 1970s was largely down to the club structure, which produced good players. The club system was strong, which was why we had such a competitive base from which to choose our players for the national side. There was strong competition week in, week out in Welsh club rugby. There was a good fixture list against the best of the Welsh and English clubs. When Cardiff played against clubs like Coventry, Bristol, Gloucester, Llanelli, Neath, Newport and others there were big crowds and a lot of tension. It created pressure and that prepared us well. It was the same for all of us in Wales.

England didn't have that kind of structure at the time; the change in the situation in England from the late 1980s onwards, when competitive leagues were introduced, created the climate for England to improve so much internationally. The club system was far better in Wales in those days.

Thomas declares himself as passionate and enthusiastic about the game now as he has ever been. It remains a massive part of his life and virtually his family's life, too. Yes, he says, sometimes it intrudes too much into your life – you need a balance and discipline there. But he believes the executive structure now in place will help that. For him, rugby is all about Wales doing well. For that to happen, Cardiff and the Premier clubs have to do well. The ups and downs, the frustrations, are all a part of it, he concedes.

'I haven't been hurt by all the criticism; I have broad shoulders. Besides, Cardiff is always in the firing line. I feel very proud to have been elected Chairman of Cardiff. It is one of the biggest honours I have ever had and I don't take my responsibilities lightly. Cardiff's name goes before you in every direction. The name Cardiff rolls out a red carpet in parts of the world like Australia, South Africa and others. That is a wonderful privilege.'

But on another more general subject, I wondered how far were England going ahead and at what rate were opponents like Wales being left behind? I discussed this aspect with Peter Jackson, rugby correspondent of the *Daily Mail* and Gareth Davies, former head of sport at BBC Wales and now chairman of the Sports Council of Wales and sports adviser to S4C, the Welsh language TV channel. Mind you, we talked only a few days before England lost to Ireland in Dublin in late 2001, a defeat which meant they had missed a Grand Slam in three consecutive seasons. But perhaps the result of the game between those two countries in the 2002 Six Nations Championship, a thumping 45–11 win for England at Twickenham in February, underlined the point.

Peter Jackson was certainly emphatic. 'England are leaving people behind at a rate of knots. Once they started to pull in the right directions, which they are finally doing, they began this process. Now they can only get stronger and stronger.

England and France should dominate the Six Nations Championship because of the enormous resources they have in terms of playing power. But if you have two teams dominating, other issues arise. How much longer will people pay to watch the matches? My fear is that people won't pay to see a foregone conclusion and there is a real danger of that. Professionalism has created a gap in rugby so that countries such as Australia, France, England, South Africa and New Zealand have moved much further ahead of others like Wales, Scotland, Ireland and Argentina. That gap is widening. But international rugby is fairly limited and the game needs more teams capable of winning a World Cup. Teams like England, Australia and France will pull away and therefore for how much longer will people fill the Millennium Stadium to see England put forty or fifty points on Wales? Not for ever, in my view.'

I think this is a valid point. There is this novelty of the stadium at the moment in Wales that is good for the game but once that becomes meaningless we will have difficulties. Wales played Bela at soccer in autumn 2001 and got only 12,000 to see the game. In a stadium that holds 75,000. There was no chance of Wales qualifying for the World Cup and people didn't want to go in numbers. Mike Burton would say, 'I can sell out Wales v England three times over because everyone in Wales thinks they can beat England.'

But if that is no longer the case and, worse still, losing to England becomes a trouncing, people won't pay £40 to see that. Jackson felt that was why what happened at Wembley in 1999, Murrayfield in 2000 and Dublin in the autumn of 2001, when England were up for a Grand Slam each time and lost all three games, was good for the Championship, hard as it may have been for English supporters. He acknowledged that England were now playing wonderful, exhilarating rugby and he hoped they would drag standards up. Ireland, he thought, were following them in this, but not Wales, sadly. That is why the Welsh Rugby Union has a duty to put in place a structure which will help close that gap.

But, I asked Jackson, what did he feel about a subject which had potentially alarming consequences for the whole future of rugby union? Who is to say that, at some stage in the near future, Rupert Murdoch won't decide to amalgamate union and league and make it one hybrid game? Jackson shared my concerns. 'It's only a matter of time, in my view. I respect rugby league as a game, I don't sneer at it. I accept it is a different game but none of that matters – it is what the moguls think. Murdoch will think it is one sport, he'll get his people to bang a few heads together and you'll end up with something that may be a 13-a-side or may or may not have line-outs. Wigan, St Helens and Bradford will make it a truly national English championship because, with the possible exception of Newcastle Falcons, you can't say rugby union is really strong in the north of England. Sale are not getting crowds worthy of their investment and ambitions. So I think it is little short of inevitable. There will be one rugby.'

Sadly, I agree with him. For only the diehards will say 'over our dead body'. But I fear it will be people like Murdoch who don't have the tradition of rugby in their hearts who will decide. Let's be fair, if you don't know what rugby is about you wouldn't know the difference between the two sports. But what bothers me is that rugby union is going to march more towards rugby league than rugby league is going towards union. We should remember this isn't a new concept. Jacques Fouroux, the former French national coach, was ostracised by the FFR some years ago for saying that it should happen and the game should become one of thirteen players. Maybe, too, as Jackson added, you could argue that as players have become fitter, faster and stronger, space is now at a premium. So if you take away the flankers you will create a little more room for the backs.

But, I wonder, what are you going to be left with if you destroy the fundamentals of the game? As Jackson said, 'Who knows what is going to happen? If we had had this conversation six years ago, and someone had said Richmond rugby club would offer £250,000 for Scott Quinnell, a player from Wigan rugby league club because rugby union had embraced professionalism and he would go because Richmond would pay him more, you would have said "off to the funny farm".'

But now this process will accelerate. Because one of the stars of the Lions tour was a former rugby league player, Jason Robinson. That, of course, is one of the main reasons the league players are coming to union because it gives them an international dimension rugby league cannot.

Already, the influence of the TV moguls can be seen in coverage of the game. Half times are longer to permit the screening of advertisements and studio discussions. And how many times have we all been to a match and been kept hanging around at the start because the TV people weren't quite ready with their coverage?

I do not dispute that TV has pumped very considerable sums into rugby football, and they are entitled to air their views. But that should be as far as it is allowed to go. I do not believe you can have the TV people telling those charged with running the sport how it must be played and what conditions must apply. Rugby is surely entitled to expect that those in charge of its destiny stand firm against excessive demands from those in television. Those people appointed to roles at the top of the sport surely know the game better and it is up to them to say eventually 'This, and no more.' If ever we have a situation where television is in total charge of the sport, then it will have lost everything.

Some may say that, as in the example of professional soccer, there has never been more money coming into that game, and television is almost solely responsible. It has, in turn, allowed a knock-on effect, too, whereby more people are going to soccer matches, requiring clubs to build new stadia and develop better facilities. So what is wrong with that?

My answer is, simply take a look at the reality of professional soccer in England. I am sure that there are lessons which rugby can learn from soccer. The problem of ITV Digital claiming it could not meet the full terms of its commercial deal with the football authorities and electing to go into administration, ought to be a warning to the game of rugby. It demonstrated the unpredictability and precariousness of relying on TV money as so major a part of your entire funding strategy.

Another salient point to emphasise is that money received from any governing body should surely be used chiefly as an investment in areas such as facilities and youth. Simply spending more on bigger name players because you are receiving assistance from your sport's governing body is not the ideal policy, I would suggest.

The winners have been the players. Many millions of pounds of television money given to football has simply disappeared out of it, into players' pockets. Never before have players been paid so much. Never have they been so expensive to buy. It isn't the clubs who have benefited from all that new money, it's the players. And they have taken the money elsewhere. Is that what professional rugby expects to see in the future? I hope not. Already the national Unions of Scotland and Wales are hugely in debt because of the new stadia they built at Murrayfield and Cardiff. England are making a profit now but only in very recent times. Go back a year or two and they, too, were in debt.

But what of the future in other respects? Well, that depends with whom you discuss it. There are still plenty of doom and gloom merchants around, people who will tell you that the great days of the game have gone for ever, that we shall never again see this wonderful game played as it can be. To which both Peter Thomas and myself say . . . rubbish.

Peter is optimistic about the game's future because it is growing all the time. He says, 'What a game the Heineken Cup final of 2001 was between Stade Français and Leicester. What a performance the Lions and the Wallabies gave when they met in Australia in June–July 2001. And what marvellous matches we saw in the next Heineken Cup campaign when Leicester, the holders, twice had to battle mightily in the pool matches against Llanelli, winning at Welford Road but losing the return fixture at Stradey Park. And then came the drama of the semi-final when Leicester pipped Llanelli by a point, 13–12, with a last-minute penalty by Tim Stimpson. With all the competitions now, it is certainly a global game. It has got an immense future and we should not be afraid of embracing it.'

I strongly echo such sentiments. What is needed is commitment and desire to make it succeed but not to the detriment of the principles of the game. Don't sell rugby's soul, there is no need to and you would lose everything if you did. The game can be hugely successful without doing that. As for Cardiff's future, we have a great history, a great reputation, despite what some may think. As we move further forward into this new era we have to try and build on that reputation. Being the club of a capital city, a city-centre club with the facilities to compete with the best in Europe, is a great challenge. We should not disregard history, we should be proud of it. You don't forget but you build on that to go forward. Having a great history is a strength.

But we have to live in the present. Years ago, lots of players wanted to join Cardiff just for that history and because it was the club of the capital city. But today these things are dictated by cash. We still have players wanting to come because of our set-up and we like to think we set standards. It was not by accident this club was successful and it was not just on the field, either. They were setting standards at all levels on and off the playing field at this club years ago. It is our duty to try and maintain the integrity and reputation achieved by the guys before us at this club, our predecessors.

CHAPTER 7

The Influence of Rugby League

They say that time heals all wounds. Fair enough. But then there's rugby. It took the warring factions of rugby union and rugby league the little matter of a hundred years to reach some sort of understanding and establish, at the very least, a courteous relationship.

What had started as a small spat between the northern counties of the Rugby Football Union in England over the question of broken time payments way back in the 1890s when Queen Victoria was still on the throne, only began to end after that historic meeting at a Paris hotel in August 1995. Even by the standards of fighting families, that's serious longevity for you. 'Broken time' payments, incidentally, concerned expenses the northern clubs sought from the RFU, the governing body, for their players' bona fide loss of time. When the RFU won an amendment vote claiming such a principle was contrary to the true spirit of the game, several of the northern clubs withdrew from the RFU. This was the start of the Rugby League – in 1895!

During the course of those hundred years things got pretty sour between the two sides. Any rugby union player 'taking the shilling', as it came to be known, to go north knew he would almost certainly be consigning himself to the world of the leper. He would be banned from rugby union clubhouses even when he returned to his family's roots, could expect excommunication from most rugby union officials and even a blank stare and silence from several of his former playing colleagues in the amateur code. Going north was no easy decision.

In those days, stories of rugby league scouts being seen in one of the towns in the Welsh valleys spread like a forest fire. It was as though they had the plague in the next village. When I was growing up as a rugby-mad kid in the valleys of south Wales, I remember the almost hushed silence when news came through that someone had 'gone north'. It was as though a favourite uncle had died, except in compromising circumstances that did not bear repeating. There was a social stigma attached to it, as though someone had crossed the great divide. Which I suppose in a way they had. David Watkins went in the late 1960s and his was an immense loss to Welsh rugby and the national side. Except that then someone just nipped up the valley to Max Boyce's famed fly half factory and out popped a replacement. In that case, his name was Barry John. And he could play a bit, too.

The rugby league people came knocking at my door one day. In fact, during my career, two rugby league clubs made me offers – Wigan and St Helens. The first thing to say is I never seriously wanted to go to league, mostly because I didn't want to leave Wales. It was my home – still is – and I love it. Also, when I was twenty-one when the first offer came from Wigan, I wasn't that worried about money, I wasn't married, didn't have a mortgage and so I wasn't under financial pressure.

Yet I still knew that the sums involved would have put me in a very comfortable position. How much was offered? Well, David Watkins had signed for £16,000 in 1967 and this was a couple of years after. So when Wigan asked me if I was interested, I replied that I wouldn't even start talking to them unless the basic was a £20,000 deal. I thought that would turn them away, which was really what I was secretly hoping would happen. But they surprised me.

They'd said originally, 'If you're not interested we won't make you an offer,' and I'd replied, 'The truth is, I'm not really.' But they persisted. 'What would make you interested?'

'£20,000.' They said they understood that.

You have got to remember, I was young and they wanted me as an investment for the future. Now £20,000 might not sound such a lot these days but, believe me, at the end of the 1960s it was serious money. Also, it was a lump sum, tax free. What would it have bought me? Probably two homes if I had wanted that, but certainly a very nice big house somewhere which would have set me up for life.

In the end, even £20,000 wasn't enough to tempt me. And their interest just fizzled out. St Helens did contact me later but again I wasn't seriously interested. By then, too, that great era of Welsh rugby was underway and the thought of walking away from that if I didn't have to was too much to bear.

But I'll tell you something I have never told anyone else. If Wigan had made me an offer that had knocked me off my feet, then I would have had to look at it. Let's say they had offered £30,000 – that would have been extremely serious money. I wonder whether I would have been able to turn that amount down.

I suppose that, deep down, I didn't want them to give me a figure that was so tempting I would not have been able to say 'No'. £20,000 I could reject, £30,000 I suspect might have been a different story. I didn't want to go north but everybody has their price.

So I didn't go, but others did. And Wales were by no means the only rugby-union-playing nation which began to lose more and more players. In Australia, the situation became critical with just about all the best Wallabies turning professional to attempt to pursue an international career with the Kangaroos, their league side. In England, many players in the two main northern counties, Lancashire and Yorkshire, had gone straight into rugby league as school kids and rarely bothered with union. And I remember the occasional England rugby union star, like Mike Coulman, the Moseley prop forward with whom I toured South Africa as a 1968 British Lion, suddenly changing codes. Ireland's rugby union side lost one of its finest ever No. 8 forwards when Ken Goodall, who had also been on that '68 Lions tour, went north.

Of course, players did it for a variety of reasons. For those based in the north, their family might have always had a strong association with league and therefore it wasn't so great a social leap for them. But for Welshmen, it must always have been a traumatic experience, in the early days. As things stood then, they knew they were turning their backs on all they had known and many of their friends. Perhaps they felt like the sailors from centuries past who boarded their ships and waved to their family and friends on the dockside, bound for exotic parts of the world like the Spice islands. They must have had a sense that they were leaving behind them all they cherished, all they had come to know and feel comfortable with. Perhaps they wondered whether they would ever see some of those people again. Don't get me wrong, going from Swansea to Salford was a bit easier than from London to the Spice islands. Even though the sailors had one advantage – they didn't have to rely on British Rail to get them there! But to those who do not remember those times, who are too young to have known the sense of anger and bitterness in so many rugby union people's hearts at the loss of a major talent from their own ranks, I say, 'Believe me, it was a huge decision on the part of a player.' If anyone doubts that, then they need only turn their minds back a few years to 1994 when Scott Gibbs left Swansea to join St Helens, thereby drawing some awful words of condemnation from a particular Swansea official. Indeed, even when Jonathan Davies returned to Cardiff after seven years in rugby league, some people said all the fuss made about his return was disgraceful given that he had been a traitor to Wales.

Like all Welshmen, I deeply lamented the loss of great players like Jonathan, Scott and so many others to the then professional code. But I refused to condemn them. It was up to the individual, as far as I was concerned, a matter for them and them alone. It was nothing to do with anyone else how they earned a living. I never wanted anyone telling me how I should go about earning a living and I felt it thoroughly inappropriate to start criticising players just because they joined a rugby league club. What saddened and disappointed me most was the loss to Wales and rugby union when so many went from our country in the early 1980s through to the end of the eighties. It coincided with one of Wales's weakest spells as an international side and, frankly, it was no coincidence.

So when, in 1995, news came humming down the lines to Wales that the decision had been taken for rugby union to become an open game, I felt a certain sense of excitement and anticipation. Because I felt that if rugby union players too could earn a living, it would eliminate the need for them to go north for a professional career. Wales would be able to keep her best players at home and the Welsh international side would benefit. Mind you, when Wales went to South Africa three years later and were flogged 96–13 by the Springboks, I felt ready to revise my optimism! But in fairness, there were several mitigating factors on that occasion. What has almost certainly been the most interesting, challenging and controversial aspect since rugby union embraced a form of professionalism is the influence of the rugby league men in the formerly amateur code. Former league coaches and players like Phil Larder, Joe Lydon, Ellery Hanley and Shaun Edwards have offered their expertise and advice to clubs and countries in union as coaches.

Larder, who was 57 in March 2002, first experienced rugby as a union player with Loughborough Colleges. Originally from Oldham, he was associated with Broughton Park, Manchester, Sale and Lancashire before turning professional in 1968 with his home town rugby league club. He later played for Whitehaven and in 1982 became the first director of coaching for rugby league in England. He was also assistant coach of the England national league team from 1985 to 1992. His league coaching career at club level involved spells at Widnes, Keighley and Sheffield before he became coach of the England rugby league team. He has also coached the British Lions league team. In 1997, he accepted an offer from the Rugby Football Union to return to union as a defence adviser for the England team under Clive Woodward. He is now an official assistant coach to England specialising in defence and, in that role, was invited to become part of the 2001 British Lions rugby union tour management in Australia. As well as all that, he has advised the English champions Leicester on their defensive structures for the past three years, a period in which they have dominated the English championship. It is hard to conceive a man with a more respected pedigree in both codes.

Why did he switch codes? 'It was the time for a new challenge,' he told me. 'Comparing the two games is impossible, like comparing draughts with chess. League is very much one-dimensional whereas union is a far more complex game. Therefore, the questions I am asked in union are much more involved and intricate than any rugby league defensive coach will ever be asked. The challenge is pushing me which is what I wanted.'

Joe Lydon, Ellery Hanley and Shaun Edwards were all highly distinguished players in the rugby league code. They played many times for the Great Britain league team and faced the impressive Australians on plenty of occasions. They, too, have more recently lent their expertise to the England rugby union structure, Joe as

Under-19s manager, Ellery as coaching adviser to the senior side before concentrating on work with Bath Rugby and Edwards as an assistant to Warren Gatland at the London club Wasps. Lydon also took the Under-21s to the Sanzar competition in Australia after the England tour of Canada in summer 2001 and, that autumn, was made coach of the England Sevens squad. Ellery, who assisted Clive Woodward on that England tour to North America in June 2001, also used to help coach Bristol's rugby union team before ending up at Bath. His motto is: 'If you give your best, nobody can question you.'

Lydon, in particular, has thoroughly enjoyed his new role. 'It's great, a lot of things are different, it's all new. I have been involved since September 2000 and I am now starting to find my feet. The geographical spread is much bigger than I am used to; it has taken me a while to settle in. The first few months seemed like a revolution. Now I feel like I have some idea of the direction I am going in. I don't miss working in rugby league because I am still involved in rugby. It has been my life and also my career. I was a league player since 1982, a long time as a player. I am thoroughly enjoying the new job. To continue in a similar mode in professional rugby was wonderful. I am contracted to the RFU and I hope my future is there with them.'

Talking with people about the sport you love is always highly pleasurable. In the case of people like Larder and Lydon it is also most instructional. Hearing their views, forged from a different background to my own and analysing their comments was a fascinating exercise for me. What, I asked Larder, was his overall impression on what he has been trying to do with Leicester and England these last few seasons? What did he perceive as the benefit of bringing into the union game someone with a strong rugby league background? Rugby union, he believes, has a lot to learn from league and an interchange of ideas is very good. He revealed a most fascinating story which, had things come to pass, could have transformed the fortunes of rugby in England a long time ago. This is what he said. 'When I was made Great Britain's director of coaching back in 1982, I went to Australia on a fact-finding mission and stayed with their director of coaching, Peter Cochrane. What surprised me was that he shared the same offices as Dick Marks, who was the technical adviser to the

Australian Rugby Union. Therefore, there was a constant inter-change of ideas among both codes of Australian rugby. Likewise, they got fresh ideas from wherever they could. Jack Gibson, the well-known Australian league coach, was watching American foot-ball for some innovative angles and all that information was passed on to Dick Marks and the Australian Rugby Union. I thought that was brilliant. I was out there two months and when I got home, I contacted Don Rutherford, the then technical adviser to the Rugby Football Union and suggested we get together twice a year to share thoughts, to swap ideas. But I got a really negative response. The RFU refused to mix in any way with a professional league and it was a great opportunity lost. England could have got considerably ahead of the world had they bought into that scheme as far back as that time.'

I have to say I was not surprised at all to hear that. English rugby has always had so much potential – we knew that well enough in my playing days – but it was held back by its own administrators. All I can say is, 'Thank God they didn't use that knowledge!' Because when you think about the information they could have acquired and the type of players they could have developed, it is incredible. Rugby league has always possessed people with a progressive way of thinking, certainly in Australia. It would only have been a matter of time before England picked it up.

Larder went on: 'We had lots of information in specific fields that could have benefited the union boys. Areas such as the importance of weight- and power-training and the skills of an organised defence. Nobody had ever done work on defence in English rugby before. Somebody could have been doing that way back in 1984. If it had happened, it would have given English rugby a big advantage because the other rugby union nations, apart from Australia, were doing nothing of the sort at that time. Australia and England could have dominated the game. Because it makes a massive difference if you get your defence organised.'

Phil believes he would also have learned a lot from union to expand and improve the league game, had they shared ideas. Union, he felt, could have taught league a lot about scrummaging, for example, and anyone from rugby union who has ever watched a rugby league scrum and the way it disintegrates without any attempt to use it as an attacking weapon would subscribe to that view. Larder remembers when he was coaching Keighley and Dai Young, the Welsh prop, had joined Salford from rugby union. When Keighley played them, they were pushed off their own ball and it was chiefly due to Young and his influence. That never happened in rugby league, it was virtually unknown. Larder said his team didn't get much possession in that game, and because of it Salford won the match and got promotion at their expense. He remembered the lesson of that experience and also the importance and role of the support player for the ball carrier in rugby union. That was also something league could learn lessons about from union, he felt.

Joe Lydon said that once rugby union went professional, it turned to its nearest neighbours that had been professional for a long time. But he cautioned against a generalisation of the word professional. 'Professional is an interesting word because when I started in rugby league, frankly, it was very amateur. We may have been paid but we still trained on an amateur basis. We trained Saturdays and Sunday mornings and I wouldn't class that as a professional attitude. Wigan took it to the next level for, with them, we were full-time athletes training during the day. So it was that level everybody in rugby league then aspired to. When rugby union went professional, they looked to the strides made in the previous five to six years in rugby league for their yardstick. From that they could take advantage of some of the lessons learned by league under full-time professionalism.'

Lydon said it was natural union should look at some of the techniques. The key aspect was defence with Phil Larder's strong input. Rugby league, he says, is a very simple game to play, watch and understand. Because defences have time to get set and organised it was very natural for a coach to structure his defence and build his entire game on that. This would be a mistake for rugby union, Lydon felt. 'In league, you have more universal-type players in terms of size, speed and power. There is very little to distinguish between the backs and forwards. Union is different in terms of the shapes and sizes of players but they are all athletes. At the lower level of union, everybody can still play but on the professional side of the game, the focus has to be on the whole not just individual parts. When rugby union went open in 1995, you had to break the game down to all parts. So what Clive Woodward did with England was get specialists in different positions. If you are lucky 50 per cent of the game will be about defence. We had specialist coaches in rugby league but it was easier to break down rugby league as a game to its component numbers because of the nature of the game. It is a very simple game – it consists just of defence or attack. All the time. There is no bigger degree of emphasis placed on anything other than those two aspects in the sport.'

So league learned lessons by watching, studying and talking to people from American football and the Australian rugby league side. It learned things like how to condition the body to achieve maximum power, speed and agility. What Joe says is interesting about picking the best out of other sports. I don't see anything wrong with that. You always look to better yourself and if you don't believe you can learn or improve your quality of play, then you are never going to progress. If I look back at an aspect of my game, passing, I recall something similar. I watched how Chris Laidlaw of New Zealand and Ken Catchpole of Australia spun the ball away from the base of the scrum. People in this country very rarely did that, the old dive pass was in its heyday. But I knew I had to do something about improving my pass and I copied what they were doing. I suppose we could have learned a lot from someone like Dai Watkins, the Newport and Wales outside half who went to rugby league. But what concerns me now is that since the arrival and influence of the ex-rugby league boys, more emphasis has been placed on defence in rugby union and skill levels have not risen commensurate with that progress. We have seen how England have utilised defensive expertise under Phil Larder's direction. For me, the game is getting more and more defensive-orientated and it worries me. Even the French Grand Slam team of 2002 had a former rugby league man as defensive coach, an Englishman, David Ellis.

Nor am I alone in this view. Some may look at individual matches and say well, there are plenty of points being scored, what's the problem? For example, Ireland's 54–10 thrashing of Wales in Dublin in the 2002 Six Nations Championship game in Dublin, featured six tries to one. Painful it was too, for Welsh eyes! Now what was wrong with that, you may well ask?

Well, I would say that Wales's performance was so poor that you could not make any serious judgements from it. The other two games that weekend, France's win over Italy in Paris and the England victory in Scotland, perhaps demonstrated better some of the poor rugby on display. There were simple, frankly lamentable errors made by all the players. That was proof for me, together with so many other examples, that the basic skill levels are just not as good as they once were.

As regards defence, the comments of the new Ireland coach Eddie O'Sullivan immediately after that win over Wales were both significant and revealing. O'Sullivan praised the contribution made by Mike Ford, the former Oldham rugby league boss who had been working with the Irish squad as their defensive coach. O'Sullivan said, 'I thought our defence was excellent. Since we brought in Mike Ford as a defensive coach, he has done a lot of hard work on that.'

I have talked with David Watkins, who is now back at Newport as an official, about this subject. Rugby union nowadays reminds him vividly of what rugby league was like when he first went north. Firstly, because it is now a game based on defence and attacking skills simply have not kept pace with improvements of a defensive nature. But secondly because rugby union is now a game where a side can keep the ball almost for eternity as long as it does not make mistakes. You keep the ball for as long as your skills are good enough. If they are, you go on and on recycling the ball, trying to batter through, setting it up and then having another go. And another. This is why matches so often become stalemates. Which bores the pants off everybody. Because, if one side is hanging on to the ball the whole time, the game becomes boring. I do not see this state of affairs changing very easily or very quickly.

Everybody wants to see more attacking play but the very nature of the beast at the moment is to be defensive. If you're not convinced, listen to the views of Joe Lydon because he should certainly know what he's talking about.

In his considered thoughts, Joe rather confirmed some of my current fears about rugby union, in terms of defence. He said the fact that such emphasis was being put on defence meant that a similar emphasis now needed to be put on attack. We must encourage players to understand the patterns and how to break down the defences put in front of them. But one thing he had found was the inability of players in the Under-19 group to do that. He said, 'We have practised going forward in a slight attack but the drifting defence hasn't been broken. But it is perfectly possible to break down these defences, that is the beauty of the sport. Certainly the same emphasis needs to be put on attack as has been placed on defence. Players have to be encouraged to express themselves. That is the key to any sport, whether it is rugby league, rugby union or soccer. Players with natural ability must be encouraged to use their skills, to express their talents. I think league players have much to offer union. I have seen some of the most gifted players in league transfer their skills to other sports, and vice versa. Jason Robinson is just one example, a player who didn't know union, had no awareness of the technical demands and had so much to learn about the union game but possessed natural skills, talent and a professional approach . . . qualities that helped him thrive in rugby union. For England and the British Lions.'

Jason Robinson. Now there's a player. Everybody loves talent and players who can make you jump out of your seat and Jason does just that. I have always respected rugby league but, as a spectator sport, it was something I could take or leave. But if Robinson was playing for Wigan or Great Britain, I would often watch it. He has brought that appeal into the union game now. The lad is learning very quickly and he has obvious talent. I have to say, he is a fabulous player to watch.

But there are two ways of looking at this question of defence. Perhaps this intense focus on it is what professionalism brings or you can put it all down to the influence of the league boys. Of course, defence has always been a fundamental part of rugby union. We were aware back when *we* played that one of the qualities of the All Blacks was that they very rarely made mistakes. If a match was very close, they invariably won it because they gave little away. Good defence and good tackling was always important but the majority of people I played with consciously went out to win and concentrated on line-out and scrums as opposed to thinking about defence. We might have worked on back-row defences but now every aspect of the game is studied for defence. It is vitally important players know what positions to take up around the tackle area. Since Phil has become such an important part of the England set-up, everyone seems to be taking rugby league coaches on to their staff.

But what of coaches in general? Is there not a danger that they are becoming too important? I sought out the former All Black, Ian Jones, for his opinion.

'There is a danger in having so structured a system and game, as in England for example. Young players can end up being over-coached in that system, thus, they will only do what they are told to do. Therefore, when a situation changes, I sometimes question their ability to handle that change on the field, during the course of a game. Sport is still about feel and enjoyment. Young players should feel happy they are training in the right way, not necessarily just how the coach says it should be done. You have got to learn the game, 'feel' the game as it were. The best way to do that is by playing, not just running around a training paddock endlessly. Maybe if you are over-coached and drilled to the extent that you can't decide things for yourself, you become somewhat numb when decision-making time arrives. You freeze. There are plenty of exciting young players out there but they need to be given their head, not coached so much they become like robots.'

I couldn't agree more. I see this as a real threat. Before coaches, the successful sides were those that could improvise, that had individuals in influential positions who could dictate the game and just as importantly 'read' a game. You had so few pre-determined moves that, even at international level, sides played rugby virtually off the cuff. I remember the first coach Wales ever had, David Nash, a No. 8 who had played for Ebbw Vale and Wales and toured South Africa with the 1962 British Lions. In a relatively short period of time the opportunity to prepare and the improvements we made were immense. But, in truth, what we were experiencing then was more about organisation than actual coaching.

Since then, the coach has become virtually the focal point of the game. I lament that because I thought the beauty of rugby was this coming together of all different kinds of skills, the thrill of the unexpected. But over the years we have seen the influence of the coach's ability to stifle the opposition with well-prepared organisational moves. As the prize became bigger so the pressure not to lose meant that too often coaches approached their task from a negative position. As the game has evolved, probably no side now is without a coach. Even the famous Barbarians feel they have to have a coach and just about every mini rugby team is coached. Yet I still hold the opinion that the basic requirements of a coach are to get the best out of the individuals, to use their strengths and subsequently be part of a team. In today's game, it is very apparent that all the sides practise set moves constantly. But that often shackles the individual's creative talents. How often do we see players of international qualities unable to grasp an opportunity or assess a change of tactics? If young kids are to be brought up to enjoy the game, to be encouraged to have the freedom to run and to assess situations, we must start loosening this stranglehold that too many coaches seem to have on the modern game. For sure, coaches have their role but that role should never be to stifle the creativity out of youngsters.

At this juncture, I would like to raise the question, 'Has the game been developed by the law-makers or by the technical approach of coaches?' With regard to the tackle area, the way the tackle law has been allowed to develop has meant coaches don't commit more than the necessary number of players, which is usually two or three, to the forward engagements in open play. Therefore, by the very nature of that law, it has meant the game has developed a very tight pattern which demands skills of a different kind.

When I was young, I and others around me were encouraged to assess situations and make decisions for ourselves and for the good of our team-mates. I don't think kids are encouraged like this any more and therefore this is a criticism of the system. Coaches, to justify their salaries nowadays, know how important it is to have a successful side, so they stick to a system that restricts mistakes. One observation of the present game is that it has developed a game plan that is quite often inflexible and staid. OK, I hear you say, England didn't play like that in the 2000–2001 season, especially once they got to the Six Nations Championship. My answer is no, they didn't – they had found a way to play fast, exciting rugby in which the players clearly had to make decisions themselves.

But what I would say is opponents and especially rival coaches will find a way to stop England playing like that. Maybe Ireland's victory over them at Lansdowne Road in October 2001, a defeat which cost England the Grand Slam, was the first sign of that process.

Perhaps what makes our defences so good now is that it is easy to organise a defence because teams string out across the field. The lack of innovation and off-the-cuff action, plays into the hands of a defence. Those qualities of innovation and unpredictability have become rare species because coaches want teams to play their way. If you don't want to play that way, you don't play. Very few professional coaches of the modern era say to their players, 'Go out and do what you think.' But you need players who can think for themselves and sum up situations. Actually giving and taking a pass and making a decision on the field is rapidly being coached out of players. Also, far too much emphasis from a very young age is put on unit skills as opposed to individual skills and that comes back to haunt us at senior level. For example, of all the three-quarters in the Six Nations Championship teams, who can you really say qualifies as an innovative, challenging, highly skilled player with the ability to decide strategy for himself in given situations? I can only think of three men and after that I am struggling. And the three? Brian O'Driscoll of Ireland, Jason Robinson and Will Greenwood of England. There are precious few others in that category.

Lydon denied that it had been rugby league people who had changed union through the influence of certain coaches. He felt it was more a natural progression and development from union itself going open. 'People in union have been thinking more about the game since it was declared open. They analysed how it could be changed slightly to make a better team. England, for example, are trying to be leaders in different areas, to be unpredictable and to let the players play the sport. It is a natural development in the aegis of professionalism. People are spending more time studying the game. There is so much more time spent in analysis and preparation that the nature of the game is bound to change. As for coaching, we don't coach players negatively. We just encourage them to better themselves. I am talking all the way through the sessions because I want to make sure the right coaching takes place. That means educating the coaches, a crucial aspect to all of this. The progression of the sport has to include development in every way. The competition, the players, coaching development and match officials. All these are just as important as each other, none is less than another.'

But what are some of the other lessons union can learn from league and vice versa?

Larder believes the role of running forwards in the ways you try to break a defensive line and also how to stand up and offload are fundamental. He says that a lot of union forwards just go to ground when they are held, and the game is slowed down allowing the defence to reorganise. For him, the thing that upsets a defence is if the ball is kept off the ground because then the game is so much quicker. That is the key to the whole game because it creates a tremendous advantage for the attacking side. We see that and see people working on it. And the league boys have had years of doing it. You can see the skills required of forwards to do that now. Getting into position to take, give and receive balls. But does it mean, I wonder, every country is going to have to have a rugby league influence? It looks like that until the rugby union guys acquire all the knowledge. Larder said that, in rugby league, defences were always very organised. For the rugby league player to make a break, he said, he needed very good footwork. It was his footwork and power that would enable him to make the break. That was something the union forwards needed to learn. Also, a lot of guys in league expected the runner to adjust his run coming on to the ball. Therefore, the player in possession really had to concentrate on the run his colleague was making and where he must serve the ball to him. 'When Freddie Tuilagi joined us at Leicester from rugby league, he had problems because a lot of the Leicester players passing to him didn't realise he was slightly changing his angle at the last minute.'

Larder insists the first step in learning is always to appreciate that there is something to learn. If a sport learns from another, it makes that sport stronger, he feels. Surely the objective for every player and coach is to progress the game and improve every aspect of it. Union players, he says, are smart and quick. All the players he had worked with had realised how important defence was. Once they were open-minded and prepared to learn quickly, they invariably learned successfully. If they learned from other sports it enabled them to step up to another level in defence and attack, he said. 'The proof of that is what has been achieved with Australia since John Muggleton worked with them. Similarly, since I have been involved with Leicester, they have won the English Premiership every year. And each year they have had the best defensive record of any team in the country. That gives them a tremendous advantage. But I feel that coaches can fully understand the make-up of defences and they could soon adopt new methods of breaking them down. But at the moment, there are not too many clubs in the English Premiership that have got their defensive acts together. Apart from Australia, there has not been another nation that has been really well organised defensively. That is one reason why Australia won the last World Cup. It is also a reason why ACT won the Super 12 tournament in 2001.'

Ellery Hanley has no doubts on this subject. 'For me, defence always wins football games. If you know how to defend, individually and collectively, your success rate will be higher. If you are a lazy player in defence you will be found out, either through videos or by coaches, and you will get turfed out. There is nowhere to hide. You have to be ruthless because you only have a short period of time as a sportsman. I believe in perfection and trying to achieve perfection.'

In 1997, Larder was so impressed with the British Lions defence in their Test series against South Africa that he sent a fax to their manager Fran Cotton congratulating him on that aspect of the Lions' play. They were getting that expertise, Larder believes, from the ex-rugby league guys on that tour, players like Scott Gibbs, Allan Bateman, Alan Tait. That, he thinks, was one reason why he was appointed by England in the first place. Cotton realised the importance of the league influence.

But what about preparation in general? I suppose in my day, we felt we were working hard and were pretty slick and well organised. I would like to think it isn't that big a difference now. I did what was natural to me, what I regarded as my preparation as an athlete. Bill Samuel led me into weight-training in the emerging part of my career but maybe a lot of people didn't do that then. Today, of course, it is part and parcel of every player's preparation. I didn't think of myself as professional but I did feel my preparation was very thorough. For example, coming up to games, I looked after my body and didn't have late nights. But I was trying to hold down a job as well, like everyone else then. That was a huge difference.

As for diet, although we didn't have specific dieticians, we became conscious of things like pasta, which was a better preparation food for players than red meat for reasons of carbohydrates and digestion. I remember on Lions tours there was concern on the part of the management that we should have a sensible intake of the right kind of calories. It was too easy to put on weight because of the amount of food we were offered.

In 1974 on the Lions tour of South Africa, the midweek team wouldn't drink on a Saturday night because they were thinking of the next game. Certainly, you couldn't have accused the 1968 Lions of not having a drink! The nearest we came to being professional was when we went on tour. You lived the life of a rugby player for three and a half months. At Cardiff, I trained twice a week, for Cardiff College of Education and Cardiff. I played Wednesday, trained Thursday, played Saturday and trained with the Welsh squad on some Sundays. I was a PE student and it was like being in the Russian Army – you didn't go on marches but you trained every day. I occasionally trained with Lyn Davies, the Olympic long-jump champion and a lecturer at my college. I did sprint work with him but I don't recall the scientific element coming into our training, which is so much a part of the modern game: things like being assessed on your running style with the help of video tape and the use of computers to assess and guide personal fitness.

Joe Lydon said that international unions had realised its players had to be athletes whereas junior club rugby union, he insisted, would always allow for everybody to play the game whatever their physical build. There were levels of the game for everybody to play, watch and take part in. But in a professional game you had to produce athletes to play the sport. In a sense, positions meant less. Jonah Lomu played on the wing but he could be a breakaway forward. In the past, the technical demands of the sport had always meant different positions produced different types of players. 'They may all be athletes but some will be less agile. Professional sport just makes sure the individual person becomes an athlete. Every player can enhance his ability by being mentally and physically quicker. But fly halves will always be nippier than props. The key thing about rugby union or league is that you should never stifle natural talent. But if you can give those naturally talented players a little more speed and conditioning that will aid them as athletes. But never stifle or take away natural talent. Because that is something you can't coach. You encourage it. It is not what he does in the gym that makes a player special, it's his ability to do what others cannot do. Players should not be robots.'

As for professionalism, Lydon had some forthright opinions on this subject. First, he said, people made a mistake here. They thought that word equalled money but it didn't. 'Sure, you can get paid and in some cases, paid very well. But what professionalism is really about is having a professional outlook and attitude. The true term means you are professional in everything you do: in the way you live your life, your preparation for your sport, what you do in your leisure time and how you play your sport. It's about improving yourself to go to the next level.

'Money doesn't come into all those things because they apply whether you are receiving £10,000 a year or £1 million a year. Gareth, you looked a professional sportsman in attitude, mental approach and preparation. And you played rugby union in the 1970s when no one ever thought it would become professional. But your attitude was still professional, in terms of conditioning, building up your strength and approaching the sport in a professional way. But of course the majority of players in your era did not.

'To be a successful professional sportsman, you must have ability. But you also need mental toughness and without that you are unlikely to be a great professional, a player who reaches the top of his or her sport.'

I agree with that. But to concentrate specifically on the rugby league aspect, I asked the guys their thoughts on whether in a few years' time we would end up with just one game. The topic certainly threw up some interesting views. Phil said he had thought that league and union could amalgamate but he knew now it could never possibly happen without one game completely losing its identity. He hoped that would never be. Union was nothing like league – it was a far more complex, far more intricate game than league. The two were so obviously different. 'The things that make union different are really special to any union enthusiast. Things like scrummaging and the importance of the wing forwards. Line-outs, too. Rugby union isn't going to take out those aspects of its game,' said Larder.

I agree the two are different games and that was a major reason why it took union players so long to settle up north. People like Jonathan Davies then took a while to settle back into union when they returned to Wales. The games are very different.

That fact was further emphasised by the case of Iestyn Harris, who joined Cardiff and was quickly drafted into the Welsh national side. Too soon, as it turned out. Iestyn is a player of very great promise but to expect him to play a role of saviour, as some clearly did, was completely unfair on the young man. I hope and believe that he will emerge in the union game as a great talent; certainly, his pedigree from league is substantial. But players need time to switch, especially when they are learning the new game completely as was the case with Harris. It is unrealistic to expect miracles overnight.

Phil Larder continued: 'As for attacks, I was a little worried after the autumn 2000 series England played against Australia, South Africa and Argentina because they scored so few tries in three Tests. I felt our attacking game needed to improve. But it certainly did that in the Six Nations Championship of 2001. Perhaps the best pointer was the England match against France when we scored five tries. I am confident that England have the ability in their players to beat a defence. You always have a spell when a team improves any aspect of its game when it gets a little bit of a stranglehold until coaches and players decide to combat it. That process is taking place now.'

I think that is absolutely right. That is always the problem. The demand of coaches is always for success, and they will demand change to achieve that if required. People look for ways to stop you. Especially if they do not have the ability to beat you with an attacking force. And, of course, no side is guaranteed success. Just twelve months after they had been annihilated at Twickenham, the French gained their revenge with a superb victory over England in the 2002 Six Nations Championship, at Stade de France. That set up their own Grand Slam that season, doubtless to the chagrin of England.

Another area that could see big change in the coming years is the northern English counties, like Yorkshire and Lancashire, where rugby league has been so popular. I wondered whether this might signal a trend of more youngsters going into rugby union in the future than rugby league. I remember Fran Cotton always used to talk about the number of boys in the north who went straight to rugby league. I suppose we used to wonder what on earth would happen if ever they chose union in numbers rather than league. Australia and Great Britain, or really England, are the two major rugby league countries playing the game which is why England would benefit from these guys coming more to union. On that subject, Joe Lydon didn't see a major drift by youngsters to union at the expense of league. It was all about market forces and opportunities, he claimed. Some, he agreed, might now decide to play union so that they could make it a career but a lot of former league boys played union when they were young, anyway. Not all players with the chance to join a union club would do so. Players themselves would choose and it was healthy that they had that choice of two professional sports. They could see which one offered the best opportunities, he felt. His hope was that Yorkshire and Lancashire did not become a rich mine of talent for rugby union at the expense of rugby league. That might threaten league in the long term if everyone started playing union. He didn't think they would – he thought it would come down to opportunities for the individual. It wouldn't necessarily mean a big drain away from rugby league in the north of England. Besides, he went on, it would be tough for league players to switch codes in certain positions. The front and back rows of the pack would take a while to adapt because it was very different, technically and tactically in those positions.

'It takes an awful long time for players to train their minds not to revert to type in severe pressure situations. You can give someone coaching in the sport for a long time and yet he will still revert back when pressurised,' he said. 'It is easier for the outside backs in league to adapt to the new game. Jonathan Davies, Alan Tait and Allan Bateman were players who proved that. Both sports have a lot to learn from each other. But I certainly don't want to see league wiped out. That is why I don't want to see a mass exodus of players in the north from league to union. I don't think it will happen although there have been a few.'

Larder felt that union had to get its act together up north, first. He noted the promotion of Leeds rugby union club into the Premiership division for the 2001–2002 season (and their spirited performances when they got there although they subsequently finished last), and the plan of the RFU to build several new academies throughout England, to nurture and develop young talent. He talked of the people in the smaller areas where rugby league was played, places like Wigan, St Helens, Warrington and on Humberside and said, 'Rugby league is like a religion to them, it is very strong. Yet I do feel a lot of players who make their name in league will come into union. Because union has a major advantage in terms of the international stage. The league people are disappointed because the international programme is so restricted. The game has not expanded in that respect. I confess I used to be absolutely amazed a few years ago at the lack of interest in league. In the late 1980s, early 1990s, the Australian rugby league team was voted the best team in any sport anywhere in the world. They played Great Britain with a team of awesome individuals yet we struggled to get 50,000 people to Wembley to see a Test match. Yet at that time, when the England rugby union team was playing such negative stuff and had Rob Andrew kicking absolutely everything, sell-out crowds of 70,000 regularly went to Twickenham to watch it. I couldn't come to terms with that.'

I have to say, he wasn't the only one. It was the same when Wales went through one of their worst ever periods. Yet they went to London because of the start of work on the new Millennium Stadium and sold out Wembley Stadium. Thousands travelled from the valleys to see a losing team. Crowds for international games at Cardiff had been down to just over 50,000 in its last years but they easily got 70,000–80,000 in London. They had found another 20,000–30,000 fans even with a poor team! It proved it didn't matter what was happening on the field of play. People just wanted to be there.

Rugby union has always been able to get big crowds; it is the tradition of the big games, whereas clubs like Wigan have enjoyed large crowds at club level, bigger than the best in union like Leicester and Cardiff. But when it has come to internationals it has been a different story. It simply hasn't happened for the league code. Larder felt it proved that the majority of people preferred union as a game. And you have to hold your hands up and say the way England have played recently has been superb. Their attacking game has been marvellous. Indeed, most of the countries have had their moments, including Wales.

But will more kids in the north take up union now? I understand that Phil and Joe have a loyalty to their old game but rugby union has a greater international impact so I think more kids will go to union. The fact is rugby league is a geographical blip because it's only really played in two major northern English counties. So many people have tried to get it into Wales but, so far, without real success. But that, mind you, does not mean it never will succeed. Never say never, might be the appropriate phrase here, because people in Wales have enjoyed the incursions into this country by the rugby league national side over the years. The strength of rugby union has given league no chance to break through here, yet I for one would never write off league entirely. They are always looking for opportunities to expand outside the north of England.

But do the union boys, I wondered, need to enhance their skills? And which of the two games is the more skilful? Indeed, has rugby union already overtaken rugby league in terms of professionalism, which was once its arch enemy? Phil Larder again. 'I felt that when I joined the England rugby union team from my involvement with the Great Britain rugby league team, I was dropping about 25 per cent in professionalism and attitude. That was in 1997 but a lot has happened since then. The league people say things haven't improved too much with them. But union is now twice as professional as league; it is immensely more professional in every way.

'What is professionalism? Well, compare the 2001 British Lions tour of Australia with the next Great Britain rugby league tour and you'd find that the Lions were three or four times more professional than league. That's a generalisation but look at the number of coaches who now work with a Lions squad or England party. Training sessions are videoed so that there is detailed analysis of every move, in matches and training. No doubt it boils down to money and the union has more than league which cannot afford so many backroom staff. The amount of research done in union is amazing. The most professional game in the world is American football and that is down to the finances. Rugby union can afford to do all it does because of the amount of money the game is generating as a whole.'

Which begs one of the key questions of this whole debate. Is the future of rugby league now under threat because rugby union has been professionalised and is marching forward in many countries? The topic alone clearly made these ex-league men very emotional, given their obvious love and respect for their former game.

Ellery Hanley says on the subject: 'I believe rugby league has gone as far as it can go. I could be wrong and I would be happy if I was proved wrong, but rugby union has the larger scope, is the bigger picture. Union has the international stage which players desire. It is that extra dimension that top players want. Whether it means the end of league, I do not know. Whether the codes come together, I just don't know. Only time will tell.'

Phil Larder shook his head, dejectedly. 'It's very sad but I do think so, yes. The greatest strength league had was that union was an amateur sport. Some of the union players attracted into league became the biggest names in the sport. The first time I started coaching was at Widnes and I inherited players like Jonathan Davies, Paul Moriarty, John Devereux, Adrian Hadley. They were outstanding union players who became outstanding league stars as well. Now, I can't envisage any union international going to league any more, because their international programme would be so restricted in league. Yet other people will follow the likes of Jason Robinson, Henry Paul, Wendell Sailor and Iestyn Harris into union, particularly those that have achieved everything in league. They will welcome the challenge of playing for England, Australia or Wales in a very exciting international scene. Iestyn's move to Wales is a further indication of that trend. It's very sad for me to say this but I get indications that league is struggling in this country. The game will never die, it's too strong. But it doesn't seem to be expanding, whereas rugby union will get even more attractive. Take the Six Nations of 2001 – it was a massive improvement on the year before. Some matches in the Heineken European Cup were out-standing, too – they became great theatre. Union can only go from strength to strength. Of course, the game will have ups and downs but union can but go forward. After all, rugby union has only been professional six years. Think what it could be like after twenty-six years. People who are serious about rugby union and determined to succeed are bound to take the game forward. That is a healthy, exciting situation in my view.'

Joe Lydon tried to be a little more optimistic about league. 'There are fewer nations that play rugby league on a world stage than a sport like rugby union. So it will always have that tag yet it still has massive potential. I don't want to see it amalgamate with union. I think both have much to offer in their own separate ways. League is an easy game to understand at the highest level. It's a hard game to play but a very simple sport, a good sport. I believe it will always have a place in this country. League gave me so much, I would never knock it.'

The well-known rugby agent Mike Burton believes that a clear path will emerge now and in the near future. 'Rugby league teams will slowly come towards union as league clubs form union sections. They will soon find that when they have attractive union sides like

Wasps, Bath and Leicester visiting them, they will get lots of support there. But it doesn't mean league will die – I don't think that's either likely or desirable.

'Rugby league has its own values and sets of traditions, its own history. There are things we can learn from rugby league. Take full-back, for example. I think J.P.R. Williams was the only guy in rugby union who spotted that if you chipped over the first line of defence or got past the first man up, you could exploit the space there. He learned that by watching rugby league but he was among the very few who did. We can learn plenty of things from league. Phil Larder's drift plan in which sides without the ball try to push attacking backlines across the field without committing many players to the tackle so that they can snuff out the attack eventually, has transformed rugby union. He has transformed defensive patterns in union.

'Let's be honest, to have withstood all that rugby union threw at it for a hundred years, rugby league must have some tremendous qualities. But what it clearly has not got as a game is an international dimension so it is doomed to remain a bit-part player to rugby union which is now flying.

'Australia and England are the two nations that will benefit the most from an imminent demise of rugby league. People said Wales lost huge numbers of players to league but nowhere near the numbers English rugby union lost because so many youngsters in the northern counties like Lancashire and Yorkshire took up league rather than union. Now they have the choice and union will pick up huge numbers of talented young players. That is the single biggest difference between those two countries and the rest of the world.

'I think the gap between England and the other countries was inevitable. England have always had by far the biggest number of rugby players and clubs, 2300 clubs. The two countries to watch in the world are now England and Australia, because of the influx of rugby league players. Increasingly, players will see union in those countries as the most attractive option and more and more will join. That will give the two nations a real power.

'We shouldn't underestimate rugby league – it was always a much bigger game than just Wigan and St Helens. Just because some league clubs will undoubtedly start to get involved in rugby union, it doesn't necessarily mean that Wakefield Trinity will want to link up with Wakefield rugby union club.'

But having said that, Lydon is very aware of the potential of rugby union as it looks ahead. 'The opportunity for union is phenomenal, it is truly a worldwide sport. But it has still got a lot to learn from other sports including league. There is good and bad in it. During my time in league, the good coaches were always influenced by other sports. American football, ice hockey . . . you can plagiarise any other sports if you are going to improve your own. I am sure union will continue to do that and I don't see anything wrong with it. It has its own direction, of course, but if it adds on the best from certain other professional sports which it thinks might improve union, why not do it? I think that path will be successful. It is good in the obvious ways – when it is played well, it is fast, thrilling and attractive to watch. But there are also bad aspects. Players play too much rugby, although that is a problem for most sports. Look at Liverpool Football Club's schedule at the end of the 2000–2001 soccer season and their start to the new season in September 2001. Of course, it is an attractive proposition to keep playing them to raise more money. The trouble is, in the long term you lessen the product if you over-play players. You end up giving the public too much of one thing. The maximum amount players should be playing the modern game of rugby union is once a week. No more. Any more than that is very tough for them. Age-group arguments also come into this. Some people assume that if a player is young, he is fitter and fresher and can play more than someone a bit older. In fact the complete opposite should be the case. When you are younger you should be playing less because it will extend your natural life as a player. It's like a new car – drive it hard and flat out for 100,000 miles in its first two years and of course it won't last as long as if someone had done around 20,000 miles a year in it. In rugby terms, it is not so much the player's body that suffers from too much use. It is the development of the player that suffers. When a player is young, he should be developing his skills in order to improve himself. That is the most important thing he can do. Because when you are under pressure in a game, you simply revert to type. That is true whatever sport you are talking about. It's only through concentrating on the basics of the game in training that it becomes second nature on the playing field, even under the severest pressure. And if a player is always playing matches at a young age, he can't find the time for the consistent quality training he will need to get those basics absolutely right. Believe me, if you have inbuilt deficiencies in your game, they will show. Rugby union has to make sure it doesn't make this mistake.'

As I said earlier, I watch rugby league on TV but I wouldn't stay home just to be able to see it whereas with a big union game, I might. But if more and more stars are going to leave league and the union clubs will have more money to bring them across, then suddenly the TV sponsors might start saying there is no point having this because all the stars are in union. I suppose that is the threat to rugby league.

Talking of threats, I am concerned at the gap which appears to be opening up in the northern hemisphere between a country like England and the others in the British Isles. That's not to say there are not a great many wonderfully talented players in Scotland, Wales and Ireland. Who will ever forget Brian O'Driscoll's marvellous try for the Lions in the first Test against Australia in Brisbane, in June 2001? Or the contribution to that fine series, in no particular order, of others from the Celtic nations like Scott Quinnell, Tom Smith, Rob Henderson, Daffyd James, Rob Howley, Colin Charvis and the marvellous Keith Wood. But England's power is a sobering reality on and off the field. The RFU were posting profits of £14.5 million for the year 2000–2001 and projecting a £6 million profit for the following year. Those sort of successful financial figures give a union a lot of room for scope in expanding its game.

Perhaps encouragingly, Phil Larder is pretty philosophical on this subject. Any sport, he says, evolves. In the northern hemisphere at the start of the 2001–2002 season, England were considerably ahead, but he felt there were some very smart people in the other nations which would enable them to adapt and catch up quickly. That was how sport evolved, he argued. I guess that, overall, I agree with that. But that is not to say you are definitely catching up, which is why Wales wanted to follow the England style of having more specialist coaches as well as more management people. I do feel Wales, Scotland and Ireland could get left behind if they don't address this problem successfully. Each country might have some smart people there but if you don't get the structure right, and the people running the Union don't see it as a concern, then you do get left behind. It happened before in Wales because the Union thought it was Wales's divine right to stay at the top of the game. Money doesn't necessarily guarantee anything, yet if you have it and the Unions and clubs are getting stronger and closer together, the clubs can use that money to strengthen their system and put a good structure in place that can give you a real chance of success in the future. But getting things past certain committees still can take a bit of doing. We in Wales know that better than most!

Larder had some interesting thoughts overall. 'I still feel very strongly that a lot of coaches and administrators in union are very entrenched in their own game. As are most journalists covering rugby union. I'm not sure there are a lot of coaches of the calibre of Clive Woodward and Dean Richards, who are prepared to sit down with people like myself and say, "What can we learn from league?" A lot of coaches in union feel their game has very little to learn from league or any other sports. But coaches like that are or should be a dying breed. It is a two-way thing: league can learn things from union. The thing I look at now more than anything else is kicking. The amount of time players like Jonny Wilkinson and Neil Jenkins spend on kicking is phenomenal. There are some good kickers in league but the actual punting skills in union are much superior. Because union is a tactical game, the art of kicking is so important. What is needed in union especially is the kind of great vision shown by people like Cotton, Woodward and Richards in "milking" people like me as much as they can, for the benefit of rugby union as a whole. I believe union has an immense amount to learn from league, because league has been professional as a game for a hundred years. You have got to be very open-minded and there are a lot of successful coaches in rugby union who are still not prepared to be. But those people will be left behind.'

I say a hearty 'hear, hear' to that; it's very true, I'm sure. At Cardiff, we have had a rugby league input since Dai Young and Jonathan Davies returned to rugby union to play for us. And Pieter Muller, our South African centre, played rugby league in Australia earlier in his career. There is no question, these boys bring a good work ethic and fresh ideas to union. People should listen. That was always one of my beliefs: listen to all criticisms because, even if you don't agree, you might pick up just one thing.

In the end, added Joe Lydon, it all came down to that extra yard of pace, the ability to beat a man with a sidestep or defend and block somebody out of the game. Natural talent would always rise to the top. I agree wholeheartedly with that and I think rugby union is fortunate to have recruited some of the best of the rugby league men, people like Larder, Lydon, Hanley and Edwards. Their knowledge and expertise should mean that union picks out the best parts of league which are suited to the union game and which can enhance it. I no more want to see union taking large chunks of league just for the sake of it than sit and watch two sides focusing solely on defence. As with all things, there has to be a sensible compromise, a balance to the equation.

CHAPTER 8

The Lions

The 2001 British Lions tour of Australia was not a success. The Lions sprinted into a 1–0 lead in the three-match Test series and when they reached half time in the second Test with the lead, it looked like Australia's challenge might be over. But that second Test turned on an interception try, Australia suddenly revived and finished the series by edging out the Lions 2–1 in the decider in Sydney.

I don't want to give great space here to the full events of that tour. They have been documented elsewhere in newspaper reports, pamphlets, books and on film. But I have found it a worthwhile exercise to discuss the Lions concept in general with some of those with whom I have met up during the course of research for this book.

Take Keith Wood, for example, Keith was at the heart of the tour as hooker and a key man. I put it to him that, in essence, it had not really been a successful tour, either on or off the field. That had to be a great disappointment to everyone involved, not to mention the legions of supporters (some said up to 20,000) who made the long trip across the world to support the Lions. But there were other, less savoury, elements to the tour than just losing a couple of Test matches. Discontent seemed to simmer below the surface with the England scrum half Matt Dawson suggesting he and certain other players felt like packing up and going home halfway through. I just could not believe that when I read it. The thought of quitting a Lions tour halfway through never entered my head when I repre- sented them – on three tours. There was also trouble with players writing newspaper columns. But what did Keith think about it all when he got home and had time to reflect?

'I was very disappointed. The management deserved a bit of flak and the players should have got more flak. International players and British Lions cannot be condescending; everybody should give everything to be involved. But that didn't happen fully on this tour. There wasn't a togetherness about this one, even from the start. Blame could be levelled all across the board for that. But it was clear some players didn't get into it as they should have done. There was a big chunk of blame on each side, players and management, in my opinion. The way it was set up didn't help that, mind you.'

Did Keith think that now, after making two tours with them, that the Lions were here to stay?

'Yes, I do but it needs to be tidied up. When the new TV deal goes around, there has to be funds for the Lions. The whole thing is creating a huge turnover of cash in other countries and some of that has to be shared at home by the Home Unions. That money doesn't have to go to the players, but the Unions. There must be proper money for the Unions up here.'

Nigel Wray, the Saracens owner, agrees wholeheartedly on this topic. 'In 1989, when the Lions went to Australia, just about a few hundred people seemed conscious of where they were and what they were doing. This time, thousands went with them from the UK and they generated big, big bucks.

'The Australian Rugby Union made all the profit from that tour but it is the last time they will do that. If you go there with one of the best brands in the world, the profit split should be 50–50. I estimate the ARU made about £15 million out of the Lions 2001 tour. That means we, the clubs and Unions in the UK and Ireland, are investing that huge sum into Australian rugby and that is clueless. Credit to the ARU for organising it that way. But it has to change.

'Maybe, too, the brand of the Lions will be developed to the point where the Lions tour every two years, not four. The Lions bring enormous profile for the game worldwide and if it means clubs have to play their star players less often, that is OK if there is an arrangement in place with the national Unions. You could have the Lions entering the Tri Nations competition every two years, or something like that. But at the end of the day, the person we must listen to is the customer. If people want to watch the Lions every two years then that is what you should do. That is what professionalism is all about – providing the right kind of entertainment for people when they want it.'

The subject of whether the Lions players should be allowed to write newspaper columns during a tour was one I debated vigorously with Gareth Davies, former chief executive of Cardiff and a British Lions player himself in 1980 in South Africa, and Peter Jackson, rugby correspondent of the *Daily Mail*. The disasters encountered in this field were twofold. First, there was Matt Dawson's column for the *Daily Telegraph*, in which he revealed he and some others had become so disenchanted with the training regime that they had thought of quitting the tour. Then came Austin Healey's ghosted column in the *Guardian* which appeared the day before the last Test and in which he called the ACT Brumbies' lock forward Justin Harrison 'a plank', among other things. Keith Wood refused numerous requests to write a column for a national newspaper during the tour and I think he was probably right to make that decision. The content hardly qualified either player for a future role in the diplomatic service!

I must admit I was very surprised by what Peter Jackson said on the issue. As rugby correspondent for the *Daily Mail*, he had ghosted Martin Johnson's column throughout the tour. But Peter had some pretty firm views on the subject of columns as a whole. 'I said to Donal Lenihan, the Lions manager, before the tour started, "Why don't you ensure there are no columns or websites from the players?" He said that you couldn't enforce it for legal reasons. But they should have said to the players, "If you don't want to accept these regulations, we understand but you will have to be left at home." All the players would have agreed to the conditions in a shot. No player would have turned down a Lions tour just to write a newspaper column. So I think you can ban these columns by making it a condition of the tour that you don't do one. The Football Association and English Cricket Board control it far more strictly. There is no embarrassment then. David Beckham did not write a column during the soccer World Cup in summer 2002 in Japan/South Korea.'

Gareth Davies wondered whether they might have paid the players an extra sum, say £5000, to keep them from writing columns in the first place, but Peter said, 'They were getting paid enough already. And they would have done it for nothing. But there was another point. The management were negligent, in my opinion, in failing to vet the material before it was published. I wrote Martin Johnson's column with him and he read every word before it was sent off. He said it had to be vetted at a high level too. But why didn't they demand to see the offending Healey article or the Dawson column? The management should have said to both players, "Where are your columns?"

'The other thing is that if, as a writer, you can't for some reason get hold of your ghost – i.e. the player whose column you are writing – then you play safe and don't become too controversial. I wouldn't quote Martin Johnson as saying so-and-so is an ape if I hadn't been able to get hold of him. The affair seemed as though it would blow up in Brisbane when I met Eddie Butler, rugby correspondent for the *Observer*, in a lift and he said there was mutiny in the air. I said, "If you're right, that will set the agenda for the next two or three days." But he didn't use the story at the time in Austin's column.'

Davies certainly felt it was a conflict of interest. 'I can't see the problem in banning them. It's like a condition of employment. If someone offers you a job from nine to five, you don't say I'll only work from ten to four. If you do, they can turn around and say, "Thanks very much but we'll get someone else who will accept our terms." What is the difference? This all comes back to the leadership of the game. Have we got the right people running the game? How strong are they? You have got to have leadership and people laying down ground rules. But I suspect nobody was really looking into this and seeing potential problems.'

Jackson said you certainly couldn't pretend that the Lions lost the series because of it. Healey's column, in his view, was much less of an offence than Dawson's. Peter felt the Northampton and England scrum half had been guilty of a serious breach of confidence and had let everyone down. 'The timing of his couldn't have been worse. It was an act of disloyalty to the management and the rest of the guys. Had I been Dawson, I wouldn't have done it because people would have accused me of sour grapes, of saying it just because I wasn't in the Test side. He laid himself open to that accusation. But to write those things on the day of the first Test was a gross error. If for no other reason, it was the fact that you were playing into the hands of the Australian media. As for Healey, I think he thought the column wasn't going into the English paper until the Saturday morning over in the UK by which time of course the game would have been in progress in Australia. Even so, he should have imposed more control on his ghost writer.'

Does any journalist like ghosting these columns, I asked Jackson? His reply was emphatic. 'No. For a start, you are making your subject sound more articulate than he usually is. Some players are very good but some are hopeless. During the 1991 World Cup, the *Daily Mail* wanted someone to write a column but the sports editor insisted the person write it himself. The person involved did so, but it was so bland. In the end, it was too much trouble for me to have to rewrite it all. The only player I know who said he wouldn't write a word for a newspaper exclusively was Keith Wood, the Irish hooker. He had lots of offers but decided not to do one and he was a wise man. But the problem is, names sell newspapers so the offers will always be there for players.' When I think back, it amuses me to think that the Welsh players of our era had to give interviews to anyone and you couldn't even take the eight guineas fee for a special TV interview. You were forced to give it to your club or to charity. But by some administrative muck-ups, a lot of clubs happened to give it back!

As regards the Lions, I believe we should not forget it was only three or four years ago there were strong noises from some, especially a few in England, saying Lions tours were finished. Many people seemed to agree with them. I said at the time, 'Don't be daft, it's the pinnacle of every player's career.' The 1997 Lions tour, like the Ryder Cup, saved it in my view. If the Lions had lost in South Africa, then maybe future Lions tours would have been doomed. That was a huge crossroads and, thankfully, the success of that tour re-ignited the appetite for the Lions. Then, in 2001, the sell-out crowds spoke volumes for the appeal of the British and Irish Lions. I would never entirely rule out the possibility of a Lions tour every two years. Because it's true, the public have to be taken notice of. After all, golf's Ryder Cup is held every two years and that doesn't seem to suffer from overkill. But if you have a Lions tour every two years, something else will have to be sacrificed unless you have a huge pot of money. Even then, it would probably be impossible to fit every piece into that particular jigsaw. My fear would be that if you have a Lions tour too often it would lose its special feeling. People would say, 'We need to prepare more for Lions tours' and then when New Zealand, Australia or South Africa came here, you would probably find them only wanting to play the Lions. So there are all kinds of implications. It's a good thought but I still believe a Lions tour should be a unique occasion. It should be like a really good bottle of wine, only opened occasionally and sipped, not gulped. I wouldn't want to see the Lions format changed so that it became stale.

Wood says there also needs to be a consensus across the board as to future Lions tours. 'My belief is that you should probably get rid of the midweek games. The game is now too intense if you have to play Wednesday and Saturday. It would be all right to have a couple of easier, midweek ones but in the main, the games should be once a week for a ten-match tour. That would mean probably an eight-week tour which would give you proper time to organise, settle and prepare. By doing it in that way, you would have the chance to go back to what Lions tours used to contain – aspects such as visits to schools and hospitals. The players would also get a proper chance to see the country they are touring, rather than just airports and hotels. It is terribly intense on Lions tours these days with little time for such things. That is wrong, I think. Also, there simply is not the time to recover from knocks and injuries under the present-day schedules. The focus should be to give everyone a good chance of making the Test side. This was one of the problems of the 2001 tour. Because there was so short a build up to the first Test, the selectors probably had most of that team in their minds before they even left London. That gives some players no chance and they become depressed by it. There were also too many players on this tour and some of the early matches were too easy which gave us no sort of useful yardstick as to how we were playing. You need at least five proper matches leading up to the first Test and then a three-match Test series.'

My feeling is that sort of schedule would certainly give the boys a chance to recover from any injuries. And, although they are now professional players, I believe the Lions should enjoy themselves and also be diplomats on a tour like that. Keith certainly felt that if you only played once a week, you wouldn't get the same number of injuries then, either, and that would help you select your strongest side.

'The 2001 Lions were without too many of their best players in the end,' said Keith, 'and that may well have been a contributory factor in our defeat. Lawrence Dallaglio is an incredible player. Of all the players who could not play for the 2001 Lions in the Test matches against Australia, we missed him the most by far. He was a heavy and severe loss to us.

'I don't think so many Welsh players should have gone on that tour. Taking Dallaglio was the right idea; it was just a pity he broke down there. But at least there was a chance of him recovering full fitness so the decision to take him was justified because he was an extraordinary player. But certain others who went were not in the same category.

'But there's another thing about a Lions tour. The guys involved should not play until the October of the new season back home so as to properly recharge their batteries and prepare for the new season. That should be a flexible arrangement, the date of your return to action dependent on the number of games you have played. I understand people want to see those guys playing but I also would stress, they must have a meaningful rest period and time for preparation. Much of this concerns the question of tidying up the season overall and I believe we still have a way to go in that respect.'

I asked Keith for his views on the Lions 'fly-on-the-wall' documentary which was made of the tour. Did the tour film bother him? Did he approve of it?

'Well, it is a different era today, that is the first thing to say. The media plays such a big part in the game. Every month, I get two or three approaches to write a book but I turn them all down because I am just too young. Rugby is particularly emotional at times and there is a special attachment which grows up when players are away together for many weeks or months. That is the nature of the beast. But do I agree with allowing such a film to be shot, to show those private moments when the players are together? Not necessarily, would be my answer. But I am aware of the media's requirements. I write an article myself for an Irish newspaper although it's an easy read and is not controversial. I just try to give a little insight into what goes on behind the scenes and I don't see anything wrong with that.'

But isn't a documentary too intrusive, I asked?

Wood admitted he was very worried about it in 1997, on the Lions tour of South Africa. 'I felt I would have thrown the cameras out of the window. I suppose it is all right if you have the right of veto over what is shown. But the cameramen and reporters keep asking you questions, that is the intrusive part. I told them on one occasion, "Don't ask me questions, I don't want to talk." I think they understood that.'

Speaking personally – and I don't want to sound old-fashioned – I do think allowing cameras to film behind the privacy of closed doors has taken away the whole mystique of the Lions. That is a price too high to pay. I feel that what goes on in a Lions dressing-room should stay there.

Keith understood where I was coming from, but he had a somewhat different attitude. 'I can see that viewpoint, and I understand it, but I don't personally feel it has been over-intrusive. But I am not a fan of documentaries. I also think they should not have done one in Australia because the 1997 tour documentary was quite good and very successful. I think there was a reason for doing one then, too. The whole Lions concept was being questioned and some people were saying the Lions was something of the past. I think that tour, and perhaps that documentary, helped the Lions no end because it proved that was not the case. The film company paid a very small fee for it in 1997, so I believe, but there is an insatiable voyeuristic view in society now. But overall, I wouldn't say the documentary has diminished the Lions, not for me anyway. I understand that people love to know what goes on behind the scenes on tours like that and, after all, we are not freemasons. I don't see any harm in giving them a glimpse of life on a Lions tour.

'The Lions is huge now, simply colossal because of the media aspect. There was a press conference after the second Test match of the series against Australia in 2001, and seventy journalists were there. That brought home to me how enormous the whole thing had become.'

Peter Jackson put the contrary view. 'With a Lions tour,' he said, 'I would insist there had to be absolute privacy. There should be no cameras behind the scenes in the private moments.'

Well, I was thrilled to hear Peter say that, as there are certain things that should remain in the inner sanctum, and this was certainly one of the most important to preserve. Jackson said: 'It does the Lions concept no favours.' Gareth Davies felt similarly. 'I totally agree.'

For me, I just didn't like the idea and I felt they were short-sighted in agreeing to allow the cameras access. If you go on a British Lions tour, you can spend your lifetime drip-feeding stories about what happened behind the scenes. The film stripped away that mystique. It left me cold, especially the foul language. Jackson pointed out that the trouble in those circumstances is you forget the camera is there in your anger. That, he said, was why they were wrong to have sanctioned such a film.

I understand the players got very little, it was the Unions that got the bulk of the money. But they have sold their soul for a few shillings. Perhaps, too, the affair confirms what we talked about earlier: the lack of vision and leadership among those in charge of the game. The problem, said Davies, was controlling it all. 'You have too many outside influences in the world of TV. It is always another set of broadcasters, another set of talks going on. It becomes difficult to control this kind of thing. Now, so many companies are dictating other elements of the game, as we said earlier. Like kick-off times.'

My old pals from the Pontypool front row all went on Lions tours. Bobby Windsor was a Lion in 1974 in South Africa and 1977 in New Zealand, Graham Price and Charlie Faulkner (the latter as a replacement) also toured New Zealand in '77 and Price went with the 1980 Lions to South Africa. But what did they think about the 2001 Lions and some of the reasons for their eventual defeat to the world champion Wallabies?

Bobby Windsor was emphatic on the subject. 'They took too many players, simple as that. The dirt trackers is not a nice place to be. You don't feel part of it if you are not even a sub. Then you had the case of that English boy Corry in the back row. Colin Charvis must have felt sick when Martin Corry got chosen ahead of him after only joining as replacement. Because Charvis had some good games. It was felt Graham Henry [the Lions coach] didn't communicate enough when he dropped players. Players should be told which parts of their game they need to improve.'

Price echoed such sentiments. 'At least on our tours, we had chances to stake a claim for a Test place. On the 1977 tour, there were six weeks spanning nine matches before the first Test. Nowadays, they have to pick virtually the Test side before they go. It's ridiculous. It doesn't give everybody a chance. I'm sure it's not fun to go on a trip like that and realise you have absolutely no chance of playing in the Test side.

'I agree with Bob, it would appear to have been to Graham Henry's benefit to tell players where and why they needed to improve. But whatever the outcome, overall, there's no doubt a Lions tour is immensely popular down in the southern hemisphere.'

Windsor agreed with that but suggested a new structure over money to reflect more fairly a splitting up of the tour receipts. 'The host country should pay all the costs of the Lions visiting their country and then give a cut to the home Unions. The Australian Rugby Union must have made millions out of their visit in 2001. The Unions over here should get some. I also think that for one season we should try playing the Lions against a touring team like the All Blacks over here. A Test match in each of the home countries would be terrific.'

Pricey concurred. 'We should see the Lions at home. You could play these games in the autumn after a Lions tour has finished and the remaining years revert to Tests between individual countries – Wales against Australia, England against New Zealand. But once every four years, have an autumn Test series based on the Lions over here. What a draw that would be.'

But would it not threaten the traditional England/Wales/ Scotland/Ireland matches against southern hemisphere teams, I wondered?

'I suppose it might but it would be worth taking the chance. A Lions tour is the greatest thing of all, it's the pinnacle for any player. But in selecting Graham Henry, they chose the wrong man to coach the 2001 Lions,' said Windsor.

I did not go to Australia for the 2001 Lions tour. But from afar it seemed to me that one commodity was greatly lacking: humour. Bobby Windsor smiled. 'Well, we had some fun on all our Lions tours. But I agree, they didn't on that one to Australia last year. It sounded like they were living in a prison, a miserable experience. I remember when I first went on a Lions tour thinking one of my treats back home was being served cod balls by the missus on a Friday night. That was special – a treat, like. Suddenly, from that, I was on a fifteen-week tour of South Africa staying in five-star hotels with all expenses paid and being invited to have any food I fancied.

'Then you read last year that some of the players wanted to come home early. They were talking about walking out and quitting. From a Lions tour. Bloody unbelievable.

'I can assure you there was never a single moment on two Lions tours that I ever wanted to go home to my council house on an estate full of thieves and robbers, for meals like beans on toast. And then to go to work at the steelworks every day at 6a.m. in the freezing cold or wet on a pushbike.'

As usual, Bobby had summed it up best. But for the Lions, I do believe there needs to be an easing up in terms of the schedule so that the tourists can get back to some of the things which gave us so much pleasure on our tours. Things like time off in the Kruger National Park in South Africa, visiting ostrich farms, and especially going to hospitals and schools to see children. All those things were fantastic aspects of our tours. The modern-day Lions tour is much the poorer for their absence from the schedule. The fact is, there should be other things on a Lions tour than just training and playing. If that is all they have come down to, then I fear for their future.

CHAPTER 9

The Overseas Players

In the summers of 1999, 2000, 2001 and 2002, Gloucester Rugby Football Club went out shopping. They must have taken a very large chequebook indeed with them on all four occasions. By the time they had scoured the world for suitable talent each summer, the club owned by Tom Walkinshaw, the Formula One motor-racing boss, had acquired a multitude of overseas players including some of the best and most expensive players in world rugby.

Of course, we will never know exactly what players like Jason Little and Ian Jones cost the English West Country club. Annual salaries ranging from £80,000 up to around £250,000 were mentioned, depending upon which newspaper and which reporter was revealing what they believed to be the facts. What we can be certain of is that neither player came cheaply. Little, the brilliant Australian centre, was born in August 1970 and forged his reputation as a young player for his state, Queensland, and then the Wallabies with another youngster who was also to become one of the world's finest players, Tim Horan. The pair of them were to become instrumental figures in Australia's World Cup sides throughout the 1990s. Little went on to win sixty caps for Australia, a fine achievement.

Ian Jones established a reputation as one of New Zealand's finest second-row forwards, long before he ever thought of playing club rugby in England. A tall, athletic lock forward who hailed from North Auckland and North Harbour, Jones won seventy-seven caps for the All Blacks and proved himself a man worthy of following exalted company of great New Zealand All Black locks like Colin

Meads, Peter 'Pol' Whiting, Andy Haden and Gary Whetton.

To have both men in the same English club side offered Gloucester not just a wealth of experience at the heart of the forward pack and three-quarter line, but also skill and quality in abundance. As a result, Gloucester reached the semi-finals of the Heineken European Cup in 2001 before losing narrowly to eventual champions Leicester.

But what about these overseas players? Have they been a waste of money, simply a wonderful pension fund for players coming towards the end of their careers in the southern hemisphere? My answer would be maybe yes, in many cases. While it is true that we have seen some outstanding players coming into the British game, it's certainly true that others have been wildly overpriced and overpaid. Those in the latter category just haven't been worth the money.

Let's take the good ones first. The main reason for bringing in top quality guys is for the influence they can have on younger players in the squad. I know just how good the South African Pieter Muller has been for us at Cardiff. No one can say he was a waste of money. But I accept they weren't all as professional, as dedicated as Muller. So some have been a waste but the reason for that goes back to the point that there was great confusion and panic when professionalism was thrust upon the game. As soon as that happened, people said, 'We want to be top of the pile, we must be the best.' And most rushed out to buy any player with a name who was prepared to listen to them. In many cases, they paid far too much for players who were not good enough. But what had happened was that people who were at the top of their own individual professions in the business world thought they could use the same tactics in the sporting world. They did not realise that it doesn't happen like that in sport. It is a very thin dividing line between being successful and failing in sport; it's not like business.

The second major problem was that there was no yardstick in terms of what a player was worth. The English clubs immediately got off the blocks and there was an almighty rush. It was, of course, an opportunity for clubs like Saracens and Newcastle who had traditionally not enjoyed the same high profile as others such as Coventry, Leicester, Bath and Bristol to seize the chance and climb to the top. What had been glimpsed was a fast-track to Premiership success and, if buying up players was the route, then so be it. However much they cost. Also, we should remember that a man like Sir John Hall had been in the soccer business and now was trying to bring the same sort of principles into rugby. That could never work and certainly when Hall paid Inga Tuigamala, the New Zealand All Black, £1 million for a four-year contract, the writing was on the wall.

Club owners were going crazy in the first couple of years and paying any amount of money to get players to their club. And even today, although most clubs are now trying to stabilise their wage bill and stick rigidly to their budgets, I still sweat sometimes when I hear what some of these ordinary players are asking for. But it all stems from what is being paid in England. So it has become the case that you can't get a good second-row forward for under £100,000. Yet I don't believe they are worth that kind of money in our game because this game as a business can't support it. In the future, I believe more and more Welsh clubs will have to let their best players go 'over the bridge', as we say, to England because they themselves can't afford such high wage levels.

I can remember that when two Cardiff players, Adrian Davies and Andy Moore, were approached by Richmond to join Ashley Levett's then ambitious club, I was staggered when I heard how much they had been offered. Good luck to both of them – you can't stand in the way of people in those circumstances. But I do recall thinking to myself, 'God help us. Because if clubs are paying all that for two guys who weren't even fixtures in the Welsh international side, then what must they be paying for the best players around?' I could foresee the problem coming and the owners therefore have to take some of the responsibility for the mess that developed.

I suppose with the whole issue of overseas players, you pays your money and takes your choice, as the expression goes. Against the experience and know-how top international players can add to your squad and the numbers they can attract at the gate, you must raise the question as to whether they are keeping out of the team promising youngsters whose rate of development might therefore be slowed. Sure, on the training ground and in match conditions, the best of the overseas players – and I'm talking here about attitudes, not just talent – can have a profound effect. But not all of them have been like that.

Jason Little felt that young players were certainly coming through in this part of the world. He reported seeing some fantastic young players running around in British rugby, players with real ability. That is why he reiterated his insistence that the biggest thing clubs over here should have in mind is the development of their younger players. That is what provides strength and a proper future.

He said, 'I see a lot of ambition in the game here. I think plenty of players want higher honours, as is the case back home. I hope it's not a problem because Ian is right, if you ever reach a stage where your young players are only interested because of the money, then you have real problems ahead.'

It's true, there are some very good young kids coming through in British and Irish rugby. Look at Brian O'Driscoll of Ireland and Jamie Robinson at my club, Cardiff. Lewis Moody, the young Leicester and England flank forward, is another. These are very talented young players. There are plenty of others, too. There is now an incentive for youngsters to get into a profession where they can enjoy a good lifestyle. But the game cannot rest on its laurels because I think what we may have is a very small nucleus of very good young players. Certainly those with potential who are given ample opportunities with elitist squads do now have a system that will keep them close to the attention of the right people so that they are not passed over. That is a clear improvement on times gone by when many countries – and England were an obvious example of this – simply overlooked, ignored or just missed players with enormous amounts of talent because the system was not offering them the opportunity to prove themselves. All that has clearly changed for the better.

But back to Gloucester. There seems little doubt that under the influence of players like Little and Jones, plus many more who replaced them in time for the 2001–2002 season, they improved significantly. Furthermore, the club's then French coach Philippe Saint-André believed that by the end of the 2000–2001 season in the northern hemisphere, English club rugby was coming towards a peak of its powers. Saint André said, 'This League is the best in Europe. The English League is much higher in quality than the French League now. Look at what England did to the other sides in the Six Nations Championship that year. Wales and France lasted fifty minutes against them, Italy were in trouble after forty minutes and Scotland were in trouble all the way through. The English League has got better and better. It has left the others behind.'

But what did Jones and Little make of it all and rugby in the northern hemisphere? Jones, although rightly rejecting the offer to make comparisons between the English club competitions and competitions such as the Super 12 in the southern hemisphere, did feel that the English League was very proficient.

'The Zurich Championship competition breeds a structured game and leads to a tough competition,' he said. 'That explains why England are dominant at Six Nations level because of the structured game all the English players play each week. But you can't compare rugby here to the southern hemisphere. Everything is different: ground conditions, refereeing interpretations, preparation etc. But it is very intense here, that's for sure, and the amount of rugby you play certainly needs to be closely looked at. Because you can only have a certain size of squad. You can't play all these games without a big squad but clubs can't afford the real size of squads they need to handle the number of games. If clubs don't have proper numbers, they end up always playing their top twenty-two players each week. I know clubs need the income but, believe me, player burn-out is a serious threat here.

'Look at the Super 12 back in the southern hemisphere. You have eleven to thirteen matches all played in one block. You live that competition for three months, you are locked into it. Here, at the start of the season, you are looking at a twenty-two match programme on a round robin basis over as much as nine months. What does that do to your mental state? After that, you have home and away in the Heineken Cup plus the domestic Cup.'

Jones believed that, from the players' point of view, in an ideal world you could halve the amount of games played domestically by banishing home and away in the League. Teams could still plan – it would just be that one season Gloucester would play Leicester home and the next season away. It would cut the number of matches and would mean, very importantly in his opinion, you would get even more intense matches. If rugby in this country was going to advance and the intensity of matches be lifted, it needed to be a real spectacle, he said.

'There are so many unconverted people in this country still waiting to come to rugby. When it's on TV, it needs to be a superb spectacle, a real show that entices youngsters to the sport and their parents, too. But you won't do it by playing too many games and exhausting the players. By playing twelve matches instead of twenty-two, you are sure to get more intense games and begin that process. But I believe this is a problem that will never go away because clubs won't want to forego major matches during a season. They want to play every other week at home and that means a heck of a lot of rugby for the players.'

Little agreed. He found his first season in England very tough. Take Rotherham out, he said, and it had been extremely hard. Every game in the Zurich Premiership had been tough. Gloucester also met two very good Welsh teams in the Heineken Cup, Llanelli and Cardiff, although he doubted whether the Welsh League had the strength in depth of that in England. Certainly it was not the case in Scotland. That, he felt, had led to a situation where England were very powerful, one of the best teams in the world.

Little talked of the competitions in which the English and British clubs had been involved. 'I think the Heineken Cup is an unbelievably good competition with enormous potential to go a lot further. But the structure of this competition like a lot of others in this part of the world needs changing. The first match played in the Heineken Cup in my first season was on 6 October and yet, with only one weekend of April remaining, the semi-finals were only just being played. The final wasn't played until 20 May. That was seven and a half months later which was crazy for a club competition. It should be condensed much more than that to create a greater intensity of support and interest. If you get continuity in a competition, especially one that is on TV, people know what is happening one week to the next. No one had a clue who had been in the competition, who had beaten who by semi-final time and so on. That is all a big down-side in what should be a hugely popular and successful event. That must be looked at and changed.

'England are a wonderful side at the moment but it worries me where countries like Wales and Scotland are going right now. Because it needs them also to be strong to make the game as a whole in this part of the world successful. All the other countries have to catch England and France, not let them get away right out on their own. That would benefit no one. I think they will close the gap, I think they will have to. Their methods will change to cope so that people will develop and set new benchmarks. It always happens. New Zealand, for example, haven't had the best couple of years but you would be crazy to say they won't reach the forefront of world rugby again. Wales can do the same.'

From my point of view and I'm sure from that of all Welshmen, I just hope that Jason is right. Because there are clear dangers of a situation where one or two countries get out on their own, go ahead so far that they regard their neighbours as insufficient opposition. This happened in soccer in Britain. The Home Internationals in soccer started way back in the 1880s. They involved England, Wales, Scotland and Northern Ireland and were regular games each year, lasting until 1984. But by then, England had made it clear that they did not want to go on with the Home Championship and since then they have shown no inclination to revive the tournament. Now I'm quite sure that when the Home International Championship was at its peak, no one thought it would ever decline and end. Yet it did. Perhaps that is a lesson for us all to remember when we look at the Six Nations Championship and its long history as the Five Nations.

I think any gap between one rugby-playing nation and another is more ominous now because of the nature of the professional game. So it is vital we don't allow that gap between England and France, and the other nations to develop. But look at England–Scotland rugby results in recent years. Every Scot points to Sunday 2 April 2000 when England went to Murrayfield in search of a Grand Slam against a Scottish side which had lost all its previous four matches in the Championship.

Of course, the completely unexpected happened and Scotland won 19–13 on a desperate day both in terms of climate and, from English rugby's point of view, decision-making. But it's worth remembering the previous ten internationals between the countries stretching back to 1991 – England won all ten. Then they avenged that Scottish defeat in 2000 with a 43–3 thumping of the Scots at Twickenham in 2001. And they followed that with a 29–3 victory over the Scots in their own backyard at Murrayfield, in February 2002. That, in anyone's language, is sustained convincing form over a period of time.

Wales, too, have suffered some heavy defeats, notably the 50–10 defeat at Twickenham in March 2002, the 44–15 defeat at Cardiff in

February 2001 and the 46–12 loss at Twickenham in 2000. But before that, Wales beat them in 1999 at Wembley (because the National Stadium in Cardiff was still being built), and in 1993 at Cardiff. Even so, Wales have lost eleven of their last thirteen matches against England.

The point is the Six Nations is still a great occasion. But to make it really worthwhile you have got to have a high standard of competition. Other countries must be able to play a highly competitive game. If they can't, if they cannot match the continued excellence and domination of two countries apart from on the odd occasion, then in my view the future success of the competition is in danger.

Ian Jones shared these concerns of mine. Maybe now more overseas players and coaches needed to go to Scotland especially, but also to Wales, as they had done to Ireland and England. Because it was not healthy for the other countries if England and France dominated the whole time. The game needed unpredictability in its competitions. 'To be a good side you need to win consistently. That's the challenge now for England. But I see France and England's dominance continuing and most results are now predictable, although there will always be the occasional upset. Predictability is a danger the authorities should be aware of and trying to do something about. The England structure is so sound at the moment and the younger players are coming through well. From France and England's point of view, perhaps they can start playing the Tri Nations teams more often. But Wales, Scotland and Ireland also need to be involved in world rugby as well.'

As for the amount of rugby played today, I agree with Ian's view about the dangers of over-playing people. The country/club debate needs to be sorted out. It's ridiculous that English and Welsh players have to play for their country one week and their clubs the next. Look at Wales – between internationals against France and Italy in the winter of 2001, Cardiff met Swansea on successive weekends in vital Cup and League games. That was daft. We need a structure that gives these lads highly competitive games, a sensible level of competitiveness. What you cannot continue to have is a system that allows the leading Welsh players to kick lumps out of each other as they always will in Cardiff–Swansea matches in the middle of the international season. Not only that but both were vital matches, one in the Cup and the other which was crucial to the outcome of the League title.

Jones also talked of the structure of the Super 12 being played in one block and in a perfect world perhaps we would arrange our competitions along similar lines. But our difficulty is that we cannot agree on everything in this part of the world. Yet surely it is not rocket science to, say, start off with your domestic competition then stage the Heineken Cup, which is the next level up, and climax the season with the Six Nations and perhaps the Heineken final? The southern hemisphere's Super 12 competition leads comfortably into the Tri Nations, thereby giving the international players of South Africa, Australia and New Zealand a robust preparation for the international programme. In the UK and Ireland it's nowhere near as simple because there are too many self interests at work. One of the earliest recommendations when the game went 'open' was to have blocks of competitions. But because the Zurich Championship in England is so important for sponsors, other dates could not be agreed. The fact is that, in each country, everybody wants a piece of the cake. No country has the same interests as the other in the northern hemisphere.

Jason Little summed up the frustrations felt by many players. 'The rugby here is quite different. For a start it's more physical than back home. In other ways, too, it is very demanding. And it takes time for an overseas player to get used to the different styles and conditions he finds over here. Pat Howard's best year by far for Leicester was his third and last season and that was no coincidence. He had time to settle in and really understand the game here and then adapt his play. My chief frustration here is that the competitions don't seem to be things you can really get your teeth into. You start one, play a bit and then break off and play another one. Then the Six Nations comes along and you don't play any League rugby for a while. Or if you do, you're playing without your international colleagues which totally disrupts your club side. That's not perfect in any sense.'

I share the view that when you stop playing the Heineken Cup for a few weeks and return to domestic competitions, you take the momentum right out of it. It would be great to have ten games straight in Europe but then some might think it was less than ideal to have a Cup final in December. But certainly I think the Heineken

Cup is a major competition that is here to stay although it is too spread out at the moment. Several teams who had been in form at some stage in the Heineken in the season 2000–2001 found that by the time they returned to the competition to play in the knock-out stages, they had lost their form and went out. The momentum had been lost. But the Heineken Cup, I'm sure, is here to stay. Already, it has produced some marvellous matches. One of them was undoubtedly Cardiff's game against Saracens in North London early in autumn 2000. It was a superb game of rugby which Cardiff just won, but if ever there was an outstanding advertisement for the competition, it was a contest like that. I would say that was as well as I had seen Cardiff play for a very long time.

Or the Toulouse–Munster match the previous season when the Irish province won in France. Or the Llanelli–Northampton semi-final the same season. Nor should we forget the drama and excitement of Llanelli's quarter-final defeat at Gloucester in 2001, a match decided ultimately by a drop goal from Gloucester's New Zealand scrum half Elton Moncrieff which bounced off the arm of a Llanelli player and somehow scraped over the crossbar for the three vital points. Then the next season, Llanelli beat the reigning European and English champions Leicester in a thrilling clash at Stradey Park to book their place in the quarter-finals of the 2001–2002 competition. At that quarter-final stage, they went to Bath and outplayed the West Country club to reach the last four, only to lose to Leicester in the semi-finals.

The English might believe the Zurich Championship is the best club competition in the world, the French doubtless think their own Championship is the finest. I reserve judgement on both because I don't want to get drawn into an Anglo-French verbal battle! But what I like so much about the Heineken Cup is that all the best clubs and provinces are involved. Therefore, there is an opportunity for supporters to enjoy the different cultures of those teams they play in locations often far removed from the cities they probably know so well from the Six Nations Championship – Edinburgh, Dublin, Cardiff, Rome, Paris and London.

However, despite having said all that, I still believe that the format of the Heineken Cup is not quite right and that we can improve it. Frankly, the present system is rather unfair, principally because those teams in the pools of four which are grouped with an

Italian club, are obvious favourites to run in a hatful of tries which can clinch the two places for best runners-up.

Let me give you an example. The day before Cardiff played their final group match of the 2001–2002 Heineken competition, at the English club Northampton, they had scored more tries than Ulster who were paired in another group with, among other teams, Treviso of Italy. But on the Friday night in Belfast, Ulster ran in eleven tries against the Italians which meant that suddenly, Cardiff not only had to go to Northampton and win if they were to have any hope of snatching one of the runners-up places, but they had to score four tries. That rendered our task virtually hopeless and in the end we lost anyway, so it made no difference. Yet look at the opposition in our group – Montferrand, Northampton and Glasgow. By comparison, Llanelli were in a group with Leicester, Perpignan and the Italians Calvisano which twice gave the Stradey boys the chance to run up a cricket score and grab a pile of tries.

Then there was the case of Newport who also failed to qualify for the quarter-finals. Yet they were in a group dubbed 'the pool of death'. They were paired with Munster, Toulouse and Newcastle. There was no chance to score a load of easy tries against any of those teams. Do you see the imbalance here?

I suggest that it would be better to have four pools of six in the Heineken Cup because that would give you five home games and five away matches. That would give you the chance to take the winner and runners-up from each pool, the eight sides that would contest the quarter-finals. There would be no relying on one team grabbing a last eight slot because they overran easy opposition to the tune of twelve tries! I think that would be a much better format. I accept that as long as you include Italian clubs, a slight imbalance may exist anyway because of playing strengths. But that is no reason to omit them; they should stay because involvement will help raise their own standards. However, we can partly eliminate the big disadvantage some clubs experience.

I understand the difficulties of the situation, because the fact is, to try and tie in everybody's demands and desires seems next to impossible. No one has really yet got a common thread. Nobody is thinking about anything except their own interests. The French and English don't want to expand the Heineken because they have strong commitments in their own domestic leagues. Some folk in those two countries would feel that ten European games would be too many.

But if we want the sport to develop properly, then we have to set aside these narrow parochial interests. And I do think it would be a fairer competition with four groups of six, with the top two qualifying. As a sport, rugby union is not yet a major player, not along the lines of soccer, for example. Yet there is a great opportunity for rugby to move to the next level. The interest is spreading but only very slowly. What is required is the determination of all the nations to buy into a common policy that could see the game develop rapidly.

On the subject of overseas players in general, Ian, as you would expect, was firmly in favour of the concept of overseas players coming into British or Irish club rugby, although he admitted that a limit on the numbers was probably a good thing. This is what he had to say on the subject.

'There should be a limit on the numbers for the development of the game over here. But in general, you can't question too much the input, the influence, of overseas players in the British game. What did Pat Howard do at Leicester, look at what Michael Lynagh and Philippe Sella did for those around them at Saracens. I believe most overseas players feed positive things into the English game. Not just from a playing point of view, but with different thoughts on aspects such as training, preparation, mental approach etc. It's too easy to get locked into what you are doing and go along with the history and ways of your club. It's good for new boys to come in and see things differently. I think overseas players have brought good new ideas to the game but you don't want too many of them. Over a period of time, players and coaches from overseas have definitely lifted standards in British rugby. On and off the field. Swansea had a New Zealand coach and then an Australian, Cardiff had an Australian coach and then a South African. Gloucester had a French coach for a few seasons, while an Australian was in charge at Bath, as the season 2001–2002 ended. A South African was in charge at Saracens, before being replaced by Wayne Shelford, a Kiwi. That is all good and healthy, in my view. New professional attitudes have been introduced and the England players certainly have learned from that.'

Jason Little felt that a short fix of lots of overseas players was not the answer. 'Not that I'm saying some overseas stars are not worth it. Clearly, they are. Look at what Ian Jones brought to a club like Gloucester. Buying major overseas players clearly has its advantages, but in tandem, you must plan for the future. That means building up and nurturing a strong youth section. Nothing is more important than that. Look at clubs like Bath, Leicester and Wasps. They are regularly bringing through players from their younger sides. Their youth programmes must be working. That is where the money should be spent. Then, by all means, bring in a talisman from overseas who can help teach the youngsters. What players like Ian Jones have been exposed to in the last ten years can be passed on to those youngsters around him and that is invaluable information.'

I share such views wholeheartedly. The boys have got it right because there is no question that we should always look to develop our young players. The clubs, by and large, have not really done enough to encourage the development of their young players. But if you put a youngster in the second row alongside Ian Jones or a young centre beside Jason Little, those lads must learn from the experience. I think there should be a limit on the number of overseas stars because everyone agrees you are far better off pro-ducing your own. How many should you restrict the overseas contingent to within a single team? Well, ideally you could say two but then someone will always find a way around that legislation. Someone will come up with a birthright which enables him to come over from the southern hemisphere to play here because he's qualified for a British or Irish nation through a parent or grand-parent. Then you have all the French and Italians who can come here and play without a work permit because they are part of the European Community.

What I am saying is that if a club owner is determined to field a side with ten or twelve overseas players, I'm sure he could and would do it. But it is a question of being sensible. I welcome the presence of some overseas players for the very good reason that as well as their obvious skills, they bring a professionalism which they have experienced and become accustomed to for a longer period of time. At the end of the day, the club owners are running a business and they have to weigh up what is the most beneficial thing for their club, their business. Personally, I think it is nice to have a little mixture of players from different countries. The individuals learn the need to integrate, to bond together, to learn about how other individuals go about tackling tasks and living life. There is nothing wrong in that.

In some ways I wish I had taken the opportunity to play overseas during my time as a player. I had the chance. Montferrand, the French club, asked me to join them around 1973–74 and I should have taken the opportunity. I would have embraced a different culture, seen a different approach to the game and learned from it. I might even have got to enjoy such French delicacies as frogs' legs! Mind you, seeing food so fresh that when you buy it in the local market place, some of it is still crawling around, is certainly unusual!

Nowadays, player movement is commonplace but it wasn't so much then, and I decided in the end to stay where I was. By then, I felt I had commitments in Wales, both in a rugby and personal sense, and I thought it would be difficult to fit it all in. But some of my peers at that time did it. Brian Price, Brian Thomas and Denzil Williams played some French club rugby for one or two seasons in the late 1960s or early seventies. I reckon they were wise to do it.

One subject Jason Little felt strongly about was the question of overseas tours. He felt that rugby had lost so much by the ending of proper length tours by national sides and he confessed he was very disappointed at the way they had gone. 'For me, I liked the longer tour where you played sides in a country midweek and got to know the country and the people. Now, teams fly in for a one-off Test and fly out. You see nothing, meet no one. What's saddest of all is I can't see how they can physically structure the longer tour into a season any more, considering all the domestic commitments everyone has.'

I echo Jason's disappointment. My fear is we will never again see the full-length tour. The fact is that the demands and therefore schedules of international rugby have changed so much. One-off internationals are arranged to satisfy the great god that is television but to those people who have created this situation I say simply, 'You have created a monster you cannot stop or control.' There is, I believe, a danger of us all drowning in international rugby. It's a case of more, more, more . . . it is a hungry mouth that has got to be fed all the time. The reason is simple – internationals produce the most money and that explains and justifies everything in some people's eyes. I disagree and Jason clearly does, too. There are some players around the world today, chiefly in the southern hemisphere I'm pleased to say, who are virtually just international players. If the attitude that created such a situation came here to the northern hemisphere, there would be a grave danger that we would lose the very soul of our game which is the club game. I think it is essential for the younger generation to have a place where they can lean over the barriers easily and see the star players close up, to tug at their sleeves and ask for their autographs at the end of a Saturday afternoon when they come out of the dressing-room. It's good for older supporters to be able to have a brief word with these guys in the clubhouse afterwards. All this still counts for a great deal in my opinion.

I am sad to say that I, too, think the proper length international tours are gone, dead and buried. Everyone is losing from that situation. For example, Cardiff celebrated their 125th centenary in the season 2001–2002 and it would have been wonderful to host the Wallabies as a highlight of that season. We at Cardiff have always done well against the Australians and it would have been a fabulous occasion, just as it would be if New Zealand or South Africa met Bath or Leicester in a midweek match on a proper tour of England. I suppose you could say it is still up to the respective Unions to say who their opposition should be if they are making a tour. But I suspect the necessities of the modern approach render the opportunity for the All Blacks to play again at Llanelli or Newport pretty slim. It is not just the home supporters who are losing out by such a scenario; the visiting players miss a key part of what rugby has meant by the loss of visits to places like Melrose, Leicester or Limerick. The pity is that, far too often, these radical changes in direction for the game as a whole have been made for one reason alone: finance. But perhaps it is also time we started to care rather more for some of rugby's traditions. Especially when they still have so much to commend them as an intrinsic part of the game.

Ian Jones came up with an interesting viewpoint on the whole question of tours. 'I would like to see England, Wales and the other countries consistently playing the best of Australia and New Zealand. Not in one-off Tests but in a three-match series. You can only really judge yourself superior to your opponents if you play them in a three-match Test series. New Zealand and Australia have been doing it for decades down under in the Bledisloe Cup and it gives everyone a proper chance to judge each side correctly. You learn little in a one-off Test match in which a side flies in and then flies out.'

I asked Ian what he regarded as the main problems of rugby in this part of the world. His reply surprised me a little, although with hindsight what he said made sound common sense. 'I'd say the grounds are one thing you must look at. There are some good pitches, Saracens for example. But grounds like those at Gloucester, Rotherham and Cardiff are just not conducive to playing good football. Another little thing which needs urgent attention is the state of training pitches – they're not good enough in my experience. It's about time and money, and those are things rugby needs to sort out.

'Weather conditions here are just not conducive to the type of game southern hemisphere sides play. From November through to March, it is inevitably a forward-dominated, territory-influenced game in this part of the world. But if you get training facilities up to speed over here then maybe the gap can start to close in terms of different playing patterns. But it's very hard to see that happening.'

Jason Little agreed. 'More money needs to be spent on training and playing facilities over here. Not in every case but certainly in some. London Irish is a good example of a club that's got it right with its playing facilities. I've never seen a better stadium than the one they're playing in at Reading.

'Kingsholm, by contrast, will need upgrading and work done on it to match what is expected in a professional sport. A true playing surface is vital in rugby nowadays and I don't believe that is impossible because of the weather over here. Look at soccer clubs like West Ham and Watford – they have a surface which has been consistently good all winter, even during the worst of the weather. It can be done. It's down to the type of surface you put down and the amount you invest in it. People want to watch a fantastic game nowadays and you need good playing surfaces to achieve that.'

I know that clubs are aware of this need but it has never been regarded as a priority in the British game. At least, it wasn't in the old days of amateurism, but now we have a professional sport, we need to improve facilities in general. The national Unions have led the way in this with smart, new state-of-the-art stadia at Cardiff, Twickenham, Murrayfield and Paris. But at club level, although some have upgraded, others have much to do. It certainly doesn't seem to me that we have progressed as far down this road as, say, the New Zealanders or South Africans. At Cardiff, we have suffered greatly from the problems of a pitch that is prone to waterlogging and we are doing our best to eradicate the problem. We want to have the best facilities we can and have been looking for a working pact with the University in Cardiff who have some wonderful facilities. We know what to aim for. When we first went to Saracens' ground at Watford a couple of years ago for one of the Anglo-Welsh friendly matches, we could see the benefit of having a quality surface and how much more conducive it was to good fast rugby. Such a facility should become a priority for all the clubs and we at Cardiff know full well the problems that arise out of having a poor standard pitch. Before the start of the 2001–2002 season, we had spent up to £150,000 for work on our pitch. The trouble is, it costs an awful lot of money. I understand the Watford pitch cost around £750,000 to put in and I know that the RFU are planning on spending £1 million in a year or so to dig up their pitch completely at Twickenham and put down a new playing surface along the lines of the West Ham and Watford examples. Both surfaces have a special woven grass and it does appear to make a significant difference. It's a chicken-and-egg situation really as far as most clubs are concerned. You can't have the players without the pitch (not playing consistently good rugby, anyway) but there's not much point having the pitch without the best players. It all comes down to cost. I think it's vitally important that good players have the right and proper platform on which to perform and demonstrate their skills. There is nothing worse than training and playing on poor pitches full of mud all winter. It just drags you down. I know that you do get wet seasons in the southern hemisphere but overall conditions are conducive to better rugby. That is one of the advantages of playing rugby in the southern hemisphere and one of the drawbacks of being involved in the northern hemisphere game. But, irrespective of weather conditions, we have to improve facilities so that we can offer players the best possible surfaces on which they not only play but also train.

We discussed whether money had been wasted on players in the

British game. 'No,' said Jones, 'I don't think it's been wasted. Clubs get huge benefits from overseas players as far as sponsors are concerned. And young supporters have come to the game, lured partly by the presence of big-name overseas stars.'

Jones's great wish was that younger players still loved their rugby, they still played it for the sheer pleasure of the sport itself. Here especially, young players were getting paid good money to play rugby but he didn't think they should see it as a job. He hoped they were not happy just to turn up and get paid and not advance in the game. That was his biggest concern in England because there were so many players and clubs around. Players released by one club could get contracts elsewhere. They just walked down the road and picked up another lucrative deal; it was too easy to get a contract in Britain, he felt.

'That doesn't lead to mental toughness. What young players need in their heads is not thoughts about money but solely the drive and desire to be the best in the game. It's too easy to get a rugby contract in England. And it really bugs me that these guys see the game just as a job now. You need to be more driven than that to be successful. A contract with a club should be the stepping-stone to higher things, not the end of a player's ambition. Every player's desire should be to play for his country. Your desire, your every waking moment, should be geared to playing for England or Wales, not Gloucester or Cardiff. Nor just to pick up a good pay cheque and drive a nice flash car. You get rewards in life if you work hard and the reward for a rugby player has to be to represent his country. Money can't drive that desire. New Zealand and Australia will never compete financially with the clubs in Britain. But the way they can compete is the lure of the black jersey, or in Australia's case, of the green and gold jersey. That is the strongest thing New Zealand and Australian rugby has got going for it. The trouble is those players who don't feel driven by that desire or who believe they won't make that level, are lured overseas, principally to Europe. And the departure of those second and third tiers of players robs us back home of the depth and therefore competition we need. Everyone must have real competition, individuals and teams.'

On the subject of whether it is too easy for young rugby players to pick up contracts, this is a widely held concern. But I don't see we can do much about it because it is a competitive scene. The top clubs want the best players and squad numbers need to be right and built up. But every encouragement should be given to these young lads to continue their education because at their young age, it is essential they balance training with studying.

So what of the future? Jason Little sees the game going forward strongly but he warned, 'It has to be managed very well. I think a balance needs to be found between the income and providing a platform for the game to develop among rugby supporters. The players here do have a big advantage in that it is much easier to combine professional rugby with their family lives. I left Australia because I was never at home during the rugby season. You travel a lot for Super 12 and when you're home you're in training camp. Then when you play for the Wallabies, you're in training camp for weeks and months at a time. You are never home. It's a big advantage to players in the UK that they don't run into those kind of difficulties. In the end, it was why I quit the Wallabies. It became quite unusual for me to sit down with Bridget, my wife, for a few weeks on end and do things like eat meals together. Most of the players here don't know how lucky they are.'

Those who played alongside Ian Jones and Jason Little during their time at Gloucester were also fortunate. Both were outstanding players in their own very different positions and their colleagues must have picked up large amounts of good advice, tips and excellent habits that will hopefully serve them well through the remainder of their careers. Ironically, though, neither player was still at Gloucester when the next northern hemisphere season, 2001–2002, began. Jones had returned to New Zealand with the intention of going into retirement, only for the London club Wasps to recruit him in autumn 2001. Little, meanwhile, had moved just a short distance down the M5 to join fellow West Country club, Bristol. And, as captain that season, he led Bristol to the final of the Zurich Premiership play-offs at Twickenham, where they lost narrowly to Gloucester. It was compelling evidence of Bristol's progress during the season, under the undoubted influence of the now retired Jason Little.

CHAPTER 10

The Referees

Given the nature of the modern game, there has never been greater scrutiny put on referees in general. Their decisions are played back, sometimes over and over again. Their lives have become like those of goalkeepers on the soccer field – any little error is highlighted for everyone's amusement. They used to say you had to be mad to be a goalie and maybe that would be a useful quality for rugby referees at the highest level these days. I have to say I have never, ever, once thought that I ought to have taken up refereeing after I left the game. I couldn't have done so, anyway, because I never qualified for having a white stick. Seriously though, I can tell you, I would never have become a ref. I have a great admiration for the men who do take on this most onerous and demanding of jobs.

Jim Fleming of Scotland was a referee for twenty-eight years, eighteen of them as an international official. He called it 'a fantastic experience, a good innings' and in May 2001 felt that it was time to finish. England's Ed Morrison never had any intention of going to the next World Cup in 2003. Rugby now is based on four-year cycles and in his opinion, the authorities were quite right in making their decision to bring down the curtain on his international career. 'I had a good run in the game and enjoyed it immensely. But all things come to an end,' he said, in a thoroughly philosophical manner.

I talked with Jim Fleming and Ed Morrison, just around the time they were stepping down from senior refereeing, and we discussed their views on the game and how it had changed in recent times. First, I wondered what they were planning for the next stage of their careers. Fleming told me he had started coaching refs. It was an amateur job with the Scottish Rugby Union (SRU). 'The idea is for us to look at five or six boys who might make international refs in the next few years. What can we do for them? How can we help bring them on? Because the fact is we, too, in Scotland are having difficulty finding and recruiting referees of sufficient calibre for top-level future refereeing.'

Morrison took up a new role in the summer of 2001, helping to coach and develop panel referees in England, i.e. those Englishmen on the IRB's elite referee list who are chosen to handle games all over the world. He was working with Colin High, the former England international referee, to pass on his experience and know-how to help younger referees. It was a full-time role through the RFU. 'The RFU has recognised this is an integral part of the game and, just like those on the playing side, we have to improve our performances. The players have taken the game on to a different plateau. Now, we as referees have got to work hard to stay with them. In terms of fitness, of course, but also performance. It will damage the game if the referees worldwide cannot keep pace with those improvements on the playing side. But I don't believe that will happen – refereeing, too, will pick up the pace and it is already doing so.'

Fleming saw that the International Board wanted full-time professional referees. But Scotland are in a minority of one: they are a major rugby-playing country without full-time, professional referees and Fleming didn't see that changing in the near future. 'The trouble is most refs in the top thirty are in their late thirties, early forties; very few are in their late twenties. But what the IB are after is changing the situation. They appear to be driving down the age level of top referees. But just because you are young doesn't make you a good referee. Nor are you a good referee just because you are professional. It would be unfortunate if we were to discriminate against more mature referees that are not professional. They can do just as good a job as full-time professional refs who may be younger.'

But what of world refereeing standards at the present time? Jim Fleming said that if you took the top twenty referees in the world it was a pretty good standard generally: you didn't have the peaks and troughs in terms of refereeing performances that you had years ago.

Keith Wood and myself, at an Eden Park photo shoot.

COLORSPORT

Two of the key players behind clubs in England and Wales: Nigel Wray of Saracens *(left)* and Peter Thomas of Cardiff, photographed with Tim Horan and myself.

DAVE ROGERS/ALLSPORT

Referees Jim Fleming of Scotland *(top)* and England's Ed Morrison, who handled the 1995 World Cup final in South Africa, were among the finest ever seen.

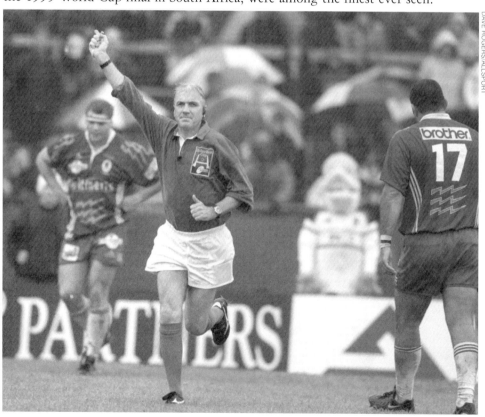

The inimitable, the glorious, the muddied marvels of the old Pontypool front row: *(from left)* Graham Price, Bobby Windsor and Tony Faulkner.

The modern-day businessman: Mike Burton has made an outstanding success of his skills in the corporate hospitality market.

DAVE ROGERS/ALLSPORT

Former rugby league men have been at the centre of England's revival: Phil Larder, the defence coach (pictured above with the 2001 Lions), and Joe Lydon, now coach of the England Sevens squad.

DAVE ROGERS/GETTY IMAGES

It's a long time ago… November 1974 and the 13–13 draw with New Zealand. But I maintain it is still essential the Barbarians continue to flourish in modern rugby.

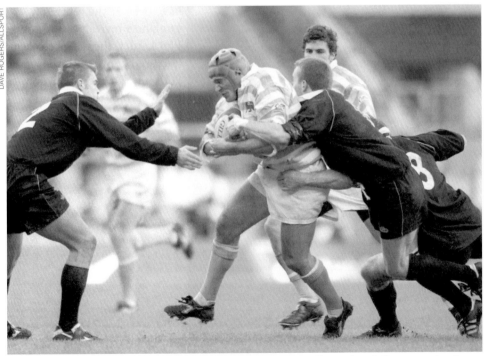

I'd also like to see the Varsity Match prosper, but it will need a different attitude to that shown in the remorseless 2001 game when so little attacking play was on display.

England's Jonny Wilkinson, of whom fellow Lion Keith Wood said, 'God, was that guy focused.'

People used to think beating England was easy for Wales in my day. I never thought that and here Leicester hooker (and now chief executive) Peter Wheeler is showing why.

Can anyone really claim
the modern-day player
has better skills than these
two greats of the past:
Pierre Villepreux (France)
and Mike Gibson (Ireland)?

'The IB are trying to get common interpretation worldwide but if you do that and go with that approach, you won't get the personalities you had years ago. People like Clive Norling, Derek Bevan and Ed Morrison won't fit the bill because the criteria the IB are pursuing will exclude such characters and referees who perhaps tried to do it their way. In a technical sense, the IB want uniformity. The people at the top are trying not to wipe out the man-management skills of the referee but if you remove the individual, you will end up doing that. Because the IB want their refs to officiate in exactly the same style. OK, not quite robots but like robots.

'But I have always felt refereeing is a very instinctive thing. You can't coach *anybody* to be an international referee. You have either got it or you haven't. It's like players. Beyond a certain level, you just won't perform if you haven't basically got what it takes. Alan Lewis of Ireland might be a good referee in the future, and Chris White of England might very well have it. I think the boys at the top now are good but not outstanding. A lot of them haven't been there that long. But I wonder whether they will ever reach the level of great referees like Norman Sansom (Scotland), Fred Howard (England) and Francis Palmade (France). Maybe the system won't let them.'

Ed Morrison reckoned there were some extremely talented referees emerging internationally. 'So much so that I believe the planning the IRB put into the international game from a refereeing point of view will bear fruit by 2003. By then, I think we will have a large pool of very good refs. The age profile of referees will be younger in the future as befits the modern game. The fitness levels of the players have changed dramatically and it is essential referees keep up. Referees like Scott Young of Australia and Jonathan Kaplan, the South African, are excellent. Kaplan has made tremendous progress. Paul Honiss of New Zealand had a very difficult match to handle at the end of the Six Nations Championship in 2001 between Italy and Wales in Rome. But he came through it in the end. In England, Chris White has come on in leaps and bounds. David McHugh of Ireland is quite outstanding at the moment. With people going into full-time refereeing, that will help no end. I think many referees in the northern hemisphere especially have reaped the benefits of the full-time process.

'I know that in Scotland and Wales refs have been amateur but all things can change. I know that in England there was a view from the senior clubs that almost demanded we had full-time refs. There will only be more in the future.'

From my own point of view, I would certainly like to see referees using their initiative far more. Yes, laws are laws but if a situation arises the referee must be allowed to make a common-sense decision. It seems to me that lots of referees now can't make a decision from their own judgement. It is written in the laws and that is it. This aspect stretches into everything a referee touches. For example, during the 2001 Welsh Cup final between Newport and Neath, Shane Williams the Neath wing appeared to score a try. Everyone supporting Neath certainly thought he'd got it but even when you looked at the TV replays, you couldn't see who had actually scored from the chip through when Williams and Shane Howarth dived for the ball. Clayton Thomas was the referee and the indecision went on for some time before it was disallowed. Then, in the same match came another example. A Neath player got tackled right on the corner flag. My first reaction was that he might have got there. Nigel Whitehouse, one of the touch judges, walked on and I think he suggested to Clayton Thomas they should use the video camera. They discussed it on the field and the decision was eventually made, without recourse to the video ref: no try. Thomas's 'feeling' was that the player hadn't scored and he didn't give the try. He was proved right, too, which confirmed my point that referees should not automatically hand everything over to the video referee. Use the technology if it is there, if you are uncertain. If you are pretty sure, don't. But what we also need is some unity on this topic. Because to have a Heineken Cup semi-final played with no video referee facility available was extraordinary. Just as luck would have it, Munster's semi-final against Stade Français in spring 2001 contained a controversial 'no try' ruling by a touch judge, yet it turned out to be a genuine score when you watched the TV replays. No wonder Munster were incensed – they lost that match 16–15. Had the third referee system been in use and the try given they would probably have won and reached the Heineken Cup final. For games of that importance, you must have the facility available.

Certainly, Jim Fleming regards the growing use of video cameras as inevitable. Generally, he is in favour of them because a referee can never be sure of everything. But he admits he would hate to see union go down the rugby league route of everything of any importance being referred back to the video ref. Was it a knock-on, was it a forward pass? He, too, believes the video ref should be used just for touchdowns. And referees should still have the power of their convictions. What worried him was that, in cricket for example, umpires bottled out of hard decision-making, and he was concerned that rugby referees would do the same. Sometimes you saw a cricketer run out by yards and it was obvious he was out, yet the umpire still called for the third umpire and that, said Fleming, was ridiculous. Referees, he warned, were handing over decision-making if they did that.

'The Ireland–France game in the Six Nations Championship of 2001 and that controversial touchdown by Brian O'Driscoll was a good example of what can happen with video refs,' said Fleming. 'I always had the feeling, watching it afterwards, that Scott Young, the Australian referee, felt it wasn't a try. You could hear the incredulity in his voice, saying to Brian Campsall the video referee: "Are you *sure*, Brian?" The trouble was, or so it later emerged, Campsall said he never saw all the angles that we saw on TV so he gave the try on the evidence before him. In my view, it re-emphasised my point that referees must have the power of their convictions and should not go to the video referee all the time.'

Ed Morrison agreed. 'We live in a modern era and a technical era yet there is never 100 per cent certainty about some incidents even if you replay them a hundred times. There have been mistakes made even with the benefit of the technology and that's why I say nothing is ever certain even with this aid. But the players seem comfortable with the technology and that is the important part. The referees must therefore adapt and by and large I think they have done pretty well. I, too, hope the authorities in our game don't go down the road travelled by rugby league in which referees can refer back to the video ref for technical things. For me, it should go only as far as a definitive judgement on the scoring of tries.'

Do we ask too much of referees? I suppose it depends on where you are coming from. But Fleming certainly believed a lot more was now asked of officials than even a few years ago.

'The pressures are clearly growing. So much so that I think rugby will eventually go down the soccer route. When players start losing money by being sent off, I suppose we could get players turning on referees and giving them abuse. Soccer referees are suffering in that respect, you can see it.

'At the top level in rugby it isn't too bad because of the players' superior discipline. But at the lower level players are not as disciplined and these things might well happen. Players there could turn nasty. We have to be very careful about that. It is up to the Unions to make sure they support referees and clamp down hard on any examples of abuse and indiscipline aimed at officials.'

There is no doubt referees are under greater pressure now that they are all wired up for the benefit of TV and the crowd. But I can tell you, if we'd had referees wired up in my day, the TV companies would have been inundated with complaints about the language. There is more pressure on referees, and on players too, for the simple reason that we can see everything today. The referee is more accountable. Rightly or wrongly, it is the way it is. It is why there should be professional referees. The more the pressures, the more should be the rewards for referees. They are open to abuse and fierce scrutiny and pressure.

But Fleming talked of other, different pressures, too. 'In the past, I refereed most of my games in Scotland. But nowadays, with the Celtic League taking off, our top three or four referees found themselves handling very few matches in Scotland between the end of August and the beginning of January. From our point of view, there will be more and more travelling, with weekends away from home. That is why the southern hemisphere boys introduced neutral referees and it's now becoming the same for northern hemisphere referees. But that might cut down the number of future recruits to the refereeing fraternity. Because there are very few employers who will let referees disappear every Friday morning and also fit in the fitness requirements to be a top official. Nowadays, you have to train a lot more to achieve the fitness level demanded. I knew that myself in my final seasons.

'I was training three or four times a week, whereas a few years ago, you were OK after a good Tuesday night session with your club and a Saturday game. That was all you needed. But the increased fitness levels and the travelling required mean so much more is asked of referees nowadays. So referees will have to become professional and we in the refereeing business have told the

SRU this. We haven't got any professional referees at all in Scotland, the only major rugby-playing country in the world without them. It is a problem the Scottish Union will have to address sooner rather than later. For me, it was sad that neither Wales nor Scotland had a single referee in the elite world list when I retired after the 2000–2001 season, although there are now full-time Welsh officials. No Scottish official handled a Six Nations match that season, which was equally sad to me. But it's a political thing now. For, out of sixteen refs in the elite list worldwide, most are from the southern hemisphere so by its very nature you are going to get a lot of them refereeing the Six Nations matches. These people are no better than northern hemisphere refs but they were professional before us, so they have a head start.

'The way I see it, there would be no problem at all having a Scottish referee taking a Six Nations match but that's not IB policy. Officials handling those games must be elite list referees. Yet, speaking personally, I think I refereed as well in my final season as I had ever done in my career. Ironically, the day I got a note saying I wouldn't get any Six Nations matches that season, I received another note giving me my assessment marks for handling a European Shield game between Ebbw Vale and Perigeux. I was given 97.5 out of 100 by the assessor and I defy anyone to say they could match that or improve on it. Yet the IB people said I was too old. I was dropped from the list because of that.'

I must admit I found the topic of referee assessment fascinating, but disturbing, especially in one remark Jim Fleming made. This is what he said on the subject.

'We have to look at this very seriously; I think we have a major problem here. Referees and assessors want to do their job at the highest level but the standard demanded from above by officialdom puts huge pressures upon both parties. If the referee or assessor doesn't do his job properly and doesn't stick strictly to the letter of the law, then he is seen to be falling short and pays the commensurate price. But that is detrimental to rugby in general because it is making people too dogmatic in terms of assessment of referees. Assessors take marks off throughout their assessment; there is no power for them to add on marks. So if I play an exceedingly good advantage law and a side scores a brilliant try partly due to my decision, I don't get any extra marks for that and to me that is wrong.

'A referee with a great understanding for the game and empathy with the players earns no marks for that. But, if he makes a simple mistake, he loses marks. It is all too negative. We have to build on the positive nature of this. At the moment, it is much too negative.'

I totally agree with Jim. It seems to me that very few referees have a 'feel' for the game. They blow the whistle because if they don't, they fear the assessors will mark them down. Most people I talk to about today's game have one major grouse – the referees' lack of 'feel' for the game and how people want it to be played. Of course, that may be seen as a criticism but in my view it is more of an observation. The point about the assessor is absolutely right. I know that even some assessors are not happy about the way they have to mark and they don't agree with it.

I always felt a good referee was one you didn't notice on the field. But now you can't help notice him and, what is more, you often notice the referee more than the players. That has to be wrong. I just wonder whether we have created an ogre and whether it is down to the assessors even though some of them feel hamstrung by the directives they have received.

Of course, the so-called laws and limits of assessment are laid down by the IRB but I know many referees are concerned about this. What worries me most is what Jim says about not getting more marks for doing *good* things. Why has that been dreamed up? Ed Morrison said that assessors could make or break young referees. But, he asked, what is the alternative?

'Like the players, everybody has to be judged or measured. So whatever system you use, there has to be a means of assessing the referee. I think assessors by and large are fair. If you have had a good game the assessor will say so.

'Perhaps sometimes though, we defer too much to the assessment system. I think you can referee at all levels but it is vital to enjoy it, to strike an understanding with the players and if possible find an empathy with them. Whatever the assessor sitting in the stand may believe. I started refereeing in 1982 and always enjoyed it hugely. I coached for a year when I stopped playing and didn't enjoy that. Now that is serious pressure! But refereeing prolongs your rugby life. Of course, everybody has bad games – players, referees, the writers on the game . . . everyone. If you can accept that, put it out of your mind and get on with the next game, I think you can

190

improve and continue to enjoy it. No good worrying about past mistakes. Learn from them, certainly, but don't let them linger too long in the back of your mind.'

Refereeing at the top level today is now a lot easier than it was seven or eight years ago, according to Fleming, principally because of the improved discipline of the players. He is probably right because you only have to go back and look at some of the England–Wales and France–England matches of the past to realise that today it is far easier. He ascribes that to the players' attitude, discipline and professionalism. But he warns: 'When the going gets tough, it sometimes shows up the deficiencies in refs. But the players generally have shown a big improvement and overall, they are a joy to referee now.'

I agree with Jim, I think there is pretty good discipline today. We all have opinions and like to tell referees they are wrong. But I think guys today very rarely jibe at the referee, because they know they will get no change anyway from him. But also because TV has robbed the game of its soul and character in many ways.

In trying to give people at home an insight into the game by miking up the refs, it actually detracts because of all the discussions. The banter in rugby used to be great and if you were a strong referee you gave as good as you got. But if you say anything now you are virtually in the sin-bin. The old saying that the best refs were the ones you never noticed doesn't seem to apply any more. Personally, I still like to see referees having a good rapport with the players. That is what is important, having mutual respect between the two parties.

The suggestion has been made that there is now too much going on in a game for one referee and that a system of two officials should be tested and perhaps introduced. Jim Fleming reminded me that two referees handling a game had been tried already, by Dr Danie Craven down in Bloemfontein, South Africa some years ago. But it did not work because it resembled a muddle and the idea was quietly buried. Speaking personally, I regard the idea as a total non-starter. I would rather see one referee make some mistakes than two referees making no mistakes. Because the game needs that human touch about it. We risk taking away the entire soul of the game. Anyway, can you imagine a world where refs get everything right? What on earth would we have to talk about the next day?

Who would we have left to slag off! It would be a great part of the sport gone.

Fleming went on: 'Rugby is a game of complicated laws and I don't believe there is any more going on now than there was ten years ago. Maybe in the future, the pressure for a second referee will come to pass and we will have to have them. The thing is people's expectation and awareness of situations have risen in recent times because of the media.

'I suppose it might work but refereeing is a gut feeling so you would have to have huge empathy and understanding between the two officials in charge. Otherwise it would be a licence for chaos.'

For Ed Morrison, one of the great things about refereeing was the challenge. He didn't think it would be so enjoyable if two people were on the pitch.

'Most of the time, I think rugby matches are refereed very well. I hope that doesn't sound presumptive but I think there's plenty of evidence to show that. Players complain that there is not enough consistency but would you have any more consistency with two referees? Or would there be more inconsistencies because a ref at one end of the field might have different beliefs to his colleague at the other end. It sounds far too complicated to work.'

Let's hope we never see it! But on another topic, one element of the game we would also have wished never to see happen is already reality: the loss of relationship between the referees and the players.

It is certainly one of Ed Morrison's big fears about the modern game. He complains that there is no longer the coming together of players from both sides after matches so the referee can't mix socially with both sides, either. He says that is much more than sentimentality coming out in him because referees could learn so much from having a natter with the players after a game. He feels players would make points, give their views, criticise if need be and referees would listen and take home some valuable lessons. For him, the referee and therefore the game was the poorer for the loss of such opportunities. It was one of the real downsides of professionalism. But he fears it is now just a job for the players and, like anyone else after a day's work, they want to get off and get home. He doesn't feel they can be blamed.

I hear what Ed says and I think it all comes down to pressure to win. Yes, when I played for Wales or the British Lions, the pressure to win was intense. But the big difference was that my livelihood didn't depend on the result. Our attitude and expectations were high and there was spectator pressure, too. But now, as the prizes get bigger in the game, it's inevitable, it's a fact of life that divisions will arise. The old friendships will suffer. These lads today are under even more pressure to perform than players just five years ago, never mind in my day. I agree that referees could learn a lot from a chat with players in the bar afterwards. But I suppose that is just one of the casualties of a professional sport. What is crucial is that discipline remains high among the modern players because kids copy these guys. Therefore, their discipline must be rigid.

Players have a great responsibility to the youngsters wanting to follow in their wake. Generally and I think certainly at international level and mainly at the high club levels, the game has advanced in leaps and bounds as far as discipline is concerned. Yet today it is just as physically demanding if not more so. Therefore, I have only admiration for the present-day players who control their emotions in what can be a very volatile game. To me, the game was about emotion, that was the way I played. But now, discipline among players must be absolutely rigid and that means you can no longer have the type of banter or communication with referees, on or off the field, that we enjoyed.

Jim Fleming agreed it wasn't a problem just for referees, but for the players as well. 'After professional games these days, players don't mix with each other very much, if at all. They just change and often get straight on the bus home. It's different for the Six Nations games with the dinners afterwards. But it's true, there is a breakdown in relationships after matches between players and referees and the game is the poorer for that. I think it was invaluable to have an opportunity to air some grievances, in either direction, amid a friendly setting once the match had finished. Without any question, the loss of that opportunity to forge understandings, perhaps even friendships, is to be lamented.'

As a former player, I too regret the loss of this relationship. It has been one of the struts that has underpinned the whole game for decades. Sure, you didn't always agree with the referee's decision but you had a healthy exchange of views and got on with it. Some referees were very gregarious, and afterwards, it was nice to have a beer with them and chat as friends. That was rugby at its best and the disagreements were forgotten long before the end of the evening. I think if refs have the human touch they should use it.

Also, we should accept their mistakes as well as their correct decisions. I go back to the years when I played and sometimes referees disallowed tries I knew were scores. Equally, they sometimes awarded tries that we knew weren't. But the bottom line was refs were like all of us, good and bad. The relationship you could have with them was a key part of the game. If that has been lost, then rugby is undoubtedly the poorer for it. We might have moaned at referees about decisions from time to time. You'd say, 'Aw, come on ref, give us a break, that can't be a try' or something like that. He'd either tell you to get on with it or explain it. The only refs I ever had a problem with were those who were less than 100 per cent straight. Yes, we encountered them, very occasionally, often on the other side of the world when we were touring with Wales or the British Lions. I could never abide those guys, never had the respect for them to strike up a relationship. In one game in New Zealand, we were penalised more in one half than I think Wales had been in the previous two years. Those who remember those times and are true rugby people can probably work out who I'm talking about. In one match, a certain referee jumped up and punched the air in celebration when the home team dropped a goal against us. When he got back to earth and the smile had disappeared off his face, he said lamely to us, 'I was only jumping up to see if the kick had gone over!' You can't have a relationship with a referee like that. We never respected him ever again. But the overwhelming majority of officials are not like that. They are decent people with a job to do and they do it honestly and to the best of their ability.

Mind you, there were times when I wanted to have a conversation with a referee to ask him what on earth he'd been up to! I remember in 1968, Ireland played Wales at Lansdowne Road, and we wondered before the start about a game in which Ireland's team had 179 caps between them, and we had the princely total of 60! During that match, I attempted a drop goal and in the wind it was blown around and I thought originally it might just have crept over, but I wasn't sure. But those behind the posts could see quite clearly it had not and saw it go wide. But the English referee Mike Titcomb blew his whistle and signalled a successful kick, giving us the three points.

Mayhem then broke out with the Irish crowd going nuts. Spectators invaded the playing area and held up the game for five minutes. Our full-back Doug Rees also kicked a goal and with time running out, it was six-all. But then Mike Titcomb started playing what seemed to us this endless amount of injury time. It went on and on, and of course the inevitable happened. Ireland got into the corner just where the dressing-rooms were in those days at Lansdowne Road, and they got a pushover try by Mick Doyle. They missed the conversion, Titcomb blew the whistle and we had lost 9–6!

I saw Mike later and said, 'What on earth happened there?' He told me he reckoned the only way he was going to get off the pitch safely was to dash straight into the dressing-room area, which is what he did the minute he blew the final whistle! We always had a joke about that whenever we saw each other afterwards. I remember him saying once, 'It comes to something when I am best remembered for giving you a drop goal, Gareth, which never was!'

Another referee I always had a laugh with was the Scottish official Bob Burrell. He took the France–Wales match in Paris in 1969 when we drew 8-all with the French. Bob had clearly prepared carefully for the game by brushing up on his French. During the game, he was prattling away in French to their players and he seemed delighted with himself. I was standing at one scrum, ball in hand, and he suddenly said something to me. In French! Of course, I didn't have a clue.

I just stood there with the ball and said, 'What are you on about?' He looked up, realised what he'd said and we both laughed. He'd got so carried away he'd forgotten one of the teams spoke English.

Ed Morrison felt all this came under the banner of relationships with players. Whether it concerned events on or off the field, it was the same topic.

'I know I've been criticised at times for calling players by their first names during a game. But I think people misunderstood my motives. I accept players are not my friends but we are all operating in an environment where we want to try and get the best out of everyone. If I can say something to someone that will assist that process, then I see no reason why I shouldn't address a player and tell him something. If you're going to talk to a player, why use his surname? If you call someone by his Christian name, that is just being civilised, in my view. I don't believe addressing players by their surname in the manner of a headmaster would assist. In fact, I believe it would be positively detrimental. I don't think it's being pally, as some people said. You are trying to create a relationship and build a confidence factor between yourself and the players so we can all get on with the job of trying to produce a top-class game of rugby that will be enjoyed by players and spectators alike.'

I had to declare an interest at this point. I was one of those people criticising Ed for constantly calling the former New Zealand captain Sean Fitzpatrick by his first name. It came over as excessive familiarity. But perhaps this is an indication of how intrusive microphones have become. People may want to hear the referees now but they hear everything and often don't understand what is behind the ref's words. It's the price you pay for the advent of this technology because it takes away the intimacy of what goes on actually on the field. What went on between the referee and the players was private and should have stayed that way. The fact that now it is broadcast to thousands on the ground and everyone watching TV creates problems. It worries me that some referees think they are now bigger than the game and treat the players like children. The good refs have a rapport with the players, but they are also strong on discipline and get what they want. But they work *with* the players to create that situation, treating them in a mature way. That has to be the best method.

The whole issue of microphones has come to the fore in the game in the last few seasons. I personally am not in favour and I understand a major debate has been going on within the IRB and refereeing circles as to their validity. The way I see it, the authorities just want to sell the game to a wider audience. I understand that the intricate laws of rugby are not always apparent, especially to new audiences. But perhaps this is the wrong way of dealing with it. Maybe the authorities need to look at other ways. Quite honestly, I wonder whether it is one reason why there are fewer referees today. Morrison and Fleming thought that was doubtful; they preferred to focus on one element of rugby in the twenty-first century which they do believe carries enormous dangers for the game long term: that of abuse to match officials. Jim Fleming had some tough words to say on the subject.

'There is no doubt that one reason why there are fewer refs is abuse from the crowds. The last thing a referee wants is to get abused all afternoon and then find nobody speaks to him afterwards. When you are refereeing largely for pleasure, the pleasure factor is all but lost. But I think that is what is happening. I admit even someone as experienced as myself was somewhat taken aback by the abuse I received at the European Shield semi-final at Leeds between Harlequins and Newcastle in April 2001. Some of the things said were very, very nasty indeed. I said to someone, "Is this normal down here?" and they replied, "The crowd response is very vitriolic nowadays." It is an even greater problem in Wales and I regard it as a cancer creeping into our game. There is also too much abuse of players by the crowds. But it is the tide of professionalism washing over the game. People have paid their money so they believe they have the right to come and give you heaps, whether you are a player or referee. It is modern society and the product of professionalism. There is nothing the game can do about it, in my view. It is sad that it has come to that, because as a referee you were always abused . . . but in a light-hearted way. It was jocular stuff and some of the cracks even had the referees themselves laughing. But this isn't funny stuff, it has become very, very nasty.'

Ed Morrison concurred. 'It is one of the biggest problems facing the game today – the abuse from off the pitch. It is aimed at players as well as referees. It has to be a concern that we have now created a soccer-type mentality in our crowds. I believe there is still great respect among players for the officials in charge of a game of rugby and it is up to all of us to protect that situation. If people step across that line, the governing bodies must deal with it. Because if we ever lose the respect players have traditionally had for referees, then the game will lose so much. Of course, referees are human and they make mistakes. Just like players in any sport. But to have a game refereed honestly and with the best intentions, you need respect from the players for those in charge. It cannot work otherwise. Abuse off the pitch is now about par for the course. I believe it is up to clubs to ban supporters found to be abusive. That is probably as much as they can do but it would be a very positive step to take. Because if we allow that sort of abuse to occur over and over again then we will be down the soccer route. There, players have pushed over referees (perhaps we had better not forget Leicester's Neil Back doing exactly that to English referee Steve Lander), they constantly hurl verbal abuse and try to intimidate referees on the field. That is the last thing rugby wants to see happen.'

I'm convinced one reason for this is the different people who are coming to rugby. Television, for example, has brought the game to a wider audience and a lot of those people whom they have encouraged to come through the gates have never been brought up in the traditions of the game. They don't understand the finer points. But they have vociferous opinions and therefore you get abuse. It's all right clubs increasing their fan base and attracting bigger audiences. But I believe everyone has to work hard at explaining certain things about this game to these 'new' audiences. They must understand this isn't a version of soccer where abuse is rife and seems to be tolerated. It's smaller, different and we don't want people like this if they're going to start abusing referees and players. Every club has a sense of duty to try and make it clear to these people that this type of behaviour isn't appropriate. Mind you, I don't know how you do that but I do know clubs have to be strong.

I think you must start with schoolkids. Tell them not to whistle when the opposition are taking a kick at goal . . . things like that. It's a question of ensuring the standards rugby always had are retained. But we'll only do that through much hard work and attention to the task. This problem doesn't just exist in England, mind you; it's happening in Wales, too. In our country you always had fans voicing their opinions, probably more so than in England. But it was good-natured banter with refs, whereas now on too many occasions it is just downright unpleasant and the language is ill-suited to a rugby ground.

On another theme, the issue of referees switching hemispheres brought warm nods of approval. Jim said he had always been in favour of referees operating in different hemispheres. He felt it gave them a completely new perspective of what people were trying to do. 'When southern hemisphere refs first came here, they were chastised. It was the same for us going there; we were called pedantic and whistle happy. But things are improving because of referees' exposure to the different hemispheres and I am very much in favour of that.'

Me, too. I am a great believer in this and its success supports my view of years ago that referees need exposure to the game in every part of the world. When sides played in the other hemisphere years ago, the biggest challenge was always adapting to the different referees they would meet. The laws were the same but it was how the referees would interpret them. But there were no opportunities for neutral referees in the 1970s. I am sure that in most cases the referees were men of integrity but some of the decisions taken left too much room for doubt. Maybe I didn't fully appreciate then the pressure these guys were under. But if these referees are neutral, as is now the case, we can at least ensure the game is not questioned from this aspect.

The questioning of match officials by coaches was something Ed Morrison felt strongly about.

'I feel there is a time and place for everything. Referees should not be wrapped up in cotton wool but, equally, I can't see it does the game a lot of good to have coaches or players firing off exocets about a referee. I understand very well that coaches can become frustrated immediately after a game and they give what they think is an honest answer to a question. But abuse heaped on a match official certainly damages the image of the sport and for sure it doesn't help encourage people to come into refereeing. A young referee starting out in the game would think to himself, "If they heap that kind of abuse on a guy like him who is so experienced, what would they say about me?" There is always a shortage of referees and abuse being hurled in their direction, from whichever source, isn't going to help change that situation for the better. I believe the place to criticise anybody is in private. I always thought it healthy if someone wanted to come up to see me after a match and chat through a decision or interpretation. I never minded. But the use of the media for criticism of referees does not encourage better relationships with referees.'

Ed thinks that if you are honest with the media, there isn't a problem in discussing things with them. He says he always welcomed chatting over a point (or should that be a pint!) with them if it helped clear up any misunderstandings or factual inaccuracies. He accepts everyone is different and some referees would be more at ease doing this than others. But he thinks we should remember that the media has a vital role to play and in general it does it very well. 'Rugby gets a phenomenal amount of coverage for a minority sport and we should be prepared to work with everybody in the game, including the media, to keep that situation and ensure it stays healthy. Besides, referees should never be afraid to state their case.

Perhaps referees should be much more pro-active than they are in this respect.

'I accept we get it wrong at times. Referees, as I have said so often, are only human. But I think difficulties and misunderstandings need to be sorted out in private. The game would benefit greatly from that approach.

'I don't like to see legislation that prevents coaches making comments. I know it exists in soccer and managers can be brought before the FA and fined. But I don't want that in rugby. I think there's already enough legislation in life and I'd prefer to see a voluntary code of conduct. Legislation is no way to do it. In my view, it's about winning people's minds over, that's the way to do it.'

In Ed's experience, when senior coaches contact the RFU's refereeing department and show evidence on video (which they usually have access to) that a referee has been well below his best and not performing to the standards required, then it is usually acted upon. The RFU are very good like that, they don't sit on it and do nothing, he said.

We all say and do things in the heat and immediate aftermath of a game. But that is not the best time. When I played, you had plenty of views about referees but you just bit your tongue. You very rarely criticised them in public, it was not done, was not part of the game. I'm not saying there should remain a wall of silence so that referees are never criticised – let's have sensible, mature dialogue to clear up misunderstandings and any errors. Referees should be big enough to admit they may have been wrong. They are, after all, human beings and if you know a human being who never makes a mistake, I suggest you clone him or her immediately because you'll sell the product for a fortune!

A shortage of refs? Jim Fleming felt that this was a widespread problem. But he said, 'It isn't just referees we are short of in Scotland, it is players as well. The numbers playing the game have dropped dramatically and it seems people are not interested in becoming members of clubs. That's a Catch 22 situation because if you have fewer players, you will eventually have fewer ex-players going into refereeing.'

I wonder if in the future there might be more incentive for former players to go into refereeing now that it is a professional occupation. It is an opportunity for the players who are retiring to further their livelihood by staying in the game whereas players who had given up years ago had to earn a living. The players of my generation and those before us had given up so much time to rugby that taking up refereeing when you finished playing was the last thing on your mind. The only young guys who took it up tended to be those who had been injured at an early age and weren't playing any longer.

The system seems to work well in cricket where the umpires' list is filled with ex-players who wanted to remain in the game. But of course the difference there is that, once accepted, they become professionals at once and are able to earn a proper living. If former rugby players have to wait years to land a place in the top group of referees that are professional, then they're less likely to do it. That is an aspect which will need to be examined by the authorities if they do want to entice retiring players to stay in rugby.

Morrison said that he had often asked many senior players about whether they fancied taking up refereeing once they finished playing, but they had never shown any interest. Yet he felt it would do rugby a lot of good if some top-quality professional players did decide to go into refereeing once they retired because there is always much respect for the views and opinions of players who have been there and done it for many years.

'Of course, some make good referees, some not so good,' he said. 'But their experience at that level has to be an advantage. The Llanelli scrum half Rupert Moon is going into refereeing and I think he will be very successful. If more players did that it would give us a glossier image which would help the game in general. Referees are easy targets and too many people like to get stuck into them. A different image would help a lot.'

But what do the modern referees feel about their job since professional officials were introduced? Steve Lander, the England referee, said that the advent of professional referees had given them more time to think about what they were doing, the role they play and how they should handle specific circumstances. 'We have more time to talk to other referees about the job and that interchange of ideas and discussion of interpretations etc. has to be a good thing.'

Lander also felt that it is a very good thing that there are now ex-international referees, like Ed Morrison and Brian Campsall in England, working in the referee performance departments now set up by most Unions to help raise refereeing standards, and that there was a good interface between clubs and referees. That side of it had never been better, he felt. 'We can work ahead in partnership and that side of things is becoming easier. People are talking about the application of the laws rather than just finding out on the day what they can and cannot do. Through that process, the players are becoming much more aware of what they can and cannot do. Consequently, decision-making in internationals is generally speaking much improved.'

I think Steve is right in this. Because in the Scotland–England Six Nations Championship match in February 2002, the tape shows that Scotland did not give away a kickable penalty until I think it was the sixty-second minute of the match. That proved the players had worked on what they could and couldn't do in aspects such as the tackle area.

Steve Lander says, 'That is all to the good. Players need to think what they are doing and why. It helps them and their team and of course it is a big plus for us, the referees. Everyone sees a better game, too.'

One of the things referees do not enjoy very much is the often cruel exposure of them by TV replays. Lander told me, 'It has always been a pretty unforgiving environment because in those replays people usually don't see the context in which the referee has made his decision. They may look at the actual incident but something else may have occurred immediately prior to that which might have a bearing on it.

'The fact is no referee will make every decision 100 per cent correctly in a game. That is impossible. But the best referees, like the players, make the least number of mistakes. I feel that the TV commentary experts and analysts all of whom enjoy 20/20 hindsight vision, are not being very fair to referees. We can all watch replays of an incident and get it right every time, anyone can do that. But a referee has a split second in which to make a decision, no more. It is inevitable that occasionally he will get it wrong. The trouble is people are in search of the perfect game and realistically that won't happen. Therefore, this is a negative because these analysers are making things unnecessarily harder for referees. Also, some of the things portrayed on TV don't particularly help the game.

'Don't get me wrong here. I don't mind being criticised, that is part and parcel of the role. But if people criticise, they should offer a solution, not just knock somebody without offering another way.'

In February 2002, Steve Lander refereed a friendly match between the London club Harlequins and the South African provincial team, Natal Sharks at the Stoop Memorial Ground, Twickenham. Natal were building up for their new season in the southern hemisphere and Steve said he found it a lovely experience. 'Just like an old-fashioned game, no intense pressure on a side to win and gain League points. Just two teams trying to play good entertaining rugby, a throwback to the past.'

But during that game, Lander still had cause to issue a yellow card against one of the young Harlequins forwards for a blatant late challenge on a South African opponent. Steve got it right in my view; it wasn't a red card offence, but the boy did deserve ten minutes in the sin-bin to cool off. And while he was off, leaving his team-mates one short, Natal scored four tries and won the game which was perhaps the greater punishment for his indiscipline. But on the entire issue of yellow cards, I asked Jim Fleming whether they were more often than not a cop-out for referees. Fleming was frank in his response.

'Yes, overall. It has always been my big worry that it would develop into that situation. I can see the value of yellow cards in dealing with repeat offences. The player who keeps trying to kill the ball merits a yellow card as the correct punishment. But when it comes to foul play too many referees are using the yellow card to cop out. I think that has been one of the problems. The answer lies in the hands of the IRB and national bodies. If we train referees properly to use yellow cards for technical offences and very little else and not lose sight of the need for red cards at times, then we will solve the problem. We have to make sure referees don't go on copping out in this manner. Sometimes you have no alternative: you have to take the ultimate sanction.'

Morrison said that, in junior rugby, it was true there had been a sharp reduction in sendings off. 'The view is that referees are hiding behind yellow cards. I don't think it's so much of a problem at the higher levels because it's not that often you see a dirty game. In fact, it's quite rare to see a brawl. But that opinion about referees at junior level avoiding sendings off, is one shared by many of my colleagues at junior level. It is a fear a lot of people have and the topic has been raised in many referees' meetings. The thing about a sending-off is that you rarely even think about that decision. You'll think about everything during a game but, when it comes to deciding whether someone should go or not, you find it becomes instinctive. My view is that if you have to think about it, you shouldn't send the player off. It should be so clear and obvious if a player has to go that you don't need to think it over. If it isn't, don't do it would be my maxim. Rugby has moved such a long way in such a short space of time. And given the increased pressures players are operating under, and knowing that their performances and the result affecting their team could have an impact on whether they keep their job or not, I have to say I have every admiration for the players and their behaviour in general on the field. You will always get exceptions but overall, the behaviour has been consistently good. It's only very occasionally you run into a game that needs an extremely tough hand to control it, or an individual or two threaten to get out of hand.'

Well, that's undoubtedly true. But I still think yellow cards are a cop-out in some circumstances. I think they were introduced originally just for foul play but now their use seems to have crept everywhere. It seems less than ideal to me.

I would remind people that rugby is still a man's game. Certain sports are, like rugby and soccer. Take the UEFA Cup final at the end of the 2000–2001 soccer season in the UK between Liverpool and the Spanish club Alaves which Liverpool won 5–4 with a golden 'own goal' in extra time. It was a marvellous match, well refereed. It was a hard game with some tough tackles. But there was a lesson for rugby in that match the way the referee had a feel for the game. To me, that is the essence of good refereeing, possessing a 'feel' for the game.

I watch a lot of football on TV and I have spoken often with Clive Thomas, the Welshman who was a leading soccer official in Britain some years back. Clive advocated years ago bringing into soccer the rugby rule that if players argued about a decision, the free-kick would be given ten yards closer to their own goal-line. Weren't we all fed up with seeing referees jostled and pushed in football? Then, the soccer authorities did introduce the ruling and it certainly helped.

That is why I say both sports can learn from each other. For me, there is nothing better in soccer or rugby than a good hard game over which the referee has control but which he will also allow to flow. Yellow cards have a role to play but their use has to be considered by the referee in each different situation.

Of altogether more importance was an issue Morrison brought up: match fixing.

'You can dismiss the notion as some sort of sick joke,' he said. 'But then, those like me who love their cricket, did much the same thing when anyone mentioned such a possibility in that sport. Perhaps we have now learned never to say never. Because anything involving money would appear to be ripe for exploitation in the minds of some people. It's not enough simply to say it couldn't happen in rugby, because it's happened in soccer and also now in cricket. So why should rugby of the future be sacrosanct from those who are willing to do anything for money?

'It might happen in the future. But we have to be very protective of what we have got in rugby.'

Ed had equally firm views on the social side of rugby. 'If you have never experienced it you will never miss it so the coming generation won't know what we're all talking about. But for those of us who have known that side of the game, I believe there would be widespread agreement with my opinion that if rugby loses that altogether, it loses so much. The social side of the game is one of the things that has made rugby special. I feel sorry for the players of the future if they never know that side of the sport. They won't make the friendships we all made and that's a matter of sincere regret. But of course, everything has changed and not always for the better. The game as a spectacle is now far greater than ever before. For example, I thought the England–France game in April 2001 was an absolutely marvellous piece of entertainment. In the years to come, it is obvious we will have a game of great pace and power. It will be enjoyable yet it will also be more cynical. Winning is everything now, losing is nothing. That adds great pressure to the match officials. Players are looking to gain any advantage by any means they can . . . that is human nature. Once money comes into it, things change.'

Jim Fleming summed it all up: 'I promised myself I would go out at the top. It has become obvious the IB want professional, full-time, fitter, younger referees handling their international matches, their showpiece games. My face didn't fit any longer. Clayton Thomas of Wales was the same as me. They didn't any longer want middle-aged, gentlemanly officials. I suppose they feel it's a young man's game and they want younger men refereeing their matches. That is why the three of us – Thomas, Fleming and Morrison – weren't selected for any Six Nations matches in our last season. I'm fifty now. There are new challenges ahead for me and for the game, but I'll work in an amateur capacity to do what I can to help.'

As I see it, as much as I like tradition, I am also for progression. If you expect the highest quality games and professional attitudes, you have to have professional referees, especially at international level. I don't see why not; it's a step forward and has to be good. So we must embrace the younger referees, wish them well and hope more will be encouraged to follow them. But let's also acknowledge the tremendous job men like Jim Fleming, Ed Morrison, Derek Bevan, Clayton Thomas, Clive Norling, Gwyn Waters and so many others have done down the years. After all, there would have been no games without them and their fellow referees.

CHAPTER 11

Junior Rugby

I an Roddan and Chris Hobbs may not be household names in the world of rugby union. Neither has any international caps on the wall of his home, there are no Barbarians ties or Lions blazers in the cupboard. Yet they and people like them have been the lifeblood of this game every since it was established and their contribution to the sport cannot be overestimated.

Both men are in their late thirties, both played rugby for their junior clubs for many years and both have been selfless in their desire to serve the sport they have loved since childhood. Both are now putting much back into their clubs, as coaches to junior sides on Sunday mornings. They are long-standing, loyal servants of the game and they have my deep admiration for all they have done. I just don't believe rugby union would have reached anywhere near the same levels of popularity but for the sustained efforts of guys like these two and so many others at clubs in every rugby-playing country.

Ian Roddan, now aged thirty-seven, first joined Stow-on-the-Wold rugby club, in the heart of the Cotswolds, as a twelve-year-old, playing for their minis. He played at centre, rose to become first XV captain, was skipper for two years in 1989–1990, helped coach the first XV in his time and is now a coach of the Under-7s.

Chris Hobbs went to Jeremy Guscott's old school, Ralph Allen, in Bath – Guscott was two years below him. Hobbs joined Avonvale RFC as a seventeen-year-old and still plays for the first XV. His is a small club based in the village of Bathford just outside the famous

Georgian city in the west of England. He has twice been their club captain, was social secretary and membership secretary. Now, because his club doesn't have a juniors section, he coaches the Under-11s and Under-15s at nearby Avon RFC and his son George plays in the Under-11s.

Both men have been more than generous in the time they have given their clubs. When Roddan was club captain, he used to train twice a week as well as being available all day Saturdays. Friday nights were spent organising a multitude of things, phoning around and generally being on hand. On Sunday mornings, he would be found at the club helping clear up from the night before. Nowadays, it is just Sunday mornings at the Oddington Road ground with the minis – and, as with Chris Hobbs, therein lies the succession for the future health and prosperity of Stow. Ian's eldest son George plays in the Under-9s and brother Charlie in the Under-8s. Last season, Ian coached Charlie and his pals in the Under-7s. All of which is probably enough because Ian works in a building firm near his Cotswolds home and does long hours of physical labour.

Chris Hobbs joined Avonvale rugby club in 1979 because a friend's father was Colts manager there. He captained the first XV from 1991 to 1993 and still does occasionally. His commitment? Sunday mornings for two hours coaching the youngsters at Avon but occasionally all day or most of the day if they're at a tournament somewhere. Then there's a committee meeting every other Monday for two hours at Avonvale, followed by two hours of training for him on Tuesdays with the first XV. He also coaches the Under-15s for a couple of hours on a Wednesday evening at Avon and he plays on Saturdays for Avonvale. He leaves home at 11.30a.m. Saturdays and doesn't usually get back until 8 or 9p.m.

Because he's in the fruit and veg business, he also needs to get up at 4a.m. every day to go to market. And the time he gives to the game? 'It's all a labour of love, my rugby involvement.'

I sought out people like Chris Hobbs and Ian Roddan because I wanted to know what people at the junior level of the game thought about its development. How did they feel about the money now available at the top end of the sport? Did they feel that junior rugby had been overlooked and how healthy was the game at their level? What were the type of problems confronting them and how did they perceive the future of clubs like theirs?

It is said that Stow-on-the-Wold rugby club was founded in the 1870s. The first players were railway workers from England and Wales who were working in the area building the line from Bourton-on-the-Water to Stow. One early account tells of the players being collected from the famous square in the heart of Stow and 'transported to Stow station by means of a horse-drawn brewer's dray'. This dray was owned by a local brewer, Mr Gus Green of Stow. The club was one of the founder members of Gloucestershire Rugby Union, formed in September 1878.

Ian Roddan's father, Homer, was a reserve for Scotland, and played District rugby just after the war. He was in the army and played as a back-row forward. As a highly qualified civil engineer, he helped the club immensely following its successful bid for a lottery grant in the mid-1990s.

Brian Warby, who has been associated with Stow since 1970 and was chairman of the Development Committee, joked, 'I and my team raised the money and Homer spent it. Seriously though, he acted as a sort of clerk of works when the job was being done and his contribution, like that of so many others, was very substantial.'

So too was the lottery grant. The club received £162,500 as the basic grant, plus another £50,000 from an organisation called The Foundation for Sport and the Arts, which is funded by pools money. The club had around £25,000 to start with in their own kitty and the entire project cost well over £260,000. It involved buying a third pitch and levelling and draining that one before work could begin on further levelling and draining their two original pitches.

'We used to play on the side of a mountain before the grounds were levelled,' Ian remembers. 'It was 16ft from corner to corner – always a game of two halves,' he smiles.

Then they embarked on radical improvements to the clubhouse, costing about £160,000. They extended the original front, built a two-storey addition and extended the changing-rooms. All told, the work took the best part of three years. Floodlights were put up and training facilities improved. Now they have three good pitches, the clubhouse is excellent and there is a delightful lounge on the first floor with a wonderful view across the Cotswolds fields and farms. It is a splendid building, offering facilities of which some senior clubs would be proud. Plenty of people, such as the secretary Nigel

Drury have played their part but two real stalwarts of the club have been John Wright, who has been involved for around fifty years, and Ian Roberts. Two great characters who played rugby for the club and have served it well ever since.

Ian talked about the changes he had seen and what had created them. 'The first thing to say is that it went from a completely amateur game where there was no real need for winning, a world in which there were no league tables, just a collection of traditional matches. The first competitive step was then going into Leagues. But Stow didn't join Leagues immediately, they kept out for the first couple of years, because they wanted to keep their local fixtures against clubs like Evesham, Shipston-on-Stour and Stratford.

'It was good for Stow that we did because it let us have a look at how things were progressing. But in the end we had no choice because we slowly ran out of fixtures as all the other clubs adopted a League programme. Joining a League became inevitable for us too.

'We joined lower down, in Gloucestershire League 4, and did really well for a few years. Promotion followed to Gloucestershire Leagues 3, 2 and 1. Because we had kept out originally, we were put into the bottom leagues when we did join and then inevitably we found our level which was higher up. Then we joined Southern Counties North but later had the option of switching areas, so we moved to South West 2 East. That means we play most of our first XV matches against teams from the M4 corridor. I think the longest trip we have is to Olney, the Northamptonshire club. Had we not switched, we would have ended up playing some of the Cornish clubs and that would have meant too much travelling.

'We had five or six years of being very successful and, of course, winning breeds interest. But now, it has levelled off and, like most junior clubs, we are now finding it more difficult to balance the books.'

Chris Hobbs reported a remarkably similar tale from Avonvale. The club was founded in 1883 and has provided almost 120 years of village rugby. The club opens its doors to the local soccer and cricket teams and the clubhouse has been made available for other local social and sporting events such as school sports, Guy Fawkes nights etc. It has always been a key part of the local community. Moreover, the club has produced international trialists, county players and numerous Bath first XV players.

The club can also claim the honour of being the oldest continuous junior rugby club in the Bath Combination. Starting life as 'Batheaston FC', strong family connections have held the club together through the years. For example, there were Blanchards playing for the club in the very first year or two and there still were just a few years ago. Avonvale have certainly made their fair contribution to the life and times of rugby in their area. For example, they were once short of a player before a game and hastily conscripted a soccer player to make up the numbers. Only trouble was, in his first ever line-out, he jumped up and headed the ball back into touch! Mind you, one local referee had a novel way of sorting out those tough Avonvale boys. During a match the club once played against Midsomer Norton, play had become so heated that the referee stopped the game and ordered all thirty players to sit down on the pitch for ten minutes to cool off.

When Chris Hobbs was Avonvale captain, at the start of the 1990s, the club was in Somerset Divisions 1–2. They played clubs like North Petherton, Wells, Minehead and a few Bristol sides. 'Before Leagues, we would play in Gloucester, Dorset, Swindon and Wiltshire. They were good local matches. Mind you, we also played a London club, Battersea Ironsides, each year because one of our members had a connection with them and that was always good fun. But you haven't got time for those sort of games now.

'I find the fun has gone out of rugby a bit now. They arranged the Leagues originally on how well you had done in the Cups. We opted not to go into the Leagues at once but when it became clear we were running out of fixtures against clubs like us, we had to join. We went into Somerset Division 3 and won that League the first season. We won the second division the following year. Eventually, we got into Division 1. We were playing teams like Weston Hornets but now they're five or six Leagues above us. Other teams in the same League as us from the Bath area were Old Sulians, Oldfield and Walcot O.B.'

Stow believe that the League they are now in, South West 2 East, is as high a standard as they have ever played in. That standard, they believe, is considerably higher than it was when professionalism first arrived. That is a real plus point. Although there have been some notable casualties of the process, overall standards have been driven up at all levels. But Roddan says there is a realisation now that the club can only go so far. Which in reality means it won't go much further than it is. 'Maybe some clubs bigger than us will come to the same realisation because you can only do what you can afford.'

There is no doubt that Leagues have changed the face of the game, especially in England. Yet League rugby was always prevalent in junior rugby levels of Wales, especially in west Wales. You had competitive Leagues there going back decades. Perhaps that was the yardstick by which Wales became strong. The arrival of a League structure in England has made their national team so much stronger because their best players are now playing in the top League rather than with clubs all over the place. Remember as recently as 1993, you had a player like Wade Dooley representing England against the best teams in the world yet playing his club rugby for Preston Grasshoppers or Fylde. That just couldn't happen any more. But in my day and even as recently as the late 1980s to early 1990s, the game in England was widespread with no central point to bring the best players to compete against one another.

So, you see, while it's certainly true that Leagues have helped England, I wouldn't say they have improved standards in Wales. A lot of people used to say playing in those local Leagues in west Wales was harder than performing at the top level. After all, a well-directed boot can find a painful target whichever team you happen to be playing for or against! Certainly, competition for places in those days was very stiff and those circumstances produced a type of guy who could really compete. But for many reasons – such as the demise of the local communities through the loss of the heavy industries and teenagers moving away far more – that competition and indeed the overall system has been lost in Wales.

But now, as the boys say, even many of the junior clubs in England are looking at what Leagues have brought them and saying, 'No more.' As I travel around the British Isles, to clubs in my own country and especially places in England such as Yorkshire and also Scotland, I hear the same message, the same call from the majority of people involved in junior rugby. They are all concerned about where the money is going to come from.

Just as an example, Pyle RFC near my home has always been

regarded as one of the best junior sides in Wales. They enjoyed a fine reputation among the junior clubs for producing many outstanding players who went on to play for several first-class sides.

But two years ago, the people behind Pyle decided enough was enough. 'Why are we struggling to make ends meet just to keep a bunch of players who want money from us?' they asked themselves. There were also whispers that many of those players were past their best anyway and weren't worth the cash. So they decided to stop paying their players and almost overnight about twenty of their squad vanished. The result is obvious in one respect. They are now way below many of the clubs they would otherwise have been well ahead of. Many players won't go there now and that has meant they have declined somewhat in terms of playing standards.

But not in terms of spirit or overall finance. The club has survived and, by their act, the committee have probably safeguarded the future of the entire club because they refused to put themselves in debt. If you ask me whether they were right to take that drastic decision, I would say yes, definitely. But I know a lot of clubs are worried about this choice.

Because the trouble is, we have created a situation where players expect some sort of reward and think nothing of moving on just for the extra few quid. OK, I hear you say, under professionalism some clubs have come together and improved. Now they have sponsorship and people behind them and they are enjoying a high profile. Which is true. But for how long can they do it without getting to the very top? The answer is, I don't know and it is clearly a topic in many people's minds at junior clubs in many countries. Several people have said to me, the sooner we revert back to what we were, the better. It is not a question of not being ambitious; it is just the reality of the situation. I get the impression they are just awaiting a directive from the Unions.

Some people might say that all ambitious clubs have to pay players. That is all well and good for them, but you have to be realistic. The fact is, 95 per cent of those clubs will never be Premiership clubs. Therefore, in my view, they have to accept their status. Perhaps one solution is to become a feeder club for a bigger, Premiership club, thereby probably ensuring they receive some assistance which would help them with their finances. More money should be given by the Union to put into the structure of clubs like this, so as to support the grassroots of the game.

Peter Thomas of Cardiff thinks that the failure of the WRU and Unions like them was in not realising the game should have been divided long ago into two sections . . . professional and amateur. They clung to power, he said, and they were reluctant to appoint a full-time professional board to run the professional game. Until as late as mid-2002, they were still running it as if there was no divide. But there was.

Should the game have been divided? Well, the big problem it all dated back to was saying the game had gone open. But what on earth did that mean? No one knew. I thought at the time that that statement was going to give us all sorts of problems. All the clubs in Wales thought this must mean it is legal to pay everyone – no one knew what professionalism really meant. More importantly, no one knew where that money would come from, either.

Junior clubs like Clydach, the Welsh club which I visited recently, are thriving on the face of it. Yet the people there told me about the problems of players wanting to go to other clubs for more money. This happened in 1995 and it is still happening. Whitland, a club on the other side of Llanelli are a typical country club, and more recently, they started asking themselves what they were paying players for. All these clubs have been stung by this. Whitland and other clubs in the region like Tenby were taking ex-Swansea and Llanelli players, guys who had virtually come to the end of their careers and were paying them £100 or £200 a week. But it didn't help the finances of those clubs and did nothing to promote club loyalty. One of the real strengths of Welsh rugby at that level has always been the competitiveness between villages and between local towns. One village team against the other meant something and the contest produced hard, competitive rugby. But the smaller clubs obviously get a smaller cash injection from the Union each year, perhaps on average something around £70,000 per annum, and since 1995 most of that money has been going into the players' pockets. Then, suddenly, the clubs began to ask themselves what they were giving this to the players for, because it was supposed to be for grassroots rugby as a whole, not a handful of players. It confirmed to me that we have all lost our way.

I believe the junior clubs would welcome a decision that said below Division 1 in Wales the game reverts back to amateurism.

You can't turn the clock back as such but perhaps you could have an agreement saying the expenses of a club at that level could not be above a certain amount. Such an agreement would take a lot of pressure away from the smaller clubs. It has become a big problem for them to try and compete. I know that in England several clubs would like to revert back to amateurism. What is destroying Welsh rugby at a lower level is a situation where players are moving from one club to another which just happens to be the highest bidder. There is no loyalty any more. I know the situation is greatly bothering the junior clubs. Peter Thomas is optimistic that decisions such as these which must be made will in fact be addressed. Crucially, one of the recommendations by the investigating commission chaired by Sir Tasker Watkins to the Union was that the game should revert to amateurism below the Premier Division.

However, Nigel Wray of Saracens suggests it might not be as straightforward as that.

Wray doesn't believe you can stop the likes of Old Millhillians, his old club, if they want to pay players and they think they have the funds to do so and become properly professional. Yet he agrees with the theory that you don't need more than a few clubs as 100 per cent professionals. He thinks we are probably talking between twelve and sixteen clubs in England and you want maybe only half that number in Wales.

I am not saying that the club which finds a backer worth millions who is prepared to spend some of those millions to see his team reach the very top should be denied eventual access to the Premiership. If their financier is sound and secure and he is determined to commit big funds to a club, then good luck to that club. But in reality, how many people are there like that out there, prepared to put so much money into rugby these days? Very few, I would suggest, certainly in Wales.

Wray warns, 'You can't compel clubs to revert to amateurism but logically that's how it is going to evolve. Because the gap between amateurs and professionals is going to get bigger and bigger. That is a good thing and it is inevitable.

'Financially it makes sense. The game can only reasonably support a certain number of professional clubs because professional sport is very expensive.

'But there is huge money in sport nowadays and as for rugby, it has a great image with the kids. It is one of the few sports where you can take your son and daughter and they will both like it. As for sponsors, they want to associate their name with a clean game that is family-orientated and rugby provides both factors. But it all requires a lot of investment in the first place on and off the field. It's not just about buying good enough players; it's to do with creating the right facilities such as state-of-the-art gymnasiums.'

Well, the trouble is it's easy to say that but how do you do it? Most people you talk to see that as sensible. It's tough having to pay players who are playing third-, fourth- or fifth-grade rugby. Maybe franchises are a way forward. But some sort of accommodation of the two ways has to be found. The role of the amateur administrator, too, should be somewhere within the amateur game which will continue to exist at lower levels.

We should also not forget the strength of the village sides was always the pride and identity they had. The competition between local sides produced a strong competitive element and clubs were the stronger for that. That in itself developed a specific background from which these players could develop and play for the better clubs. The senior clubs all benefited from this structure. But now a lot of players are in the comfort zone – quite satisfied to play for money without having to perform at the highest level. And they just move on when offered more money. But who does that benefit? Is it good for the game as a whole? I doubt it.

Most of the junior clubs in west Wales have had their moments in the last few years. Clubs like Tenby, a cracking little club, recruited some ex-first class players, in their case some ex-Llanelli first-team boys. Not surprisingly, two or three players from that level transformed them overnight and they became a very difficult side to beat. But you can't sustain that. Now clubs like them are just waiting for the money to come from the Union to pay the players. And instead of using that money to benefit the club as a whole, it is all going to pay older players who are nowhere near as good as they once were. Is that a realistic, sensible way to run a club at this level in these times? Personally speaking, I don't think so.

In junior rugby, the whole thing was run for fun because there was nothing else. You weren't beating the likes of Leicester, Coventry and Bristol so you played for and existed for fun.

Fun was one word Chris Hobbs felt very strongly about at junior level. It wasn't, he said, anything like as much fun as it used to be and I think that's true. That is probably because the preparation is almost as demanding as in the professional game. Every club has a coach and we all know the demands they make on players. The club's results are paramount which means the position the coach achieves in the League dictates how he is measured. It's not about the health of the club in general, just the results, and that's a huge problem which has been created at all levels. Because at these levels we're talking about, the boys have still got to hold down a job.

The game itself, Hobbs said, was a hell of a lot cleaner than before and I agree with him on that. That is a good thing, too. I only ever played one or two games for my old village side back in Wales, Cwmgors, but people used to say that rugby was the toughest in Wales. My word, it was a battleground, too. You had men who worked in the colliery taking on their rivals from up the valley; steelworker against steelworker, too. I was very young then, still at Millfield school, but I remember playing a junior club match at Lampeter once, and it was probably one of the toughest matches I had in my whole career! I was taken aside before the start by one of our craggy old forwards and warned, 'Stay out of the way, son, when the action starts. Don't get involved.' I was glad of the advice because just after the kick-off, the most almighty punch-up started. That was par for the course, nothing at all unusual. There was probably more fighting than playing in those days. But now, of course, the game is far cleaner and at the highest level, you can hardly get away with anything.

Chris Hobbs remembered Avonvale used to play a lot of country clubs full of farmers. 'All they wanted to do was fight you all the game. Now, they play. I remember we went to North Petherton one year and we always knew what to expect down there, in Somerset. You'd get a good old kicking! They were big up front, the crowd of around three hundred would always be very vocal and you'd get plenty of stick. On and off the field.

'But this particular day, they got the ball from the kick-off and ran us off the park for the first ten minutes. I called the boys together and said, 'What's going on here, I'm absolutely knackered?' What we didn't know was that they had just changed their style of play from nine-man to fifteen-man rugby. In the end, we stuffed the ball up our jumpers to try and keep it away from them for a bit while we recovered! I think we only lost by about five points.

'But days like that in places such as that were what rugby was all about, they were fun times. We went down there one year on their carnival day. We silenced their noisy crowd and won the game. Afterwards, someone said if you don't leave the club by 5p.m. you'll never get out because of the carnival. So we stayed until midnight and had a marvellous evening, the highlight of which was one of our boys jumping on to various carnival floats during the procession down the high street. It was a cracking night. But I have to say, it's not as much fun playing them now in League matches. Now they're all "must win" games and that's never as much pleasure.'

Roddan acknowledged that point. Rugby, he said, used to have a whole ethos. Amateurism produced a social camaraderie between clubs, not just within your own club. At Stow, they used to have very close ties with local clubs such as Cheltenham Civil Service, Cheltenham North, Stratford, Evesham, Shipston-on-Stour and Old Cryptians. Those were real local derby matches and the social scene was strong between the clubs. But now, they don't even play them and he believed that was a loss.

He also felt that everything was friendlier when it was amateur, and I agreed with that. Off the field, it was more sociable and it was almost a case that the harder the game, the more you enjoyed the evening together. You always stayed at the clubhouse having a few beers.

Going back to the question of pressures on junior clubs through good results in the League, Roddan said, 'Today, you are deemed a failure if you are not at least in the middle of your table or above. So it has changed the game, but whether for good or bad depends upon your viewpoint. I don't know how it has affected some of the lower clubs because it is a dangerous thing when you start to stretch yourself beyond your sensible limits financially. If you go along that road but don't have success, you don't have people going to your club.

'A lot of the clubs in the Gloucester area are like that now and players have become more nomadic. If a club is doing well, the better players are drawn there but if it starts losing, those players leave for somewhere else. There isn't the same loyalty now.

'When professionalism arrived, we realised that we didn't have any players who were going to make a living out of it. You still need an organised structure but most sides got drawn into winning at all costs. That wasn't healthy.'

All this reminded me of a story from years ago, when I was in New Zealand with the 1971 British Lions. I remember Barry John and myself went along to watch a schools game somewhere in Auckland, and I can tell you, we were very impressed by the standard on display that day. Yet there was something else we would hardly believe – the amount of shouting and pressure from masters and parents, watching on the touchline. A kid got the ball on the halfway line, started dodging and weaving and then threw a marvellous dummy which beat the opposing full-back to send him in for what we thought was a wonderful try. We cheered like mad as he touched down.

But one man wasn't impressed. The PE master gave the boy an absolute rollicking, yelling at him, 'You should have taken the man and passed to the support.' Instead of being encouraged, he was ridiculed in front of everyone. Barry and I just looked at one another, we couldn't believe it.

Well, after the game, we were invited into the school to meet the headmaster. We passed rows and rows of photographs of former boys in their rugby shirts and we then spent some time talking to the head, in his study. Just as we were about to leave, a young man knocked at the door, came in and was introduced to us. The head said, 'This young man was the biggest disappointment of my school career. Potentially, he was the best young player this school produced but now he doesn't even play the game any more.'

We left the head's study soon after and were crossing the school yard when we saw this young man again. 'Why on earth did you pack it in?' we asked him. His reply stunned us both. Fingering his temple, he said, 'I've had it up to here with rugby. I have been playing competitive rugby for thirteen years and I am totally fed up with it.'

I think junior rugby in Britain risks losing a lot of players for the same reason if there are these constant pressures and demands made of amateur players by a League programme. But the dangers of losing players at this level are serious because the junior clubs they represent are the bread and butter of the game.

Neither Roddan nor Hobbs had a problem with professionalism

at the top end of the game. They felt, too, that their views probably reflected the general opinion throughout the world of junior rugby. Roddan said, 'The game had to go professional at the higher level, definitely. Proof of that is the way the gap between the northern and southern hemisphere nations has closed considerably since the influence of professionalism started to be felt in the northern hemisphere. Watching England is a good attraction now and they have worked hard to make sure they produce an attractive game for the spectator. The days of England winning 6–5 or 12–3, by kicking goals, have gone and that is good.'

Hobbs agreed. He felt that the introduction of Leagues was good for what they wanted to do at the higher level of the game. 'The effect can be seen in the England squad now and the number of top-class players available to England. But I feel sorry for the teams in Divisions 2, 3 and down. It's a money thing today and most of those clubs won't make it any higher just because they haven't got the finances to get up there with the rest. I also feel sorry for the clubs who have lost so many players over the years, perhaps because of injuries or other reasons. Combe Down, for instance, in our area dropped six Leagues, going from South West 1 to Somerset 1. I regarded them as the best junior club in Bath over the last twenty years but they've lost their way and I know it hasn't been easy for them.

'I don't think people in junior rugby resent the top level and the focus on it. The junior clubs around here accept they will only get a limited amount of coverage and that's OK. As for money at the top level, I don't mind guys getting paid. It's always been there but now it is above board. I think the England players are worth as much as they get. If you are good enough, you get well paid and that's fair enough. I don't see why good players shouldn't earn money out of the game and it's certainly more honest now than it used to be.

'At our level, we get an end-of-season free barrel of beer. But that's OK, that's the way it always was and remains.

'What annoys me is the ridiculous pressure put on people like Martin Johnson and Clive Woodward. Woodward has put together an England squad that has produced perhaps the best rugby in its history. Yet when they lost a match, to Ireland, some were calling for his head. You have to give people time. I think Clive Woodward has the backing of the majority of the English rugby public. OK, he made a mistake with his team in Ireland but he held his hands up and admitted it. Fair enough. My view is fair play to the bloke, he's done well for England.'

Which is true, but I do believe that these guys are professional and they have to expect a certain amount of honestly given criticism. They are, after all, handsomely paid, players and coaches, and they are expected to produce results. England have missed out on a few games, especially key ones such as the Grand Slam defeat in Ireland in autumn 2001. Then the next season, 2002, they lost to France in Paris, another defeat in another big game. I think professional people understand there is a certain amount of pressure to deliver and I don't see that is wrong. This argument was used when Graham Henry lost his job as Welsh national coach in February 2002.

One thing that did annoy Chris Hobbs concerning the top end of the game was when he saw a guy like Zinzan Brooke going to Coventry and perhaps keeping out a young fellow in their team. Yet, said Chris, Zinzan finished playing top-line rugby for the All Blacks years ago. He didn't like that, but I have to say I rather disagree. I can understand why people say this but I do think these guys can bring a lot into a club.

'I also think that the senior professional club in an area should do everything it can to help clubs in their local patch. Bath are just down the road from us but in my view they don't do enough for the Combination clubs in the area. I'd like to see that change, because it would lift everyone at the junior clubs around here. But I suppose some people would say it's a professional game now and they are under no obligation to do it. Maybe, but I'd still like to see it happen.

'A senior Bath player coming to our club to coach us just once in a while would make a huge difference. It's not just this area, either – I think the top-level players need to be aware of this and play their part. They should remember their roots, and where they came from.'

I am sure they do but I also acknowledge that the time a professional player has is limited. Many clubs are aware of their responsibilities and try to send players to local schools or clubs. Establishing a relationship between the senior club of the area and the junior sides can be mutually beneficial, especially when a junior club unearths a little gem of a player. From what I know of most senior clubs, coaches do go out into their local area to offer some tips and guidance from time to time, which is good because, as Chris says, nothing gives the junior clubs a bigger lift than seeing well-known, international players coming to their club for a short visit as some of the Bath stars did at Avon in 2001–2002. That is something all the senior clubs and players should be striving for.

But, I wondered, what has been lost at junior level, through the advent of professionalism? If you go back to the 1960s and 1970s when I played, junior clubs were the heart and soul of the game. Their clubhouses were blazing with lights, bonhomie and goodwill late into a Saturday evening and they seemed to epitomise the spirit of the game. Is it different now? And how did Ian and Chris feel about the financial side of the game as it had affected their clubs?

Roddan said, 'Stow, as a club, is financially sound. We don't have a whopping mortgage yet our facilities have improved beyond recognition. They have at most clubs. And you have to say most sides are now playing attractive rugby. That has filtered down from the top. But all this has been achieved at a cost which is the loss of the camaraderie which was so integral a part of rugby. The social side of the game has been greatly reduced.

'At Stow, for example, players and supporters used to stay most of the evening at the clubhouse, drinking in the bar, having a meal and generally being with friends through the club. Years ago, 50 per cent of the rugby was social. You looked forward to playing your local clubs, seeing some old friends and opponents and having a few beers with them. But people don't stay late on Saturday nights now. It is not the same tight-knit social club that it used to be. By 7p.m. now on a Saturday evening, most people will have drifted away to do other things. But that may be a reflection of changes throughout society, as much as rugby. There are other attractions now open to people. Perhaps too, some players come from further away and you can't stay drinking all evening and then drive home.'

This, of course, is a problem that strikes at the heart of all amateur sports clubs, not just rugby. Amateur cricket clubs are just the same; the notion of the captain going around the bar all evening with a jug of beer and constantly refilling everyone's glass, is heading for extinction. In some cases, it has already died out.

Firstly, because not many people would think about staying all evening at their sports club nowadays and secondly because, as Ian says, most people are at last taking seriously the problem of drinking and driving. And that has to be a good thing, whatever the cost to rugby. For those who want to stay drinking all evening, that is still perfectly possible. But they must make alternative arrangements to get home, such as calling a taxi.

The trouble is, as Ian Roddan says, this creates a difficulty because the main income for any junior club is the bar. The finances start to struggle if you're not getting the numbers in there.

He says, 'I think once the Leagues arrived with the intensity and drive they produced to win, things changed. Nowadays, there is a lot at stake in pretty much every game you play, even at junior level. I am comfortable enough with that; after all, nobody plays the game to lose, but equally you have got to guard against winning at all costs. Especially at junior levels where people still have to get up for work on a Monday morning. You can't afford to be off work because of injury caused deliberately during a game of rugby on a Saturday. You're there for some fun, some enjoyment, after all. It's not a dirty game but we need to ensure it doesn't go that way.

'I suspect that some people drive their clubs on too much. Because Leagues and professionalism are wonderful things if you are winning but very difficult if you are not. Before Leagues and professionalism, you were never judged to the same extent whether you were a player, coach or administrator. It's different today.

'I do think professionalism has brought one major bonus. The game at both senior and junior levels is much cleaner than it used to be. Without a shadow of a doubt, it's better from that point of view. It's a good thing too, because it is a hard enough game without deliberate acts of foul play. That should not be part of it at all. Throwing punches is not clever.

'Today, people are much fitter, the will to win is much stronger and the commitment is far greater. All that makes it a very demanding game these days.'

Chris Hobbs echoed such thoughts with regard to the drinking culture at junior club level. And, he said, that had had a knock-on effect on numbers attending and participating.

'In our heyday, we had nearly four sides but now we are struggling for two. Numbers have declined generally throughout junior rugby. Drinking and driving is a big issue – the days when you stayed at the club until 10 or 11p.m. and then made your careful way home by car are over for many clubs.'

True, but socially everything has changed and I suppose every generation changes. But that camaraderie formed the platform from which we used to have so much fun. It produced a whole world of characters. Yet I can remember when I was young, one or two gnarled old players moaning that 'the young boys go home too early nowadays'. Drink-driving is undoubtedly a factor today but maybe things change whatever the reason. It is just society continuing to evolve.

But Hobbs felt another reason for some of the changes had been the edict that you must have three front-row forwards available as replacements. That, he said, takes players away from other teams. 'In the old days, you would put your wing forward up into the front row if there was an injury. Sometimes a wing would play hooker, just to get a side together but that cannot happen now.

'Another problem we have at our level is getting the proper treatment for injuries. If you do ligaments in your knee, you have had it for a year or two unless you have private insurance and that is expensive. A lot of people are injuring themselves and realising then that they can either work or not. But work comes first and some don't return after injury.'

I believe this has been a dilemma for rugby players from the year dot and it concerns me that it remains the case. The game is getting harder and more physical all the time. Lots of guys are being hurt. But the NHS is under so much pressure that ideally clubs need their own private health insurance yet apart from the leading clubs in each country, it is far too expensive for the majority to afford it. So the injured rugby player at a junior club has to join the queue at his local hospital to get an examination, and then be referred to a specialist whom he might not see for weeks. All that time, the injury could be getting worse. This is a major problem. The sad part is I don't believe there is any real answer unless a player takes out private medical insurance himself and by no means everyone can do that.

There isn't any doubt whatsoever in my mind that the way the game is being played now will take an enormous toll on the health of players in their later lives. At Cardiff last season, twenty members of our first-team squad had some sort of surgery all within the space of a year. That is no coincidence and plenty of other clubs would tell a similar story. Players won't last as long as in our day and, if my experience is anything to go by, we are breeding a future elderly generation that is going to be half crippled by the time they reach fifty.

I say 'if my experience is anything to go by' and what I mean by that is this: I retired from rugby having suffered no serious injuries whatsoever in a career of about eighteen years. I never damaged any ligaments, still today have my original cartilages, I never broke anything and hardly had even a stitch put in me. That was after fifty-three caps for Wales and more for the British Lions on two tours to South Africa (in 1968 and 1974) and one to New Zealand in 1971. Yet, despite all that, there have been times since I turned fifty, when I have hardly been able to get out of bed in the mornings. I have struggled to get around a golf course on my own two legs. Furthermore, there isn't a day goes by when I don't meet up with someone from an earlier rugby-playing generation who has had a hip or knee replacement. Those seem far more widespread than I ever thought. But when I complained about it to my brother-in-law who is an orthopaedic consultant, he said, 'Well, what do you expect? The body was not designed to take the sort of impacts which you subjected yours to.'

All I can say is that if he thinks the impacts *we* experienced were too much for the body, then those being dished out today are probably twenty times harder. Some of the tackles that you see today make you wince from your armchair. Even backs are making them; England's Jonny Wilkinson is a good example. But at what cost for the future? Because it is only years after you have retired that suddenly it comes back to haunt you. And it is going to be much worse in the future because the hits are so much stronger. Some doctors might say that with the improvements in surgery and rehab, players won't suffer in the future. But I think they will.

But for the junior rugby clubs, there are other problems to consider. 'I have been on our committee for fifteen years and sometimes sit down and think, "Where will we be in ten years' time?" We sometimes have to beg, steal or borrow boys from other clubs even though the local rivalry is still there,' said Chris Hobbs.

'Avon, one of our local rivals, have gone up the divisions in the last couple of years and are now in Somerset Premier, the League above us [Somerset 1]. They have had some very successful years. But Avonvale is a club full of dedicated, determined people. It's a small, village club but I suppose it's a typical English junior club.

'There are some people in every club like me – Dave Ball is someone from our club who has done everything at Avonvale. He's been captain of the first, second, third and fourth teams, president, chairman, general maintenance man, bar manager . . . everything. He's in his early sixties now. We have a couple of others in the club like him.

'Clubs need these people, guys who hold the whole thing together. They're the ones the police call at 3a.m. when the club's burglar alarm is ringing and someone needs to get up and go and turn it off.

'My worry for Avonvale is that we are now down to two sides. Last season it was three. There are fifteen players in their forties and we haven't got the players to replace them. Tony Box is fifty-eight and still playing as prop for the second XV. We certainly don't have the young kids. I suppose ten years ago I would have said the same thing, so maybe things sort themselves out. But the lack of young-sters worries me because there are so many more things they can do with their leisure time these days. They have a lot more money and travel the world. Plus a lot of the young local village people have moved away. They go to university and often don't come back. After all, we are only a small village side.

'Places near us like Trowbridge, Devizes and Melksham are all towns, they have more people to draw from. We try all kinds of things to recruit players. We do poster drops around the villages and at Bath University.'

At Stow, they run four sides and a veterans' XV. They have about 240 non-playing members, more now than ever before. The other thing is the minis side of the club which is, as in so many clubs, a great success, which, thought Ian, seemed to have all the hallmarks of being very good for the game long term.

'The number of kids playing junior rugby is testament to the fact that it is a healthy sport and the system is working. We have age groups from Under-7s up to Under-17s. Turn up on a Sunday morning and all three pitches are divided up and there's a sea of young faces playing, which is great. I suppose on average there would be up to twenty youngsters in each age group.

'I coach the Under-7s at our club and we get over twenty of them turning up on a Sunday morning. It's the same at most minis age-group levels. But one problem the game does have is transferring youngsters from minis to seniors. If you don't run a Colts team – and we don't at the moment – you lose those youngsters, they go and do something else. But with a Colts team, the next year they should go into the third XV, perhaps the second XV the year after and then the firsts. There is a natural progression, a series of stepping-stones for them to follow through.

'The game is losing too many youngsters at sixteen to eighteen. Some leave and go to university, some get a job, others get involved in plenty of other interests. They disperse at that age and, unless you have a very good structure which offers them something, you will lose them. Colts rugby is something that needs to be looked at closely because it is essential in the progression from junior rugby to the senior game.'

I agree that it is very important that you have a system, a continuity in place where you can bring these kids right through. It's really only those who are going on to play the game at a high level, or a few others who just want to play on in junior rugby, who keep going. Too many don't and just drift away from rugby. The only hope clubs have of keeping these kids is a thriving Colts section which covers ages from sixteen to, say, twenty – important years for keeping players for the future.

Chris Hobbs made a very sobering point which all coaches at junior level these days ought to be aware of: 'We have got nineteen kids in the Under-11s at Avon and I am aware of my responsibilities. In more ways than one. I try not to think about being sued if there is a serious injury. But, like all coaches, you must be aware of it. If something went wrong and it happened, I would have to look to the club for help. A lad in a schools side not far from Bath broke his neck some while back and the referee was sued. The ground was wet, the scrum kept going down and he broke his neck in one. He was a hooker. But I haven't been put off it by such thoughts even though we live in times where people are suing others much more often.'

I understand the concerns of people like Chris because we are now in litigious times. I know that the IRB are very concerned about this whole issue and have been anxious to try and eliminate as far as possible aspects of the game such as collapsed scrums. It is a game that is getting faster and harder and you have to try to apply the laws that help keep those serious situations to a minimum.

Of course, experience is important and Hobbs has a lot. 'I did my first coaching course back in 1988, one evening a week for six weeks. Mini rugby was underway then and I helped coach kids aged between 6 and 12. In 1997, I did my first 12–18 age group coaching exam and in 1999, I did the intermediate and then adult level 2. Now I'm on Adult level 3. Ideally, I prefer coaching 18–19 year olds or adults but I took on the Under-11s because it's nice to feel you can do something to help. Now I'd like to take them through to the 15-a-side game.

'One thing I don't like about youngsters' rugby today is the pressure they are being put under by their parents. Some parents are OK; they're not trying to get their kids to play to a certain level and that's good. But too many are demanding everything from their kids, it's absurd. Coaches get stick for not selecting children. That's wrong. The RFU guidelines say clearly that winning is not everything. It is also important to have fun. As a coach, you should not give young boys a rollicking. They're doing their best and they should be enjoying it. It's different if you're older and playing more seriously but at minis level it's wrong to shout and scream at them.'

So what of the future for Stow-on-the-Wold and Avonvale rugby clubs, and indeed all the clubs like them? How do they see themselves in a few years' time?

Ian Roddan said that his club was in a better position now than ever, even though finances often raised some concerns. More people were involved, that was for sure. But he felt they had reached a crossroads. They had gone as far as they could go in senior rugby, and many of them at the club were saying 'No more, we don't want to go higher.'

'We are a small town playing at a high standard so if we slipped down a little, I wouldn't necessarily see that as a bad thing. Success breeds success but the social side of the club has changed. Match fees at £3–£4 and a year's membership at £25 are much as they were years ago [the same amount as at Avonvale]. But it's a very small amount financially. When you think of what you get for that and you compare that with prices at some tennis, hockey and squash clubs, it's a world of difference. The membership fees are laughable really and all clubs need to look at avenues of making money. A useful source of revenue to us is the caravan rallies they hold on our ground during the summer.

'As for the future in other respects, I don't think you can un-invent Leagues and frankly, they're not a bad thing. It has taken the junior clubs a while to find their feet in this so-called professional era but I am quite sure the majority of clubs will go back to where they were, before 1995. Frankly, they can't afford to do anything else.

'The players will have to help out behind the bar again, the guys will have to take home the shirts to wash them on rota . . . all the things that you did before you went down the professional road. We have had all those things done professionally at our club and things like the teas were contracted out, too. The bars were run by paid staff and all the catering was run on a contract basis. The pitches were mowed by the council and paid for by the club, instead of someone from the club doing it themselves.'

But wasn't that the whole spirit of club rugby? Players and officials did come together and help in all manner of ways. It wasn't just at junior clubs, either. The trouble is a lot of guys have very quickly moved on from there under professionalism. So, whether or not people will go back to doing those chores willingly remains to be seen. Because once you have developed a culture that is not used to those things, I think it will be difficult to get it back. Perhaps some players will take the attitude that they'll find a club which will continue to do those things for them. I believe the message with all of this is that it will be difficult to turn back the clock. Some clubs will be forced to by financial circumstances but a lot won't find it easy.

Roddan says that Stow are no different from anywhere else. He believes that once people start to try and balance the books they will realise they are going to have to give up some things. 'You must look at the things you can't afford. It is amazing when you analyse it, but what was done for nothing now costs a lot. That revenue has to come from somewhere and the fact is most junior clubs can't afford to spend that money. In the old days, the clubhouse was cleaned for next to nothing, shirts were laundered by wives of players or officials. Professionalism changed so much of that. But we will have to return to it if clubs are to remain viable.'

Among other things, Hobbs is also fundraising secretary at Avonvale and organises many events to raise money for the club. But with all things, he said, it was difficult to get manpower. They have been looking for someone to do a Sunday afternoon bar shift at the club but can't find anyone.

'Financially, we are quite well off. We have a very good committee and, strangely, raising money is not as big a problem as raising a team. We have events on during the week and at weekends and, of course, membership is the main money earner. The bar doesn't suffer here as much as at some clubs because we are a village side and people can walk home from our clubhouse on a Saturday evening, if they live locally. Other clubs out in the country are not as fortunate.

'Football and rugby at our ground on Saturdays and Sundays makes the place very vibrant. We often take quite a few hundred pounds over the bar on a Saturday night. Almost everything there is done voluntarily, apart from getting the kit washed in the village. We also get good local sponsorship and that helps.'

Hobbs said that when people asked him if he was worried about the future, he felt his answer was probably yes. Not just for his club but for other clubs too. 'We personally haven't got any youngsters coming through and it's very hard to set up a junior section. I don't know where the players are going to come from in the future. Unless we can tie ourselves into a local school, we are struggling yet we are not as badly off as some clubs. We do a family membership and have around 150–200 members including wives. We would have had up to 80 playing members in the past but now it's about 50. But at least the decline has come to a halt. We allow three or four football junior sides to use our pitches – it helps with funds. And they will become associate members.'

But how had professionalism affected them? Did they pay players to play or could they simply not afford it? Hobbs admitted there were people playing at their level getting paid. Not at his club, but at a few others. But not a lot.

'They get £20 or £30 a game, some of them. The most we do is pay the expenses of two students who travel from Exeter to play. But most clubs haven't got the money to do anything. One reason is that a few years ago some club members would put their hands in their pocket and give their club money for certain things, perhaps a few hundred pounds. That doesn't seem to happen as much now.'

Ian Roddan said that it was a path Stow had gone down in the past, but not with conspicuous success. And no longer. 'We had two overseas players, Western Samoans, playing for us a couple of years ago. They certainly had an impact on the side, because of their size. A lot of the sides Stow played had one or two either ex-first class players or overseas guys. But overall, it was of limited success and didn't really work for us and we haven't got any now. We wouldn't go back to it, it's too expensive. It causes problems within the team and the club. It's very difficult to get it right.

'Another thing that has already changed is that Stow have gone back to an in-house coach after trying outsiders for a while. I always argued that if you paid anyone, then it should be the coach because, while players will come and go, a good coach is the one person who can really make a difference to a side.'

Roddan felt that something else may change, too. What would be ideal, he thought, was to reduce the Leagues, by eliminating home and away and just playing teams once in a season on rota as to venue, and bring back the traditional, local, friendly fixtures. He believed a lot of clubs would like to see that happen. 'Those fixtures have virtually gone out of the window but we need them back. If we could maintain some sort of League structure but also maintain links with local clubs, then I think many clubs would benefit.

'I think the very local fixtures are the ones supporters want to come to. It is a good social day out and there is some reason to go and watch. Shipston-on-Stour was a good local fixture we used to have, but lost when Leagues became serious. I think that maintaining these old ties would strengthen the game at grassroots level. Because all the so-called successes of League rugby have often been at the expense of the social side of the game. If the game loses that, it has lost a very big part of its tradition. The local derby fixture is at the heart of the social side of the sport.'

I must say, I agree that there is something very special about playing local fixtures. Also, it is an interesting point Ian makes about the possibility of freeing up some part of the season for local matches against teams even if they are from different Leagues. As for travelling, I think clubs like Stow which elected to stay at this level so as to avoid the prospect of going down to places like Cornwall too often were quite right. In Wales, travelling is not so much of a problem, yet some north Wales clubs like Wrexham and Bangor want to play south or west Wales teams in Leagues. If you had to go up to north Wales every other week, it would be a huge commitment and much too much for most people for more than a couple of fixtures.

Yet you have to ask yourself, would you *really* get many more people if you played more local fixtures? Apart from getting together a few more local officials from the two clubs, I wonder. I understand there was a survey into crowd support at cricket's Lancashire Leagues, which documented the declining support at lower levels. I am sure soccer would say the same at the lower levels. Unfortunately for sports clubs, and it is a fact of modern-day life, parameters have been vastly extended in terms of entertainment available to people in their leisure time. When sports clubs were in their heyday, potential entertainment was far more limited. There were no computer games or internet chat rooms which fascinated and occupied the minds of children for hours at weekends; transport was nowhere near as easy because fewer young people had cars, and therefore lacked the freedom and greater independence they enjoy today. When you add on other social aspects such as cinema, shopping, weekend travel, family responsibilities etc. you perhaps begin to understand why numbers at sports clubs have declined dramatically. The world has opened up to a far greater degree than ever before and clubs have to compete for the attention of young people with so many other attractions.

Chris Hobbs could see the point about what had been lost in terms of social fixtures. But he didn't think it would work to turn the clock back in that sense. 'I don't think going back to half a season without League games now would work for us. Because I think some people in our club would only play the League games, not the friendlies, apart from the local derbies. They'd say the friendlies didn't matter. Some would only play so many games in a season, and that's wrong; when you get to my age you should play every game if you can. After all, you're a long time retired. When people say "I want to have a rest" they start to lose me, unless they're carrying an injury. But each to his own.'

232

But, I asked both men, were they basically happy where their clubs were? Did they have any other strong feelings about the game in general? Roddan admitted that the national Leagues were somewhere he couldn't see Stow going to, nor would many of his fellow members want the club to be there. 'Once you get into Leagues, you start travelling but supporters won't travel. And if you lose them, they won't necessarily come to home games after that so the social side of the game and your club starts to diminish further.

'Stow moved from the original South West Leagues to the South Midlands because of the geographical problem. We would have found ourselves going to places like Penzance and players are not prepared to do that. You have to go on a Friday night to be competitive which means the problem of commitment in terms of time and also finance. Like a lot of other things now, it's just not practical for a club at this level of the game.'

Chris Hobbs felt it was wrong to say, as some people did at junior level, that the game was dying. He didn't think it was. But what didn't help, he said, was the RFU signing a long deal with BSkyB a few years ago to show England's home internationals only on satellite television. The game was not being advertised to all people because not everyone had BSkyB. It was all right the RFU saying they had received a lot of money but at what cost to the game at junior level, he asked?

He also pointed out a flaw in the system at youth recruitment level. 'I know the RFU have got Regional Development Officers now [RDOs] and the coaching is much better. More clubs now have minis playing and coaches have to do their basic coaching courses. More people are taking up coaching.

'But Somerset Youth Development Officers [YDOs] were missing so many kids a few years ago. They weren't going to junior clubs looking at young players, they only went to the famous rugby schools, like Millfield and Colston's. Now they pick a schools' side and a club side and it's better because there are a lot of kids out there. They should go to all schools, public and private, plus the junior clubs.'

Hobbs also brought up a point I have heard mentioned by a great many other people, from all levels and areas of the game. The question of the cost of going to watch England play top international matches. I think I'm right in saying that it is now more expensive to go to Twickenham than any other international ground in the northern hemisphere. I know for sure it's a lot more than the Stade de France, Paris, or the Millennium Stadium, Cardiff.

I suspect that Chris's view is widely held. 'It still costs too much money to watch a game at Twickenham – £42 and £45 to see Australia in autumn, 2001. There are a lot of youngsters out there who would love to go and see those games but they can't afford to. Again, the sport is perhaps losing them by failing to give them the opportunity to go.'

But what has raised prices is the old issue of supply and demand. England, especially since their growing successes in recent times, know that they could sell out Twickenham two or three times for a match like the one against Australia in November 2001. On a day when only 39,000 went to Cardiff to see Wales lose to Argentina, England were beating Australia before a 75,000 full house at Twickenham. So as long as the English team continues to be successful and play exciting rugby, then I'm afraid I can't see the situation changing.

Hobbs's final point was one with which I sympathised. He estimated that at Avonvale, they play twenty-two League games in a season with four or five Cup matches, depending of course on how far they went. Then, he said, you had the Combination Cup games, the local event. It was too much high-pressure rugby for people at these levels. 'That's good for the top end of the game, but not for us. Overall, of course, it is still hugely pleasurable, like it used to be. But my chief problem now is that it is always a "must win" game, everything is geared to that. I find that a shame and I don't know that it suits this end of the game. I think it is putting a lot of pressure on players who just want some fun on a Saturday afternoon.'

I understand his viewpoint. Expecting intense pressure and all the necessary preparation involved for matches like Cardiff v Swansea or Leicester v Bath is perfectly natural, given the fact that the game is now professional. But I'm not convinced it suits those at the junior levels to be trying to aspire to such professional attitudes.

For those junior clubs who wish to be ambitious and climb the

Leagues, then the structure and opportunity is now there for them to do it. You have got to provide opportunities for clubs like Worcester, Rotherham and Plymouth Albion to find their way through, if they want to. But I don't believe the majority of junior clubs want to rise to the Premier division in their country. They're perfectly happy running a healthy, prosperous club which is a focal point for the community in their area. Perhaps it's time more provision was made for clubs like those who, let's face it, probably make up about 95 per cent of the clubs in each country. Because I think the sooner the majority of junior clubs go back to what they were, junior sides enjoying the game as it was meant to be played, then the quicker we will be rid of this ridiculous situation we are currently in.

Paying so much attention to the top level of the game is all very well. But if we forget the cares and considerations of the junior clubs, ignore the issues that affect them, and the people who search out, find and coach the Brian O'Driscolls and Gregor Townsends of the future, then we risk serious damage to the future structure of the sport. It is an issue that will demand very careful consideration by those charged with the administration of our game.

CHAPTER 12

The Media

'The newspapers!' wrote Sheridan, the great playwright, in *The Critic* in 1779. 'Sir, they are the most villainous – licentious – abominable – infernal – not that I ever read them – no – I make it a rule never to look into a newspaper.'

Well, if Sheridan thought that of the newspapers then, I wonder what he would have made of today's offerings. How about page 3 of the *Sun* or the exposés frequently served up by the *News of the World*? The mind boggles as to what the man might have written about them. Whether we like it or not, the newspapers – indeed nowadays all the media – play an increasing part in our everyday lives.

Media organisations want to get a closer, more exclusive insight into the players playing the game and some of the major matches and tours. How else can you explain Will Carling's move from an ordinary rugby player to a media-created celebrity? Why else would the British Lions allow cameras to film behind the scenes throughout their 2001 tour of Australia to make a so-called 'fly-on-the-wall' documentary? The public's appetite for these pictures would appear to be insatiable, and not just in rugby. But is all that the media brings to the party healthy for the game itself? Or is the truth that many of its influences are downright bad for this great game? It is obvious that every major sport will have to learn to cope with increasingly inquisitive media in the years ahead. TV cameras and microphones will pry where they have never been allowed to go before, cameramen and the reporters will snoop where they once never envisaged going. It may well be that everyone becomes fair game, every institution is put firmly under the microscope of public examination. But is that good for any sport, particularly rugby? And what do the media men themselves think about this whole business?

To debate this issue, I sat down with two people who have worked in television and newspapers and have extensive experience of rugby football, as both player and observer. The journalist Peter Jackson came to live in Wales from his Northern Ireland home nearly forty years ago and has extensive experience of television, through his work on BBC Wales for whom he presented a Friday night sports magazine programme, 'Sportfolio', for six years. Of course, today he is better known for his newspaper work as rugby correspondent of the *Daily Mail* for whom he is arguably the most distinguished of the national newspaper rugby correspondents. Gareth Davies, fly half for Llanelli, Cardiff, Wales and the 1980 British Lions during a fine playing career, was head of sport for BBC Wales from 1988 until 1994. He then joined Cardiff RFC as the club's chief executive until 1999 and since then has been chairman of the Sports Council of Wales. Gareth is also a sports adviser to S4C, the Welsh language TV channel.

As I was to discover, both men have some intriguing and forthright opinions on the game. I thought what developed in our discussion touched on some of the most pressing and important issues that are facing rugby. Looking back, said Gareth, you could argue it had been the media that had kept the sport alive. Certainly it was true that there had been no really vitriolic attacks from the media towards the game. Yet from 1995 to the end of the millennium, there were some desperate moments in the game's history. But TV money kept it afloat, broadcasters were always scrambling for TV rights, and newspapers filled more and more space with rugby stories.

I think that was true. Yet there have been changes in the personnel covering rugby matches these days because many of the correspondents have come from a soccer culture. Gareth agreed but, generally speaking, he felt that the coverage had been very positive. But, he warned, there were bound to be changes as rugby gained in credibility as a professional sport. This I agree with. Indeed, we have already seen the first signs of it with BSkyB TV's glitzier, more commercial, more tabloid-type approach in covering the sport. The recent Lions tour was a case in point, in that it was so different from earlier years.

Gareth felt that the whole set-up of the game had changed. 'Take the first weekend of the Heineken Cup in the 2001–2002 season – there may have been as many as twenty different kick-off times over the course of that weekend. Because you had so many different TV companies covering matches in the six countries – companies like Eurosport TV, Canal Plus in France, S4C in Wales, ITV 1, TG4 in Ireland, BBC in England . . . you have got to appease all those different companies. It does change the nous of the game. But, you wonder, are we taking the crowds for granted? With decisions like starting Bridgend against Harlequins at 7.10p.m. on a Friday night, I'd suggest we're pretty close to doing so.'

Of course, this is something I have some experience of through my work with TV and also Cardiff. And, yes, there is a price to be paid for welcoming the TV money. Yet Gareth Davies believes if it had been football, it would have been different because he senses that soccer audiences are willing to be flexible and bend to TV times. He feels they understand there is a quid pro quo with the sums invested by the TV companies in their sport. They have to give something back. Perhaps he is right. After all, Liverpool often play Manchester United at 11.30a.m. on a Saturday morning and Tottenham played Derby County on a Monday night with an 8p.m. kick-off in October 2001. Such things seem to have been accepted. But in rugby, he said, there were still too many different camps with people trying to push in different directions. That didn't happen in soccer, he felt.

The trouble is, I suspect, that people supporting rugby have voted with their feet when it has come to a major game being played with a 5.30p.m. kick-off time. The frightening thing, admitted Davies, was if you alienated your core audience, you would have real problems. The older generation brought along youngsters whom all the clubs wanted as their future. If the older guys became disenchanted and stayed away, so did the youngsters, he warned. That was the danger of allowing TV companies to dictate kick-off times too much. 'What worries me is that there is no real coming together of everybody involved. The last contract S4C signed with Welsh rugby, they tried to ensure it was a partnership which was worked out. Because each side needed the other. We on the TV side didn't want people complaining about kick-off times because that was endangering the game and its future.'

But how have all the major changes at the highest levels concerning television affected someone like Mike Burton, for example?

He told me, 'All the big sporting events these days are staged quite differently compared to the past. The first thing the sports organisations do now is set up the TV contract. As we go ahead, pay-per-view is going to happen more and more. It will be a huge thing and affect us in all manner of ways. Don't forget, the TV talks are now crucial to every major sports body and their premier events. Because once you have the TV contracts, everything else follows. Then you put in place title sponsors followed by the lower level sponsorship packages.

'Once TV is involved, it is a whole new ball game. That is what has changed rugby so much, the money TV was prepared to pump into it. There is no getting away from that. Soon, all those boards around the rugby grounds will all be sold under the TV contracts. I don't see TV as the great evil, it's definitely showing us the way forward.'

Yet Burton shares my view that simply selling rugby's TV coverage to the highest bidder and ignoring those who do not necessarily have access to every form of TV coverage, would be disastrous for the sport long term. Who knows how many potential long-term recruits, either as players or followers, it might cost the game in the years ahead?

It's all right for those of us who have satellite coverage in our homes saying it would not matter whether all rugby in one country was on satellite or terrestrial television. But many rugby followers and supporters do not have satellite and therefore, the game would be guilty of a gross dereliction of duty if it sold only to satellite without considering those who have only terrestrial television.

Burton agrees, saying, 'I'm the first to say that you have got to have a balance between terrestrial and satellite television. I think that balance is crucial because any sport needs to reach as wide an audience as possible. But what I see as a greater danger is when you have the TV people dictating how long the break will be between halves in a match and that sort of thing. I call that intrusive TV and

I don't like it, it's a real danger for the game.'

Burton said that another thing about dealing with television was that Unions must decide how they wanted to portray their sport. Because TV would overrun you if you let them, he warned. They would ask for everything from access to the players' dressing-rooms immediately after a game, on-pitch interviews at half time and at the finish and many other things. Through those methods you get inside the sport, according to the TV people. But rugby had to decide whether it wanted those things, whether it wished to see its game covered in that manner.

Burto thought it an inevitable consequence that TV would become increasingly influential in rugby union. It was already in the sense that when you go to a major game now and something controversial happens, you are looking around for the TV replay on a giant screen. You did that automatically and it was one way that TV had had an influence over all of us. 'TV will drive the game forward and drive upwards the sums of money coming into the game. I don't see any evil in that as long as the governing bodies are in charge and are making sound business decisions and have the interests of everyone in the game in their minds. Sure, we have to be careful in the way some things are introduced but given that, I think the game will continue to grow.

'More and more it is a show we are discussing here, there is no getting away from that. People who watch, whether on TV or at the match, want to be entertained; they want to see a spectacle. It is an on-going show in which the rewards are high and the demands great. Rugby union has to be good and entertaining. Because you can watch all manner of sporting events from Spanish and Italian League football, to live cricket from the West Indies, to tennis in Australia and golf in America to athletics around the world and a host of other sports events. In a market as competitive as that, rugby union will need to be a spectacle now and in the future.

'I say to rugby and those who run it, "Embrace the future, don't be afraid of it." Because the fact is, we are still in control of it – Mr Murdoch doesn't run rugby, not in the northern hemisphere anyway. Proceed with caution, certainly, but let's embrace what has happened and enjoy professionalism and the future. But for sure, make certain the people at the top remember there is another game that has to be catered and cared for,' said Burton.

But one thing quickly leads to another. On the subject of kick-off times, Friday night rugby has been suggested for the Six Nations Championship. Gareth Davies and I agreed that is nonsensical. He reminded us that the Ireland v Wales match in the 2002 Six Nations Championship had been given a 4p.m. kick-off time on a Sunday and that totally messed up the entire weekend. I must say I completely agree with him because people have to go to work the next day. By that decision, the authorities probably lost thousands of supporters who otherwise might have been able to go to Dublin.

Peter Jackson has probably been to more Five or now Six Nations Championship matches than Messrs Edwards and Davies put together! Nowadays, of course, Peter will think nothing of covering a French international in Paris on a Saturday afternoon, working late that night after endless interviews to write up his report for Monday's *Daily Mail* and then catching an early-morning flight to Edinburgh, Rome or Dublin to report a Championship game being played on the Sunday! Thus, his experience is extensive and I thought his words on this topic were especially apt. 'The first time I went to a Six Nations game on a Sunday was in Edinburgh in March 2000 for the Scotland–England game and the atmosphere was funereal. The game itself wasn't too bad but afterwards the whole place was deserted. It completely destroyed the ambience of the weekend. A Friday night international would be the same. I can't believe they will do it. There is talk of France playing on a Saturday night in Paris and I think that has some value. For a start, Paris and the restaurants and cafes and bars are open most of the night anyway. And a Sunday afternoon in Rome for an international is all right because fewer people travel there anyway and also because sport on a Sunday afternoon is a tradition on the Continent. But going back to Gareth Davies's point, a 5.30 kick-off is a difficult time for the community because people want their Saturday night out.'

The venue was the key, according to Davies. If it was a run-of-the-mill League match in Wales starting at that time, he said you would only have 1000 or 2000 there. But it was to some people's advantage because they could watch two games like that. They would go to a 2.30 kick-off match to start with and be home by 5.30 to watch the other one on TV. That, he said, was the attraction for the TV companies. He knew from a broadcaster's point of view, 5.30 was a slot both ITV1 and Eurosport wanted.

But Gareth felt that overall the game just hadn't been very good at selling the changes that had happened since professionalism. 'Clubs, players and broadcasters have had to be dragged to the table. I'd ask, is that a lack of leadership in terms of pro-actively selling the game? We have to move this product on and that means finding new people to come through the doors. In England, they have been more successful at bringing in a new audience. In general, though, you'd have to say the sport has been dragged into this new millennium. It has been a very fractious time, not conducive to building a business. In England and Ireland it is settling down but in Wales, it appears the rifts are still there. That is down to different agendas, and a lack of leadership.'

Jackson said that he too felt much was attributable to the little tribal splits within the WRU. 'They don't look at what is best for the game, it's their own little parish they are interested in. One shining example of someone being successful in selling the game is Peter Deakin, when he was with the English club Saracens as their commercial and marketing expert. Saracens are a great success story of professional rugby because they have gone to a rugby desert called Watford and turned crowds of around 400 which they used to get at Southgate into 8000 or more. Even when they're struggling, they get 6–7000 and for the big matches against a side like Leicester, they have had 15,000 plus. Now you can say they give some tickets away to kids, but they're still going and they've still transformed their support base. Peter Deakin, who has now incidentally re-joined them as chief executive, was outstanding for them but that was down to his rugby league background.'

There has been a disturbing lack of planning throughout rugby, said Davies. 'In Wales, for example, it seems to me we should be saying, "Where do we want to be in 2003 or 2005 and how do we go about ensuring we get there?" You would have two or three years to sort things out, that way. But no one is doing that to the best of my knowledge.' Well, I know personally that the clubs themselves are saying they can't go on like they are. But the General Committee of the WRU overturn decisions they don't like and that sets things back. There is a constant contradiction and that is what has been holding back the game in our country. In many ways, you could say that the entire process of professionalism and the first few years of its difficult progress, has been a saga of unhappiness and missed opportunities. Peter Jackson highlighted a case in point when he said that Wales missed a glorious opportunity when it could not come to an agreement with the RFU for an Anglo-Welsh League. The WRU wanted nine teams in it, which was obviously far too many.

This was a subject with which Gareth Davies had been closely involved during his time as chief executive of Cardiff. He went on to tell a revealing story about what had happened. 'I was involved with Cardiff RFC at the time of those discussions and got roped into a sub-committee. Tom Walkinshaw, the Gloucester owner who was leading the English clubs, asked me to go to a meeting in Tewkesbury with the English and Welsh rugby unions to discuss this project. The discussions went on and the English Union said they could look at four or five Welsh clubs in it, but no more. The WRU called a time out and I was left wondering which side to go and talk with. But the WRU turned it down flat, there wasn't even a debate. Again, it was the WRU agenda driven by individual clubs which wrecked it and lost the opportunity. It was a shame – sponsors were lined up and everything. It would have been invaluable for the game in Wales, in terms of lifting standards.'

Jackson said it was a real opportunity missed for Welsh rugby, because it was the ideal competition in his view. He said that he never subscribed to the idea of a British League because he felt it was too close to a European Cup, in basic concept. But he was sure the public would have liked to see the return of those traditional England–Wales club fixtures, and I agree with him wholeheartedly. Of course, it was what the Welsh public wanted, an Anglo-Welsh League. When Cardiff and Swansea left the WRU for a year in the season 1998–1999, those first two or three months saw the English teams put out their best sides and crowds in Cardiff were the biggest seen since professionalism arrived. We had 10,000 for the match against Saracens and then when we played a second-string Bath side, we had to delay the kick-off because so many people were trying to get into the ground. On more than one Saturday, Cardiff's attendance exceeded the total figures for the entire WRU Premier Division. As for an Anglo-Welsh League, at least the players would have played their club rugby at a far higher level in preparation for the international game. As I said earlier, one of the reasons why Wales were successful during our time in the 1970s was that we had a series of hard club fixtures, sometimes on midweek nights, against teams like Bristol, Coventry and Gloucester. The club rugby then was so tough; today it's not.

Davies agreed. He remembered when he was eighteen and went to Coventry for a match with Llanelli and they had an all-international backline out; names like Peter Preece, Richard Cowman, Peter Rossborough, David Duckham etc. It was, he said, a fantastic experience for such a young lad. But then in those days, there was such a passion in our land for the game. Peter Jackson summed it up best. 'When I first came to Wales from Northern Ireland all those years ago, I felt rugby was the number one discussion topic in the land. Bus conductors, taxi drivers . . . everyone talked about rugby. I had come from a place where it was only a middle- to upper-class recreation, the working man wasn't much interested in the game where I'd grown up. Even quite recently, all those years after I first experienced it, the support for Wales at Wembley was phenomenal and everywhere you looked there was passion. I think the passion is still here to some extent but inevitably they have also lost some of it. Things changed with professionalism. Pontypool were the biggest casualty, a club that was far bigger than any in England. Indeed, they were the number one club in the British Isles at one stage but their decline seemed to reflect the diminishing of the game generally in Wales. Having said that, I found Llanelli's performances against Leicester in this season's Heineken Cup very uplifting. They played so well and the passion was certainly there in that Welsh team. There's no doubt, when the Welsh teams are motivated, they do rise to it. We should also remember that there is a tendency in Wales to swing from utter despair to total ecstasy. "I am never going again to watch that load of rubbish" suddenly changes to "I think we will win the World Cup". The look and expression on ordinary people's faces when Ireland beat Wales 36–6 at Cardiff in October 2001 and then thumped them 54–10 in Dublin a few months later, was incredible. You could swear it mattered so much to them. They had just witnessed awful performances and they were drained. There was a look of complete disbelief on their faces.'

I did believe that we were losing our passion for the game generally and this seemed to be confirmed by the fact that the crowds weren't there. We had Newport here at Cardiff for one match a few years ago and just 3000 turned up. Llanelli were getting 2000 for some matches and I thought the game was going out of the door. People were not turning up, they didn't seem to be interested. What changed my mind was when we went to Wembley. The numbers that went up there convinced me the Welsh still felt a passion to some degree about the sport. But Peter is right, we go from one extreme to the other. The media play their part here, too, because one minute the team is the best in the world, the next they're the worst. But it's their job to sell newspapers. The trouble is too many of the Welsh players believed it when they said they were the best!

I know one thing. Regular fixtures against, for argument's sake, the top half-dozen English clubs in a meaningful Anglo-Welsh competition would have helped raise standards significantly in Wales by now. Perhaps six Welsh clubs would have been involved, and from those six, imagine the number of potential international players exposed to a higher level of club rugby each week. With all due respects to the clubs involved, Cardiff against Caerphilly and Llanelli against Ebbw Vale could hardly compare with Cardiff against Leicester and Llanelli against Gloucester.

Jackson thinks the reason why rugby means so much to the Welsh psyche when more people in Wales play soccer is that the game has been the one sport where Wales have been if not the best in the world, able to challenge the very best and almost match them. It's the one sport where Wales have been able to say, 'We can take on the rest of the world.' That is either a millstone or an inspiration. But that is why he thinks rugby will always matter more than in England. They don't have the same passion about rugby there that they do in Wales, he argues. 'In Wales,' he said, 'there was this huge passion for the game. Perhaps only in areas like Gloucester and

Cornwall could you rival that. Club rugby in Wales was the envy of the world. That was why English clubs tested themselves on Wednesday nights against teams like Newport, Pontypool, Cardiff and Llanelli. England suffered partly because it is a bigger country and is more fragmented. But what England have at last got is success and they are all pulling roughly in the same direction now. Given that situation, they should dominate for years to come. The English First Division always had a greater depth of competition, now the English League is superior in every way.'

The loss of such an opportunity was lamented by all of us. Gareth Davies said that he felt every year Welsh rugby had stumbled from one crisis to another. He provided a classic example of failing standards to underline his point. 'I'll never forget, some years ago, Cardiff played Abertillery or Aberavon, I can't remember which one, and they beat them something like 95–20. Yet there was the ridiculous sight of the officials on the visitors' bench jumping around in delight, late on in the match, because a try they scored – you couldn't call it a consolation – meant they got one more bonus point. Now that single point meant they sneaked above Caerphilly in the table and they survived relegation. I knew then something was seriously wrong in Welsh rugby. No one in that team was thinking about conceding 95 points. One try meant survival and somehow they turned that into a triumph. It was absurd.'

As Peter Jackson said, it is certainly wrong to reward failure.

But going back to the media, Peter feels – and rightly so, in my view – that rugby is still very lucky with the media it has got. He thinks it has had a terrific deal from the media in this part of the world. He says that most of the writers love the game and the people in it. Therefore they are less inclined to savage people as happens so often in soccer. The media have been very fair. The only problem is that, in my view, at the moment we have a generation of writers, in Wales particularly, who suffer by comparison with the doyens of the past. This brought to mind some great names from the world of sportswriters and some memories. Jackson remembered J.B.G. Thomas, esteemed late rugby correspondent of the *Western Mail* and spoke of the tremendous stature and authority he had in the game. He said that he would be critical of him only in the sense that it was only after an abysmal Welsh performance that

Thomas was ever prepared to criticise. But he did have tremendous authority and influence. Indeed, he was called the sixth selector.

I believe there comes a time when you need to be constructive in your criticism. I also think we now have too many weak writers. I suspect a lot of them do not really know and understand the game; indeed, many have come to rugby, as it were, from days as soccer writers. It is hard to compare them with the likes of J.B.G. Thomas, or many other what I would call proper rugby correspondents. Too many just put out the official line, it seems to me. And for games that are so important, you feel we deserve better. It is a point Gareth Davies had some thoughts on. He felt there was a huge lack of investment in some areas of the media now. For example, the *Western Mail*, the national newspaper of Wales, wouldn't send their own reporter to the match between French club Montferrand and Cardiff in the Heineken Cup tie early in the season 2001–2002. As he said, you would have thought a paper of that stature would have had their own man there. Apparently, even when Bridgend played Harlequins in the same competition, there was no *Western Mail* staff man at the Brewery Field. The paper arranged to take a report from someone else who was going to be in the press box. I must say I find that hugely disappointing from Wales's national newspaper.

Jackson said that he had always admired John Billot, J.B.G.'s deputy on the *Western Mail*. Life in J.B.G.'s shadow couldn't have been easy. But Billot was free to say what he thought and he was courageous. There were many great characters and decent writers around then, men like Lloyd Lewis (who was to die so tragically in the Paris air crash of 1974), Dennis Busher, Tudor James, who was a wonderful man, and Malcolm Lewis. Tudor James's batman had been Jimmy Murphy, who went on to become Sir Matt Busby's second-in-command at Manchester United. I myself remembered Tudor coming on the 1974 Lions tour. He used to say he had deadlines that were almost an impossibility. It all seems so long ago now.

Jackson put it into perspective, before we became lost in a ramble through the past! Everything changed for ever, he insisted, when the game went open. 'Now there is a totally different attitude. In some cases it has become like soccer. The sacking of John Hall and Jon Callard's departure at Bath, player power rearing its head at a place like Sale, a factor which cost John Mitchell his job as coach at the club. Yet Mitchell is now All Blacks coach. So although things are not as bad as in soccer, we are certainly heading in that direction. Wasps lost five of their first six League matches of the 2001–2002 season and the media were immediately saying, "What about Nigel Melville's position?"

'But I have to say, if I was Gareth Edwards, I would be envious of what players are picking up today in terms of salaries. Because he would be earning an absolute fortune out of the game and he would be worth every penny of it.'

I laughed. I can still remember things like the Cardiff club refusing to pay me £1 worth of petrol for my expenses on one occasion. But I have no regrets. We knew things had to change because the demands on the amateur players were so great it was virtually immoral.

Jackson certainly subscribed to that opinion. He recalled the example back in the 1970s when – no names, no pack drill! – a Welsh international player had an offer to go to Widnes rugby league club for £15,000. He turned the offer down and said to anyone listening, 'I couldn't afford to turn professional for those sums, I'd be losing money.' Remember, that was in the 1970s! There was another story on this subject, from Gareth Davies. He remembered sitting on the bench at Stradey Park for a Llanelli match against the touring Tongans. He had been to Stradey to watch Llanelli ever since he was a boy. He was sent on for the last few minutes of the game and afterwards in the dressing-room, someone gave him a little brown envelope. He said, 'What's this?' and the person said, 'That's your expenses.' Being so young and naïve, Gareth told him he didn't need them because he'd got a lift to the ground that day! Anyway, he was told to keep them and when he opened the envelope, there was £8. Not bad for a 17-year-old schoolboy but, as he says, 'I remember thinking, "Blimey, what's 'Benny' (Phil Bennett) on, then?" '

But of course there were huge crowds there in those days and they used to joke that the money from that enormous Stradey car park went straight into a pot to pay the players. All totally erroneous, no doubt! Gareth Davies felt that it was a contradiction in terms that Wales still expected to be good and you had to bear in mind the numbers. Yes, he said, there was tradition and inherited talent in Wales. But as he said, 'We are not going to keep up with

England because we have about 3 million people and they have over 50 million. New Zealand also has only 3 million and they are starting to struggle to keep up with Australia and England. I know Australia don't have large numbers playing but they have been fantastically forward-looking in their approach to the game. Wales had a great side in the 1970s but it was a one-off. At that time, we had ten world-class players and five nearly world class. That was a freak of nature, of circumstance. There was also the innovative coaching structure under Ray Williams.'

For that period, I personally think our system was superior. By accident or not, it was ahead of other countries and therefore the comparative lack of numbers in Wales was not a factor. Now it is, because our system is no longer better. In fact, it's fallen behind other countries. But, wondered Peter, could we have done what we did in the 1970s had the collapse of traditional industries and education systems occurred thirty years earlier? How big a contribution were those factors to the demise of Welsh rugby? Those were certainly key factors. But we should also remember, while Rome burned, Nero fiddled. In other words, the WRU did nothing for the future because they believed they had a divine right to the attention and support of the entire nation for their game in perpetuity. They were seduced by facts like we used to beat Australia regularly, sometimes even New Zealand (although not for half a century). England, we hardly lost to. Yet this was by players who all came from a strip of land 90 miles long by 40 miles wide. It wasn't even the whole of Wales that was supplying players. Local identity gave strong competition at all levels, and that helped. You had town against town, First Division club against First Division club. Rivalries were fierce – for example, Aberavon would throttle Neath for sixpence!

Gareth Davies said that it was all about people with natural ability exposed to a higher level of competition. In England, he said, it was the other way round. 'When Bill Beaumont played for his club Fylde, there were probably less than 400 people there and they might be playing Birkenhead Park or someone. It was no wonder England's players couldn't make the step up in class for so many years. In Wales, on the other hand, our top players were having fiercely competitive rugby every time they played. Given their natural talent too, that made them fine players. In England

250

now, that problem has been overcome and the numbers game starts to be decisive. I just feel that even with only four or five Premiership clubs, we still wouldn't have a sufficient number of greatly talented players.' Peter Jackson felt that it would be a calamity to cut the number of clubs in the Premiership in Wales down to that few. He said it should be no lower than six. Remember, he went on, what did Glasgow and Edinburgh bring to the table in recent seasons when the Scottish Rugby Union cut their club scene down to two provinces? The club game there now was destroyed and for what? Ireland, he said, had had the best of the Celtic League set-up; it had been a good season for them.

We moved on to other subjects and Jackson talked about what he termed 'a defining moment' in the relationship between rugby players and the media. It came in Cardiff in 1991 when England won 25–6, their first victory in Cardiff for twenty-eight years. 'The England management and captain, Will Carling, refused to speak to the media and it was one of the most abysmal episodes I have ever witnessed in my professional career. It was an appalling blunder and Geoff Cooke and Carling were hauled over the coals for it by the RFU. It was like something out of Monty Python. They said they weren't going to do interviews and talk about the match because the RFU had stopped them doing stuff for the BBC for which they would be paid. None of them would speak to any media guy. The guy I felt most sorry for was the player who never had a finer hour for England, Simon Hodgkinson. He kicked all the goals that won the game and in normal, sane circumstances, would have been 'the' story for the next 48 hours. As it was, he never got the credit for that victory because England's self-imposed gag became the story of the whole match. I believe that what professionalism has done is lose the close relationship between the press and the players. That had survived longer than in cricket or soccer. But those days have now long gone in rugby, too.'

Peter was right. There used to be a trust between us and the majority of the journalists. There were very few you wouldn't have talked to. Yes, I agree, everything has moved on but having that trust was significant in the way the game was played. Journalists still wrote critical reports when they felt they had to, and I felt as a player you learned from those reports. It was a very important part of your growing up. But what did Peter think, did he believe the players respected the media as much now or was there now a fear, a divide between the two? 'It's different now because the game is enjoying a popularity never known before. There are more people involved in every sense. You used to get one TV crew maybe at a training session; now the whole world has become a local radio station. If you ask a young player to come to a press conference and suddenly he has a mass of microphones stuck under him, he would be less than human if he didn't think "I have to be careful here." The media now is an enormous operation. All you can do as an individual journalist is work on your own relationships with players and because you have trust, you can ring them up. But another difficult thing to do is talk with players whom you have occasionally criticised. We all take criticism personally.'

Gareth Davies suspected that the way players reacted was no different to yesteryear. But, he wondered, was there more onus on them to take criticism? He thought they had more responsibility to listen to the words people spoke. Certainly, you are not beyond criticism as an amateur or professional. But I believe that criticism should always be tempered. Criticism when constructive is fine, you have to accept that and you would do well to heed it. But negative criticism can be different. We played at a pretty high level and you expected there was media attention in all its different guises. Sometimes you had some harsh criticisms from the media and you thought, 'I don't get paid for this, do I deserve it?' But now of course they are paid so it is probably different. Jackson said that his sports editor would say, 'Encourage players.' He added, 'You don't go out to slam people. You look for something positive to say. But maybe in a professional game the guys are there to be judged. The greater the reward the more you are entitled to say "Was that good, was it not?" '

I wondered what responsibility did the TV media have? Because after all, it's trying to sell the product. Is there a conscious effort to portray rugby in its best light?

I sought Gareth Davies's views on this one because he was best qualified to comment. 'Well, there is a feeling that big money has been paid into the game. There is a nervousness about the money being paid because that money goes straight into the players' pockets. We said the arrangement had to be a partnership in growing the game but there is an acknowledgement that too much money is going to the players. The idea wasn't just to up the fees for the players but to try and make the whole product stronger. We still haven't got to grips with that.'

Jackson said that there was no doubt that rugby union now got more column inches than ever before in terms of coverage in the national media. 'Twenty years ago, Terry O'Connor wrote a rugby column on Tuesdays for the *Daily Mail* with a little news piece on Fridays. Now there is major concentration every day. But it is folly for people to sell out to the media. Bath did a fly-on-the-wall documentary but were very naïve to think the TV crew wouldn't film absolutely everything. What was produced was to the great embarrassment of many major figures at that club.'

It would be, as Peter Jackson suggested, very difficult to quantify how much England rugby lost by selling out to BSkyB. But the truth is, great numbers of people haven't seen any of England's wonderful rugby played at Twickenham since and how much has that cost the RFU in terms of future support? There is nothing to beat a big TV terrestrial audience for your live games. Such a policy is short-term reward, I believe. If kids cannot see the cream of the sport, your entire future is imperilled. Fewer kids go and watch what we all continue to think is a great game. These are England's glory days and if you don't have their home games on terrestrial TV showing to millions of people, you are losing a glorious opportunity to capture people for life as supporters and followers of the game.

But Gareth told us a remarkable story about how TV can manipulate sports like rugby for their own commercial purposes. 'I was watching the Lions' first Test in Brisbane in a TV studio and saw the local Australian Channel 7 programme. I realised that it was not even live – they were showing it two or three minutes late. That delay was deliberately done because if there was an injury, they could time the injury to run adverts.' This, of course, was the ultimate fear, that once TV started to run professional sport, they would call the tune. You also risked having half-empty stadia because the aim and intention of the TV company was to have people watching the game on TV, not at the ground. Now they do interviews at half time in France and there are already signs that that is creeping in here, too. Also, cameras are already in the dressing-room. We should be aware that soccer crowds are suffering from live TV. I watched the Aston Villa–Fulham match in October

2001 and Villa knew if they won, they would go fourth in the Premiership. Yet there were thousands of empty seats there. It comes back to the point, people don't want to go to live matches when they can watch the games in the comfort of their own homes. Or at least, they'll only go when Aston Villa play Manchester United or England play Australia at rugby. But neither clubs nor countries can survive on a big crowd just once here and there.

There are so many games to watch on TV now. Will it have an adverse effect on the future of the game in England? At the moment, it is all rosy in English Premiership soccer but what does all this TV access do for the traditional fans? Gareth said that they had cameras in the rugby changing-rooms only until five minutes before the start of the game. No microphones were allowed. But yes, he agreed it was the thin end of the wedge. As he said, who would be the next producer to make a name for himself by doing something innovative and pushing the barriers back even further? Jackson saw that as the danger, that the TV people would have more and more of an influence in rugby, as in soccer. 'When the fans don't know what time the kick-off is, that is when you begin to realise the dangers of selling out to TV. The danger is that television has too great an influence. Now they're saying, "We will tell you when to play, when it suits us, not you." That can't be good for the game.' We all shared the worries of this situation.

Perhaps, by way of another view, we should finish these reflections on the media with the thoughts of Mike Burton, with whom I discussed the role of the agent, earlier in this book. Of course, Burto has known media men all his life, and you could say he has learned shrewdly how to handle them, how to manipulate them towards his point of view. Burto had some strong opinions about the media and their role in the modern game. Frankly, he was less than enchanted about the standards of the fourth estate.

'What does disappoint me today is some of the standards in journalism and rugby writing. Years ago, you had some real authorities on the game, people you respected and looked up to. They promulgated different views, views that they firmly believed in and were prepared to defend. They prosecuted those views whether they were popular or unpopular. But today, these guys are no longer authoritative.

'I believe the reason for that is that rugby has lost much of its exclusivity. In 1955 when the British Lions toured South Africa, just two journalists travelled from the UK to cover the whole tour – Vivian Jenkins of the London *Sunday Times* and J.B.G. Thomas of the *Western Mail*. Even as recently as 1983, *The Times* did not send a reporter to New Zealand with Ciaran Fitzgerald's Lions, preferring to use a local Kiwi to write the reports. All that seems unthinkable today. So when the Lions left for Australia on 1 June 2001, virtually an army of media men went with them. You had national daily, Sunday and evening newspaper reporters, regional UK newspaper writers, TV crews, radio reporters for national and local radio, magazine reporters, internet reporters . . . just to mention a few. It all reflected how the game had changed.'

Burton went on: 'It has all helped to grow the sport but the price we have paid is to see many more writers going on tours such as the Lions who really have no basic understanding of the game, its history and traditions. Many of them were disenchanted soccer reporters who took up rugby probably because it seemed like a more pleasant environment in which to work. Of course, many of those tabloid newspapers would only ever have three or four lines of report on the game itself. But what they would refer to as the "spicy stuff" would be the focal point of their stories, the main reason for their presence. Now, however, these non-traditional rugby newspapers are falling over themselves to cover the sport. Especially in England. In Wales, it was different because you always used to have a lot of media attention – after all, it was your national game and very important.

'On the Lions tour I made in 1974, you had well-established journalists who understood the game and therefore stayed in that role on a paper for a long period of time. Whereas in recent years we have seen some dramatic changes which have brought in numbers of non-rugby journalists, who have followed their journalistic traditions for sensationalism. The game had not seen those people before. We can lament the loss of the old days when only people who really knew the game wrote about it. But the truth of the matter is, these people are not going to go away; having them around is a fact of life. There are always going to be changes in life but not always as you want them. The game has sought a wider audience and has tried to market its presence around the world and not just in the traditional rugby nations.' Therefore, says Burton, it is inevitable that you will attract all types. You can't have one without the other. But, he warns, it might not do the game a great service because although these 'new' reporters might tell a good game, they won't necessarily understand it.

Summary

We have heard them, met them and talked to them. Privately, away from intrusive eyes, we have quietly shaken our heads and thought, 'No way will I be like that.'

I am talking about those from previous generations who speak only of the failings of things in the modern day. 'Oh, of course it's not as good now as in my time,' you hear them say. Or, 'Well, they try but they're nowhere near the quality which we took for granted.' You can apply this to whichever group of people you happen to be discussing – gardeners, craftsmen, writers, designers . . . even rugby players.

I do not intend to fall into the same trap. I know my playing generation is now a quarter of a century older and therefore we have to accept that circumstances change, things move on. None of us can be surprised by progress nor should we scorn it.

Besides, the fact is that some things about the modern-day game are infinitely better than in my day. I will give some examples of that in a moment. Yet some are not and I make no apologies for putting them down in print and suggesting where perhaps things have gone wrong.

Please, I ask the reader, do not confuse this with some old fuddy-duddy moaning that everything was far better in his time. I do not think that for one minute. I have tried throughout this book to give a fair and balanced appraisal from not only those people within rugby whose views I sought but also from my own stance. Where praise has been merited, I have not hesitated to give it, but where something has been lacking, I have tried to point that out. I could not see the point of writing a book such as this unless it embraced a diversity of views, good and bad, about modern-day rugby.

The good things? For a start, the people I talked to about this book. To me, they epitomised what continues to be great about this sport – people who give freely of their time, through their love for rugby football. It is a game that has spawned lifelong friendships and I trust will always do so. I make the point, and I stand firmly by it, that if professional rugby means there is no longer the time or desire to make friends, often among one's opponents, then the game will be much the poorer in the future.

Then, what are we to make of the wonderful deeds of charity which continue to be carried out in the name of rugby football? Jeremy Guscott, the former Bath, England and British Lions centre, walked the length and breadth of England to raise funds for leukaemia research, nobly assisted by two close friends. All three men walked an average of 30 miles a day for a month, by the end of which their feet were almost in shreds. Yet they raised around £200,000, a magnificent achievement. Then there was the way rugby friends rallied around when Alistair Hignell, the former Cambridge University and England full-back, was diagnosed with multiple sclerosis. Thousands of pounds were raised to help pay for his treatment, a similar scenario to that experienced by Andy Blyth, a former Newcastle player, who was seriously injured in a game. Rugby goes on doing this, rallying around, helping out, raising money, looking after its friends. You feel humbled by such acts of care and friendship.

I have to say, I am more encouraged about things in general after speaking to Keith Wood and hearing what he had to say. You might say he would be positive, he's a modern-day player but he was upbeat about the future. I have a lot of respect for Keith. He knew the game before 1995 and has been a champion player during the early years of professionalism. As far as I am concerned, he deserves all he makes from his very considerable efforts.

Indeed, this is one clear example of progress from my time. In a sense, it was dishonest in my day because there were the Unions, raking in hundreds of thousands of pounds from sponsors and encouraging them to believe in the great spectacle on view, yet in the same breath telling us, the players, that we couldn't have a penny of it. More than that, they began to insist on ever more time being devoted to the game by these unpaid players because quality had to be ensured. Was that right, was it honest? I don't think so.

Today, much is asked of the leading players yet much is given to them. A fair exchange, an honest one too, many might say. And through that professional preparation which was made possible by paying players, has come some outstanding examples of rugby football. Look at the difference between England now and the England of my era. Never a pushover even then, despite what some of my fellow countrymen thought. But today, England are producing a brand of rugby which is on a different planet from most of their displays in the 1970s and 1980s. They have scored tries, produced some outstanding attacking rugby and offered wonderful entertainment. The same can be applied to a country like Australia who won two World Cups in the 1990s alone and produced marvellous players like John Eales, Tim Horan, Jason Little, Matthew Burke, Stephen Larkham, Joe Roff, David Wilson and many more. These countries could say that things have been far better for them in recent times than twenty-five years ago and they would be correct.

Keith Wood is very bullish about the state of the game and I hope he is right. But I wouldn't say that I am completely convinced by his views. I have not changed my mind that much. I continue to believe the game needs careful nurturing now. It cannot be allowed to go from pillar to post which has happened much too much since 1995. It needs a certain overview, someone who can look at it objectively and say, 'Now, we made these particular changes: are we in any danger of losing the basic principles of the game?' In other words, a type of rugby 'Tsar' responsible for the overall health and prosperity of the sport.

My feeling is that the law-makers have fiddled and tampered with the laws too much in recent times. They have been responsible for developing an unsatisfactory situation especially in the tackle area. Keith Wood touched on this and the importance of rucking to the game. Certainly, ways need to be found to get more forwards into the tackle area. I know what everyone is trying to do, namely, keep the ball moving. But sometimes, a mania for that and for constant movement has really led to nothing but the play going sideways across the field, with ball carriers running into lines of solid defenders. That cannot be construed as attacking rugby or entertainment. Sometimes, part of the game was about just keeping possession, not necessarily using it all the time. I enjoyed certain parts of the old game and I insist we need to tie in more forwards in the modern game, thereby releasing more space out wide for the backs to run into. The game would benefit, of that I am certain.

In part, it probably comes down to refereeing, for surely that is the factor which can help create that. Referees could start by allowing fair, legal, vigorous rucking. The guy who lies all over the loose ball on the ground to prevent the other side winning fast possession is cheating and deserves little sympathy if he gets a good shoeing. But a good shoeing may not be enough to deter these players and, if that proves to be the case, then the law-makers need to give referees powers to hand out firm punishment. Yellow cards already operate and they do not seem to be sufficient to solve the problem. Maybe harsher penalties will be required. For these players cannot be allowed to change the whole nature of the game by denying the opposition any chance of free-flowing movements.

It may sound like a contradiction when I talk about open, back play but I would like to see guys competing for the ball a bit more up front, so that there is a genuine contest for the ball among the forwards. Plainly, that is not happening in too many matches nowadays. Forwards are afraid that powerful sides will just keep the ball in the maul, and therefore too many stand off among the backs to try and hold a defensive line. Too often, I believe, that is threatening to strangle the game. I don't want to see the game becoming so defensive-minded that there is no space for the backs. There is a real danger of that and it is happening already. I ask the question, if this trend has developed within the handful of years since professionalism, what is it going to be like in a few years' time when sides have really had time to perfect their defensive strategies? Will we be seeing any tries scored then?

If the defence is cluttered, it is extremely difficult for sides to do anything much in attack. Tactical kicking is one answer, of course, but no one wants to see the backs kicking all the time because they have no chance of running with the ball. That would represent no sort of progress whatsoever for the game. It seems to me that whatever different moves or tactics a side works out today, it is limited by the sheer lack of space available for attack.

The trouble is, when you change the laws so often, you perhaps create one thing to the detriment of another and I suspect that is what has happened. This is the price we have paid for too much mucking around with the basic laws of the sport.

In the tackle area especially, we have changed the laws almost year by year. It has become a very loose area and people just don't commit to it. The 2001 Varsity match demonstrated this problem in the game with stark clarity. Oxford kicked three penalty goals and then sat back and defended. Few players were committed to the rucks and mauls and Cambridge, for all their efforts, could do nothing about it. It was dreary stuff to see. Now if that happens at the Varsity match in a game between students, what hope has the rest of the game got? If Varsity rugby is going to survive then they are going to have to produce something better than that. You can't expect to fill stadia playing the game that way.

What I am trying to say in all of this is, if there are problems, let's recognise them because it is still a wonderful game when played at its best. There has been great movement in many international, provincial and club games. Look at some of the fantastic games on display in the Heineken Cup. Yet too often there are the mundane performances, and the main reason for that has been an intense focus on defence.

Defence is the name of the modern game, a point which we discussed in the chapter with ex-rugby league coaches like Joe Lydon and Phil Larder. I was interested to hear them say the focus in coaching needs to switch from concentrating on defence to attack. I agree wholeheartedly with that. Coaches set out to stifle and stop before they thought about creating and scoring tries. That has to change. Defence has always been a part of the game, sure, but it is now dominating it and that is wrong. We have to find a way of shifting the emphasis back to attack.

Junior rugby is another area where I believe there need to be changes. A friend of mine is involved with Monmouth rugby and he confirmed what Ian Roddan and Chris Hobbs of the Stow-on-the-Wold and Avonvale junior clubs had said. He told me they played up the valley against a club whose officials said they paid a bonus to their players but the club was now in huge debt and worried where the next payment was coming from. It seems to me the answer is unanimous at this level – the sooner the game goes back to complete amateurism, the better. There are intelligent people who know what is required. That return to amateurism will surely come, it has to. It would be far healthier for the game in all but the top levels.

It is one of my most rigid beliefs that we must encourage people to show the kids how to play the game. We must ensure the youngsters coming into the game are given the opportunity to develop their skills at an early age.

The important time to develop individual ball-handling skills is at a very young age, from five or six upwards, because then kids grow up with them, and they become second nature to them. But for too long there has been an emphasis on unit skills rather than individual skills, like handling and passing the ball correctly.

I mentioned the value of friendships made after matches and which last lifetimes. I am proud to say that I have many good pals and contacts all around the world whom I forged links with soon after the intense heat of battle had subsided. I value those friends now as much as ever I did, even though I may see some of the more distant ones among them only once every few years. No matter, the bond is strong, the friendship is true.

Teams don't spend the time now with opponents and I find that a shame. The loss will be theirs. They have to do other things as part of their professional approach so they don't stay behind very often for a chat with opponents or supporters. But it would be sad if we lost that completely. I am encouraged that they still have a few dinners after some of the Six Nations Championship games and I urge them to keep that tradition alive at least, for those dinners are an important part of the whole occasion.

Injuries are another aspect of the modern game that demand close examination. The game was always played on a knife-edge, always had the capacity for serious injury if discipline was not paramount. The ability to hurt people and be hurt was never more than just a fraction away all the time. But there used to be a mutual respect, a determination to play hard but still enjoy and respect the camaraderie that developed after the matches. If that mutual respect has been undermined by professionalism, then it is essential that those in authority come down hard on any players who step beyond the line of hard but fair physical challenges.

Summary

I feel we were very professional in our approach all those years ago in our desire to win. We were certainly miserable for ages after we lost. You didn't feel like talking to the opposition after you lost but you did it and it was good for you. It was so important because it created not only character but also lifelong friendships and relationships. Maybe I am naïve to think this can be maintained, but I do firmly believe every effort should be made to keep it. If players do not uphold that tradition, it will be a big loss. And when their boots are hung up, who will they have to talk to about the old days and the great games!

The benefits we have all had from this marvellous sport have been tremendous. Much has changed, some good, some bad but one thing that encourages me no end is that the Barbarians have survived.

The Barbarians have been through possibly the most difficult period of their history but they seem to be winning the argument about their future. I am certain their fixtures still have a place in the modern game. I think having some Tri Nations players helps to strengthen them because they must have a team of substance when they play. Maybe that means the Barbarians are only left to play international sides or special matches against club sides. But whoever they play they should have quality players, a side that is representative of the Barbarians tradition. It has been encouraging that the southern hemisphere boys love the opportunity to play for the Barbarians and want to play for the right reasons. They clearly know the tradition and background of this great club. Everybody thought the Barbarians had breathed their last. It is a wonderful encouragement to rugby's ability to move into new eras and different times, that they have kept faith with one of the great bastions of the amateur era.

The Barbarians is more than just a link with the old amateur days. It is a club that epitomises the great pillars on which the game was founded – friendship, care for your colleagues, working together as a team and having fun. Rugby should always be about that.

The Barbarians is a unique club. But in general, too many clubs in too many countries are in deep trouble. In South Africa, from what I hear, many are in dire straits. Many clubs are broke. In late 2001, I received a request to go out to South Africa to speak at one such club. They told me that their club was basically broke and they were desperate to raise some money for it. I hear a similar message from too many clubs around the world. Yet for too long in our part of the world we have thought that everything was hunky dory in the southern hemisphere. Plainly, it is not.

So I ask, is the game as great as the IRB would lead us to believe? Or are even the southern hemisphere countries, which received all that money from the Murdoch empire back in 1995, themselves struggling? Where is the next batch of money coming from if we are not producing the type of rugby people want to see?

Then, on the plus side, I am delighted to have seen such a vivid demonstration of the popularity of the British Lions as was shown in Australia during their tour in 2001.

To hear that as many as 20,000 supporters followed the Lions on that tour, so much so that they completely swamped the home support in Brisbane for the first Test against Australia, was surely a stirring testimony to the enduring appeal of the Lions who, like the Barbarians, are a unique outfit. Not even I, so ardent a supporter of the Lions concept, could have forecast so huge an upswing in the Lions' popularity.

Yet, as with all things in the modern game, which seems to comprise a remarkable mixture of the good, the not so good and the downright bad, nothing is ever straightforward. Even concerning the Lions. As we discussed earlier, some of the newspaper columns written by the players and/or their representatives, were downright ill-advised and unwise. It was interesting to hear so eminent a British national newspaper journalist as Peter Jackson of the London *Daily Mail* say that columns by players could and should be banned on future Lions tours. As Peter said, if players insist they want to write them, then perhaps it is time to say to them, we respect your view and your right to insist but unfortunately we cannot invite you to come on the tour under those circumstances. As Peter went on to suggest, how many players would then reject a Lions tour just to uphold that point? Very few indeed, I believe.

There were, too, other aspects arising from that Lions tour which I would like to mention briefly. Keith Wood made an interesting point about Lions tours, concerning playing fewer matches. He said basically the players should enjoy it more and I agree. One of the great privileges and benefits of going on a Lions tour is getting to know people from different cultures. If you do it the way the 2001 Lions did it, training, playing, travelling and little else, you are striking at the whole basis of what a Lions tour is for, which is about cultural exchange and goodwill as much as it is about rugby.

I don't want to appear too long in the tooth in these matters. Of course, there were things wrong in our day. One that used to drive us nuts on Lions tours was the constant round of embassy receptions and functions with the local mayor wherever you went. It bored you to tears in the end. But when you look back and think about it, you realise it was all part of a great education. In 1974, on the Lions tour of South Africa, Syd Millar, our assistant manager, said that we would not go to as many functions as usual. We cut out a lot of the cocktail parties. I agreed with that but we certainly didn't cut them out altogether. I am not saying go back to the old days because they were best. What I am saying is, 'Don't just train all the time; broaden your minds by meeting outsiders, going to schools and hospitals, putting yourself in environments with which you are not familiar.' That is how you develop yourself socially as a person for the rest of your life.

I bet the 2001 Lions in Australia would have loved to have gone to some cocktail parties, to break the tedium of constant training, watching videos and thinking about rugby all day long. The trouble is, in a professional era, the most important thing is results. So when those Lions ultimately failed to get the result they wanted, namely victory in the Test series, their coach Graham Henry was firmly in the firing line.

Henry's credentials for the job have been questioned, his right to be there put under the microscope. But I can tell you that Graham Henry was prepared to give his right arm to be part of the Lions. I also know he was greatly influenced by the 1971 Lions in New Zealand and what Carwyn James taught us as coach of that tour. Those '71 Lions made a strong impact on his rugby psyche as he has told me on several occasions.

He desperately wanted to be Lions coach and he felt very proud to have been associated with them. You can argue for ever and a day whether he was the right coach. Personally, I think he was, once Ian McGeechan turned it down. McGeechan was the obvious candidate but he was not available. Without him, the Lions were limited in other choices. Warren Gatland of Ireland? Graham Henry? Clive Woodward? Gatland was no more of an Irishman than Henry was a Welshman. Woodward had changed from being England coach to director of England rugby. Andy Robinson, the coach, was inexperienced in international rugby but he was eventually chosen as number two to Henry for the tour. Also, Woodward had attracted plenty of criticisms for his style of man-management, things like apparently being too distant from the players. Would he have been able to front up to them, face to face as you must do on a Lions tour? Would his approach have worked? Also, under Woodward's overall control, England failed in three successive Grand Slam attempts so was he the clear and obvious candidate to take the Lions? Perhaps not.

There was another factor. There were a lot of England players on the tour. Would it have worked with an England coach, too? Remember the criticism of the 1977 Lions in New Zealand after they had lost the Test series. The team had more Welshmen than any others and a Welsh coach, John Dawes. People said it was too 'Welsh'.

So the point was, at a crucial time, the Lions had very few obvious candidates for the role. Yes, England were the best side in the Championship but that should not necessarily be the deciding factor. It's easy to have the knives out for Henry, but who else was there? Remember too, it is a very thin dividing line between success and failure. There is no doubt there would have been some mumblings, with questions raised about the management's style, had the Lions won the series. But they would have been quickly answered by the results. They wouldn't have seen the light of day, those criticisms.

Yet we should also remember, the Lions and Graham Henry came exceedingly close to success. After their win in the first Test, I personally couldn't see Australia recovering. I thought they looked completely confused by the Lions performance in that Test. The second Test could have been won by half time by the Lions but for the lack of a killer instinct. They didn't put enough points on the board after a very positive first half. Maybe Australia took heart from that, but there had been a great opportunity for the Lions to wrap up the series before the Australians had drawn breath. But they didn't do it and one mistake by Wilkinson turned the whole game and the entire series. After that, the Australians were like sharks to blood.

I have heard the criticisms made of Henry and, although I wasn't there, I have spoken to enough players with sufficient authority to say that Henry's approach was probably too inflexible. That is a weakness of his. Maybe he should have changed a little, but that was perhaps the schoolmaster coming out in him. Yet at the end of the day, it is the players on the field who turn territorial advantage and superiority into points, not the coaches. If the players fail, the team fails, it's as simple as that. The coach provides a framework, detailed for sure, but still only a framework.

If there was a criticism that future Lions management should learn from I'd say it was that the training was so intense it left a lot of people mentally stale. Also, too many players felt very early in the tour that they had no chance of being in the Test side. They felt that had been decided before the Lions even left home.

I understand it was a short tour compared with the long ones we were involved in. But it must be demoralising to the rest of the squad who realised very quickly they would play no significant part in the Test side. They were used mainly as cannon fodder from far too early in the tour. But players need to go out and do different things. If you are training all the time and all you are is cannon fodder, suddenly you think, 'What am I doing here?' All the guys would have gone there with the ambition of making the Test team.

Thus, as with so much of modern-day rugby, there are lessons to be learned from the experience. There is nothing wrong with that as long as those in authority make sure that those lessons are carefully digested and any changes deemed appropriate are made for the future. To my mind, the need for 95 per cent of all clubs to revert back to amateurism is a classic example of this.

Beyond dispute, this has been the most traumatic time for rugby in all its history, probably even including the split with the northern clubs in 1895 in England. The game has been buffeted and a lot of people are asking 'Where does rugby go from here?' This book has been an attempt to answer some of those questions, to remember some of the things that made the game great and perhaps to nudge a few of those in important positions within the sport as to what should remain of paramount importance. Even in a professional era.

For me, rugby remains one of the great loves of my life, an enduring passion which will never die. If there are criticisms of it in this book, they have been expressed purely with the best intentions in mind, namely that this wonderful game that has given me and countless others so much should continue to prosper for the benefit of future generations. It always was and still remains a truly special sport. Long may that be the case.

Index

Note: all references are to rugby union unless otherwise indicated. The names of countries and places refer to teams or clubs unless otherwise indicated. Page numbers in **bold** refer to major text sections.

administration (of game) *see* IRB;
  Pugh, Vernon; Unions
admission prices 234
agents 50–51, 65
All Blacks *see* New Zealand
amateur game 19, 54, 59–60, 262
  see also junior rugby
Andrew, Rob 143
Anglo-Welsh League, proposed 244–5,
  246
Association Football
  as grounding for rugby skills 39
  Home International Championship
    169
  media influence 121, 239, 253–4
  players' wages 53, 80
  referees 204–5
  young players 39
attacking game 141
Australia (country)
  interchange between codes 128–9
  Lions tour (2001) *see* Lions
  Pacific island players 57–8
Avon RFC 208, 226

Avonvale RFC 207–8, 226
  see also Hobbs, Chris
  finances 230
  future 230–31
  history 210–11, 217–18
  lack of young players 226
  League rugby 211

Back, Neil 15
Bahamas (country) 60
Ball, Dave 226
ball skills 10, 39, 62–3
Balshaw, Iain 5
Barbarians 263
Bastiat, Jean-Pierre 63
Bateman, Allan 26, 138, 142
BBC (British Broadcasting
  Corporation) 99
Beaumont, Bill 49, 250
Beckham, David 80, 153
benefactors, clubs **67–86**
  for individuals *see* individual entries,
    especially Thomas, Peter;
    Wray, Nigel
  motivation 71–3

Bennett, Phil 39
Bevan, Derek 185, 206
Billot, John 248
Blanco, Serge 62
Blyth, Andy 258
Boniface, André 10
Borthwick, Steve 65
Bowring, Kevin 24
Box, Tony 226
Boyce, Max 49, 124
Bracken, Kyran 73
Bradshaw, Keith 70
British Broadcasting Corporation
   (BBC) 99
British and Irish Lions *see* Lions
Brooke, Zinzan 221
Brown, Tony 41, 71, 115
Bunce, Frank 57
Burke, Matthew 259
Burnett, Mr (referee) 48
Burrell, Bob 195
Burton, Mike ('Burto')
   on agents 50–51, 65
   business 50, 52, 65
   on club funding 53–4, 55–6
   on future of rugby league 145–6
   on media 240–42, 254–6
   Never Stay Down (autobiography)
      49
   on overseas players 57
   as player 47–50, 63
   on players' wages 50–51
   on professionalism 54–5, 63–4, 65
   on rugby in general 51–4, 61–2
   on tickets 60–61
   on Welsh decline 119
Busby, Sir Matt 248
Busher, Dennis 248
Butler, Eddie 154
Butterfield, Jeff 10

Cabannes, Laurent 19
Callard, Jon 97, 248
Campbell, Ollie 10
Campsall, Brian 187, 202

Cardiff 122
   facilities 179
   Heineken Cup 172–3
   kick-off times 113
   and Peter Thomas 67, 70–71,
      115–16, 118
   and WRU 68–9, 78–9, 244–5
Carling, Will 52, 237, 251
Carmichael, Sandy 40
Castaignede, Thomas 72, 73
Catchpole, Ken 131
chairmen *see* benefactors
charitable activities 258
Charvis, Colin 148, 159
children, players *see* young players
Clements, Bill 22–3
clubs, funding *see* funding
coaches
   disproportionate influence of 37,
      133–6
   questioning match officials 199–200
Cochrane, Peter 128
collapsing of scrums 35–6
Cooke, Geoff 251
corporate hospitality 53, 61
Corry, Martin 159
Cotton, Fran 138, 141, 149
Coulman, Mike 125
Cowman, Richard 245
Craven, Dr Danie 191
Critic, The 237
crowds
   abuse of match officials 196–8
   comparison between codes 143

Daily Mail 153, 155
Daily Telegraph 153
Dallaglio, Lawrence 157
Davies, Adrian 165
Davies, Gareth 118, 238
   on lack of planning 244, 247
   on Lions tour of Australia (2001)
      153–4
   on media 159, 238–40, 242, 243,
      248, 252–3, 254

as player 153, 238
on players' wages 249
on Welsh dominance 249–50
on Welsh passion for rugby 245
Davies, Gerald 10, 28, 63, 109, 215
Davies, Jonathan 126, 140, 142, 145, 149
Davies, Lyn 139
Dawes, John 266
Dawson, Matt 151, 153, 154–5
de Beer, Jannie 73
Deakin, Peter 243
Deans, Colin 42
defensive game 131–3, 138, 260–61
defensive-offensive style of play 41
Devereux, John 145
diet 138–9
Diprose, Tony 73
dirty play *see* physical nature of game
Dooley, Wade 212
Doyle, Mick 195
drinks (water), during play 30
du Preez, Frik 62
Duckham, David 245

Eales, John 259
ebb and flow of play 41
Edwards, Shaun 127–8, 150
eligibility (to play for countries) 57–8
Ellis, David 131
England 77–8
    attacking game 141
    dominance 82–3, 100, 118–19, 148, 168–70, 259
    fitness of players 5–6
    gate prices 234
    players' wages 77
    strike action 58–9
    v Ireland 6–7
    v Scotland 169
    v Wales 169–70, 251
English rugby
    agreement between RFU and clubs 83–4
    benefits of League rugby 166–7, 212

composition of Premiership 56
structure of competitions 86, 167–8, 170, 171–3
European Cup 96–100, 168, 171–4
European League, possibility of 18
Evans, Ben 29

FA (Football Association) 52
facilities 178–9
Faulkner, Tony ('Charlie') 49
    favourite players 42
    on format of Welsh rugby 32
    on mental fitness 40–41
    on over-coaching 37
    as player 23–4, 26–7, 40, 42–3, 159
    on punching 33–4
    on referees 37
    on scrummaging 29–30, 33, 37, 42
    on toughness of modern game 41–2
    on training and fitness 40
Fenwick, Stevie 39
fighting *see* physical nature of game
financing *see* funding
fitness *see* training and fitness
Fitzgerald, Ciaran 255
Fitzpatrick, Sean 196
fixtures, number 17, 25–6, 55, 147, 167–9, 170–71
    see also season, structure
    internationals/tours 17, 115, 265
Fleming, Jim 183–4, 206
    on abuse of match officials by crowds 196–7
    on idea of two referees 191, 192
    on player discipline 191
    on pressures of refereeing 187–9
    on referee assessment 189–90
    on refereeing standards 184–5
    on referees switching hemispheres 198
    on relationship between referees and players 193
    on shortage of referees 184, 200
    on video referees 187
    on yellow cards 203

football *see* Association Football
Football Association (FA) 52
Ford, Mike 132
foreign players *see* overseas players
Fouroux, Jacques 120
France 82–3
    possible World Cup host 105
friendships, formed through rugby 205,
    262, 263
front-row game 28–9, 34–7
    see also scrummaging
full-backs 62
funding, clubs 53–4, 55–6
    junior rugby 209, 213, 214, 222, 230

Galthie, Fabien 42
Garvey, Adrian 32
gate prices 234
Gatland, Warren 128, 266
Gibbs, Scott 26, 126, 138
Gibson, Jack 129
Gibson, Mike 8–9, 10, 63
Gloucester, overseas players 163–4,
    166, 181
Goodall, Ken 125
grass roots *see* amateur game; junior
    rugby
Green, Gus 209
Greenwood, Will 136
Grewcock, Danny 73
Grey, Ken 38
Griffiths, Glanmor 109
grounds, standards 178–9
Guardian 153
Guscott, Jeremy 207, 258

Haden, Andy 164
Hadley, Adrian 145
Hagler, Marvin 49
Hall, Sir John 75, 78, 165, 248
Hanley, Ellery 150
    career 127–8
    on defensive game 138
    on future of rugby league 144
Hansen, Steve 109

Harlequins 203
Harris, Iestyn 25, 26, 140–41, 145
Harrison, Justin 153
Healey, Austin 42, 153, 154, 155
Heineken Cup *see* European Cup
Henderson, Rob 148
Henry, Graham 98, 112
    as Lions coach 24, 159, 160, 265–6,
        267
    as Wales coach 24–5, 109, 221
Hewett, David 10
High, Colin 184
Hignell, Alistair 258
Hill, Richard 73
Hobbs, Chris
    see also Avonvale RFC
    on costs of attending internationals
        234
    on effects of professionalism on
        junior rugby 217–18, 223
    on future 230–31, 232–3
    on Leagues 211
    on media 233
    as player 207–8
    on professionalism at top of game
        220–22
    on young players 225–6, 227–8, 230,
        233–4
Hobbs, George 208
Hodgkinson, Simon 251
Holmes, Terry 14
Home International Championship
    (Association Football) 169
Honiss, Paul 185
hooking 10
Horan, Tim 72, 73, 163, 259
hospitality, corporate 53, 61
Howard, Fred 185
Howard, Pat 171, 174
Howarth, Shane 186
Howley, Robert 19–20, 148

ingratitude, of modern players 25
injuries 224–6, 228, 262
International Rugby Board *see* IRB

internationals
see also individual national sides
costs of attending 234
number played 17, 115
one-off 176
IRB (International Rugby Board) 11,
56–7, 102, 105
and refereeing standards 184–5, 189,
190
Ireland 6–8
fitness of players 6
passion of players and supporters
6–7
Six Nations Championship 6–7
v England 6–7
v Wales 194–5
Irvine, Andy 62, 63

Jackson, Peter 238, 242
on amalgamation of codes 119–20
on England dominance 118–19
on lack of planning 244, 251
on Lions tour of Australia (2001)
153, 154–5
on media 153, 154–5, 158–9, 242–3,
247–8, 251–2, 253, 254, 264
on players' wages 249
on Saracens 243
on Welsh decline 250
on Welsh passion for rugby 245–7
James, Carwyn 265
James, Daffyd 148
James, Mike 71, 115
James, Tudor 248
Jenkins, Gareth 24
Jenkins, Neil 149
Jenkins, Vivian 255
John, Barry 8, 34–5, 39, 124, 219
Johnson, Martin 17, 153, 154, 220
Jones, Ceri 32
Jones, D.K. 109, 215
Jones, Gwyn 109
Jones, Ian
at Gloucester 163–4, 166, 174–5, 181
on England dominance 170

on facilities 178
on international tours 177–8
on over-coaching 133–4
on overseas players 174, 179–80
on structure of competitions 167–8
Jones, Ken 10
journalists
see also media
for individuals *see* individual entries,
especially Jackson, Peter
relationship with players 251–3
standards 254–6
junior rugby **207–35**
see also amateur game
for individual clubs *see* individual
entries, especially Avonvale
RFC; Stow-on-the-Wold
effects of Leagues/professionalism
19, 210–20, 222–4, 231, 233,
234–5, 261–2
funding 209, 213, 214, 222, 230
future 228–33
injuries 224–5
local fixtures 231–3
New Zealand 219–20
physical nature of game 217–18
pressure 234–5
young players 33, 207–8, 226–8, 230,
233–4

Kaplan, Jonathan 185
Keane, Roy 80
Kennedy, Ken 22, 43–4
kick-off times 113, 239–40, 242–3
Kiernan, Tom 99, 100

Lagisquet, Patrice 28
Laidlaw, Chris 131
Lakin, Bob 71
Lander, Steve 201–3
Larder, Phil 131, 133, 150
on amalgamation of codes 13, 140
on attacking game 141, 261
career 127

on drift of young players to rugby
      union 142–3
on England dominance 148
on future of rugby league 144–5
on interchange of ideas between
      codes 14, 128–30, 136–8, 149
on professionalism across codes 144
Larkham, Stephen 259
Lauder, Wilson 58
laws of game 12–13, 259–60, 261
League rugby 166–7
   effect on junior rugby 210–12,
      218–20, 223, 233, 234–5
   reform 231–3
Leighton, Samuel 31
Lenihan, Donal 153
Leopards (team) 49
Levett, Ashley 75, 165
Lewis, Alan 185
Lewis, Brian 22
Lewis, Lloyd 248
Lewis, Malcolm 248
line-outs 28, 62
Lions **151–61**
   see also tours, international
   brand 152–3
   fixtures, format 152–3, 155–7, 160,
      265
   tour of Australia (2001) 151–61,
      264–7
      discontent 151–3, 153–5, 160–61,
         264, 267
      documentary 157–8, 159
      Graham Henry 24, 159, 160,
         265–6, 267
      profits 152, 160
      reasons for defeat 159–60
   tours, other 38, 49, 265
      documentaries 158–9
   v New Zealand 38
litigation 228
Little, Bridget 181
Little, Jason 259
   at Gloucester 163, 166, 168, 181
   on England dominance 168–9
   on facilities 178

on future of game 181
on international tours 176
on overseas players 174–5
on structure of competitions 168,
      171
on young players 166
local fixtures (junior rugby) 231–3
Lochore, Brian 38
Lomu, Jonah 139
Luger, Dan 7, 74
Luyt, Louis 92
Lydon, Joe 150
   career 127–8
   on defensive game 132–3, 261
   on drift of young players to rugby
      union 141–2
   on future of rugby league 145
   on interchange of ideas between
      codes 130–31, 136
   on professionalism 139–40
   on rugby union generally 128, 147–9
   on talent 139
Lynagh, Michael 73, 74, 174

McGeechan, Ian 265
McHugh, David 185
McLaren, Bill 49
McLauchlan, Ian 40
Madden, Matthew 29
Marks, Dick 129
Mary (sister of Peter Thomas) 70
Maso, Jo 10
match fixing 205
matches, number played *see* fixtures
Matthews, Dr Jack 71
Meads, Colin 38, 163–4
media **237–56**
   see also journalists
   newspapers 237, 247–8, 253
      lack of investment 248, 254–5
      players' contributions 153–5, 264
      standards 254–6
   and referees 199–200

television 237–43
  and Association Football 121,
    239, 253–4
  European Cup 99
  increasing influence 120–21, 241,
    253–4
  Lions tour documentaries 157–9
  replays 202–3
  responsibility 252–3
  satellite, access to 240–41, 253
  and scheduling of games 113,
    120–21, 239–40, 242–3
Melville, Nigel 249
mental fitness 40–41
Mesnel, Frank 3
microphones (referees) 196
Millar, Syd 265
Millennium Stadium 52
Miller, Mike 100
mini rugby *see* young players
Mitchell, John 248
Moncrieff, Elton 172
Moody, Lewis 166
Moon, Rupert 201
Moore, Andy 165
Morgan, Cliff 10, 58, 63
Moriarty, Paul 145
Morris, Dai 37
Morrison, Ed 183–4, 185, 202, 206
  on abuse of match officials by
    crowds 197–8
  on former players taking up
    refereeing 201
  on idea of two referees 192
  on match fixing 205
  on media 199–200
  on questioning of match officials by
    coaches 199–200
  on referee assessment 190
  on refereeing standards 185–6
  on relationship between referees and
    players 192, 195–6
  on sendings off 203–4
  on social side of rugby 205
  on video referees 187
Muggleton, John 137

Mulder, Japie 84
Muller, Pieter 41, 149, 164
Murdoch, Rupert 92, 119–20
Murphy, Jimmy 248

Nash, David 134
Natal Sharks 203
Nathan, Waka 38
Nelmes, Barry 58
Never Stay Down (Burton) 49
New Zealand (country)
  junior rugby 219–20
  Pacific island players 57–8, 106
  referees 194
New Zealand, v Lions 38
Newman, Bob 71
newspapers *see* media
Nicholson, Geoff 23
Norling, Clive 185, 206
Norster, Bob 62

O'Connor, Terry 253
O'Driscoll, Brian 63–4, 136, 148, 166,
  187
Offahengaue, Willie 57
offensive game 141
offensive-defensive style of play 41
O'Gara, Ronan 97
Olympic Games 106
O'Reilly, Tony 10
O'Sullivan, Eddie 132
over-coaching 37, 133–6
overseas players 18, 32, 41, **163–81**
  for individual players *see* individual
    entries, especially Jones, Ian;
    Little, Jason
  Gloucester 163–4, 166, 181
  limiting numbers 18, 174–5
  Pacific island players 57–8, 106–7
  success/failure of 41, 164, 179–80
  wages 81, 163, 165
Owen, Michael 153
owners (clubs) *see* benefactors

Pacific island players *see* overseas
      players
Packer, Kerry 90, 92
Palmade, Francis 185
passion for game 6–7, 63, 245–7
Paul, Henry 145
pay *see* wages
Pearce, Malcolm 71
Penaud, Alain 73
Perkins, John 34
physical nature of game 14–16, 47–9,
      262
   see also rucking
   junior rugby 217–18
   punching 33–4, 47, 49
   stamping 34
   yellow cards 203–5, 260
Pienaar, François 73, 81
players
   ingratitude of modern 25
   newspaper columns 153–5, 264
   overseas *see* overseas players
   relationship with journalists 251–2
   relationship with referees 191, 192–6
   wages *see* wages
   young *see* young players
Plumtree, John 31
Pontypool 21–2
Preece, Peter 245
Premiership, English *see* English rugby
pressure
   junior rugby 234–5
   referees 187–9
Price, Brian 176
Price, Graham ('Pricey') 49
   on drinks during play 30
   on front-row game 28–9
   on Lions 160
   on number of matches played 25–6
   as player 21, 22, 23–4, 35, 42–3, 159
   on professionalism 27
professionalism 63–5, 74–5
   see also individual aspects of
         professionalism
   at top of game 220–22
   benefits 88, 96, 259

comparison between codes 144
double standards 88, 258–9
effect on junior rugby 19, 210–20,
      222–4, 231, 261–3
introduction 27, 54, 87–9, 90–96
Prosser, Ray ('Pross') 21–2, 30, 40
Pugh, Vernon 67, 68, 87, 113–14
   career 89
   on England dominance 100
   on European Cup 98–100
   on future of game 102–3, 105–6
   on game in general 107–8
   on IRB 102, 105
   on laws of game 12–13
   on Pacific island players 106–7
   on principles of game 11–12
   on professionalism 88–9, 90, 91–6
   on rugby's losses 106
   on Six Nations Championship
         101–2
   on Welsh rugby 103–4
   on World Cup 104–5
punching *see* physical nature of game
Pyle RFC 212–13

qualifications (to play for countries)
      57–8
Quinnell, Scott 110, 120, 148

Ralston, Chris 49
Read, Geoff 75
Rees, Dai 195
referees **183–206**
   for individual referees *see* individual
         entries, especially Fleming,
         Jim; Morrison, Ed
   abuse from crowd 196–8
   assessment 189–90
   Association Football 204–5
   dictating how game is played 36–7,
         260
   dishonest 194
   elite list 189
   former players 15, 200–01
   and media 199–200

microphones 196
New Zealand (country) 194
pressures 187–9
professional 201
questioned by coaches 199–200
relationship with players 191, 192–6
shortage 184, 200
standards 184–6, 189–90, 201–2
switching hemispheres 198–9
and TV replays 202–3
two 191–2
video referees 186–7
yellow cards 203–5, 260
relegation 84–5
Renwick, Jim 63
Resolven (club) 69–70
RFU (Rugby Football Union) 52
see also Unions
agreement with clubs 83–4
club funding 53–4, 56
drags heels on professionalism 93
and England strike action 58–9
ticket allocations 60–61
Richards, Dean 85, 149
Rives, Jean-Pierre 63
Roberts, Ian 210
Robinson, Andy 266
Robinson, Jamie 41, 166
Robinson, Jason 120, 133, 136, 146
Robinson, Nicky 41
Roddan, Charlie 208
Roddan, George 208
Roddan, Homer 209
Roddan, Ian
see also Stow-on-the-Wold
on effects of professionalism on
junior rugby 218–19, 222–4,
231
on future 228–9, 231–2
on League rugby 210, 218–19, 223,
231–2, 233
as player 207, 208
on professionalism at top of game
220
on young players 227
Roff, Joe 259

Rossborough, Peter 245
Rougerie, Aurélien 42
Rowlands, Clive 35
Rowlands, Keith 43
rucking 14–15, 16, 259–60
see also physical nature of game
Rugby Football Union *see* RFU
rugby league **123–50**
amalgamation with rugby union 12,
13, 119–20, 140
defections from rugby union 123–6
drift of young players to rugby
union 141–3, 146
future 144–6
interchange of ideas with rugby
union 128–31, 136–7, 146,
149–50
origins 123
professionalism compared with
rugby union 144
relationship with rugby union 123–6
wages 124
rules of game 12–13, 259–60, 261
Rutherford, Don 100, 129
Rutherford, John 10, 63

Sailor, Wendell 145
St Helens (rugby league club) 124, 125
Saint-André, Philippe 166–7
salaries *see* wages
Samuel, Bill 138
Sansom, Norman 185
Saracens 73–4
influence of Peter Deakin 243
and Nigel Wray 67, 71, 72, 73, 74,
75, 79–80, 81
satellite television *see* media
Scotland 64
v England 169
Scottish Rugby Union (SRU) 53, 83
see also Unions
scrummaging 14, 28–30, 33, 34–6,
37–9, 42
season, structure 85–6
see also fixtures, number

Sella, Philippe 73, 74, 176
sendings off 203–4
 see also yellow cards
Shelford, Wayne 174
Sheridan, Richard 237
Six Nations Championship 17–18,
  100–102
 see also individual teams
skills, playing 10, 39, 62–3
Skrela, Jean-Claude 63
Smith, Ian 52
Smith, Tom 148
Snow, Rod 32
soccer *see* Association Football
social side of rugby 205, 262, 263
South Sea island players *see* overseas
  players
SRU (Scottish Rugby Union) 53, 83
 see also Unions
stamping *see* physical nature of game
Stimpson, Tim 122
Stow-on-the-Wold 207, 209, 218, 222–3
 see also Roddan, Ian
 finances 209, 222
 future 228–9
 League rugby 210, 211–13, 233
 paid players 231
 young players 207, 208, 227
strike action 58–9, 110
Stringer, Peter 7
substitutes 8–9
Super 12 competition 167, 171
Swansea 68–9, 78

tackle law 12, 259, 261
Tait, Alan 138, 142
talent 139
Taylor, Bob 63
television *see* media
Thomas, Brian 176
Thomas, Clayton 186, 206
Thomas, Clem 23
Thomas, Clive 204
Thomas, Delme 62
Thomas, J.B.G. 247–9, 255

Thomas, Peter 69
 and Cardiff 67, 70–71, 115–16, 118
 on club benefactors 71, 72
 on future of game 122, 215
 and Mary (sister) 70
 as player 70
 on players' wages 116
 on professionalism 115, 116–17
 on Welsh clubs 111–12
 on WRU 81, 113–14, 214
Thomas, Stan 70
throwing-in 28
 see also line-outs
tickets 60–61
Titcomb, Mike 194–5
tours, international 176–8
 Lions *see* Lions
training and fitness 5–6, 16, 26, 40–41,
  138–9
Tremain, Kel 38
Tuigamala, Va'aiga ('Inga') 165
Tuilagi, Freddie 137
Turnbull, Ross 92
Twickenham 52, 234

Unions 53, 82, 83
 RFU *see* RFU
 WRU *see* WRU

van Straaten, Braam 84
video referees 186–7
Villepreux, Pierre 10
violent play *see* physical nature of
  game

wages, players 77, 80–81, 116, 249
 agents' role in negotiating 50, 51, 65
 Association Football 53, 80
 overseas players 81, 163, 165
 rugby league 124
Wales
 see also Welsh rugby
 approach to game 63–4
 Six Nations Championship 31
 threatened strike action 59, 110

v England 169–70, 251
v Ireland 194–5
Walkinshaw, Tom 71, 163, 244
Wallace, Paul 73
Wallace, Richard 73
Warby, Brian 209
water, drinking during play 30
Waters, Gwyn 206
Watkins, David (Dai) 124, 131, 132
Watkins, Sir Tasker 109, 215
Watt, Dave 48
Welsh rugby **109–22**
    see also Wales
    clubs 109–13, 117–18
    decline 31, 103–4, 109–10, 117, 119
    dominance 249–50
    failure to come to terms with
        professionalism 115
    League rugby 212
    passion for 63, 245–7
    structure 30–31, 59, 68, 109–10,
        170–71, 244
    young players 32, 103
Welsh Rugby, the Crowning Years
    (Thomas and Nicholson) 23–4
Welsh Rugby Union *see* WRU
Wembley Stadium 52
Western Mail 247–8
Wheel, Geoff 39
Whetton, Gary 164
Whineray, Wilson 38
White, Chris 185
White, Julian 73
Whitehouse, Nigel 186
Whiting, Peter ('Pol') 164
Wigan (rugby league club) 124–5
Wilkinson, Jonny 6, 149, 225, 267
Williams, C.D. 71
Williams, Denzil 176
Williams, Harry 97
Williams, J.J. 28
Williams, J.P.R. 43, 62, 146
Williams, Leo 91
Williams, Ray 250
Williams, Shane 186
Wilson, David 259

Windsor, Bobby ('The Duke') 49
    anecdotes featuring 43–5
    on defeat 41
    favourite players 42
    on format of Welsh rugby 31–2
    on Graham Henry 24–5
    on Lions 159–61
    on love of game 25, 26–7
    on overseas players 32, 41
    as player 22–4, 42–3, 45, 159
    on punching 33
    on referees 37
    on scrummaging 28, 35, 37–9
    on training and fitness 26, 40
    on young players 27, 32, 33, 39
Wood, Dudley 93
Wood, Keith 3–4, 258, 259
    on European League 18
    favourite players 19–20
    on hooking 10
    on Ireland 6–8
    on Lions 152, 156–8
    on love of rugby 4
    on number of matches 17, 265
    on overseas players 18
    on physical nature of game 14–16
    as player 8, 9–10, 42
        Lions 148, 151, 152, 153, 155
    on principles of game 14
    on professionalism 19
    on referees 15
    on Six Nations Championship
        17–18
    on substitutes 8, 9
    on training and fitness 5–6, 16
    on young players 20
Woodward, Clive 127, 128, 130, 149,
    220, 266
World Cup 61, 104–5
Wray, Nigel
    on club benefactors 78, 79, 81–2
    on England 77–8
    on future of game 82–3, 86
    on internal wranglings in game
        75–6, 81, 82, 83–4
    on junior clubs 215–16

on Lions 152–3
as player 74
on players' wages 80
on professionalism 74–5
on relegation 84–5
and Saracens 67, 71, 72, 73, 74, 75,
    79–80, 81
on structure of season 85–6
on young players 79
WRC 92
Wright, John 210
WRU (Welsh Rugby Union)
  see also Unions
  club funding 53, 56
  dispute with clubs 67–9, 76–9,
    109–14, 244–5
  lack of planning 214, 243–5, 250
  and Millennium Stadium 52

and Welsh club structure 59, 68,
    109–10, 244

yellow cards 203–5, 260
Young, Dai 130, 149
young players
  Association Football 39
  development 20, 27, 32, 39, 79,
    180–81, 262
  drift from rugby league to rugby
    union 141–3, 146
  junior clubs 207–8, 226–8, 230,
    233–4
  lack of 33, 226, 227, 230
  over-playing of 147–8
  recruitment 166, 233–4
  Welsh rugby 32, 103
Young, Scott 185, 187